DIRECTIONS IN DEVELOPMENT

Agriculture, Trade, and the WTO in South Asia

DIRECTIONS IN DEVELOPMENT

Agriculture, Trade, and the WTO in South Asia

Merlinda D. Ingco, Editor

THE WORLD BANK
Washington, D.C.

© 2003 The International Bank for Reconstruction and Development / The World Bank
1818 H Street, NW
Washington, DC 20433
Telephone 202-473-1000
Internet www.worldbank.org
E-mail feedback@worldbank.org

All rights reserved.

1 2 3 4 06 05 04 03

The findings, interpretations, and conclusions expressed herein are those of the author(s) and do not necessarily reflect the views of the Board of Executive Directors of the World Bank or the governments they represent.

The World Bank does not guarantee the accuracy of the data included in this work. The boundaries, colors, denominations, and other information shown on any map in this work do not imply any judgment on the part of the World Bank concerning the legal status of any territory or the endorsement or acceptance of such boundaries.

Rights and Permissions

The material in this work is copyrighted. Copying and/or transmitting portions or all of this work without permission may be a violation of applicable law. The World Bank encourages dissemination of its work and will normally grant permission promptly.

For permission to photocopy or reprint any part of this work, please send a request with complete information to the Copyright Clearance Center, Inc., 222 Rosewood Drive, Danvers, MA 01923, USA, telephone 978-750-8400, fax 978-750-4470, www.copyright.com.

All other queries on rights and licenses, including subsidiary rights, should be addressed to the Office of the Publisher, World Bank, 1818 H Street NW, Washington, DC 20433, USA, fax 202-522-2422, e-mail pubrights@worldbank.org.

Cover photo credits: Foreground—Curt Carnemark, Pakistan, 1994. Background—Anonymous, Ghana, no date. Both photos owned by The World Bank.

ISBN 0-8213-5159-1

Library of Congress Cataloging-in-Publication Data has been applied for.

Table of Contents

Preface x

Contributors xii

Glossary of Abbreviations and Acronyms xiii

1. Introduction 1
   Merlinda D. Ingco and Tonia Kandiero

2. Bangladesh 38
   C. A. F. Dowlah

3. Sri Lanka 96
   Saman Kelegama

4. Pakistan 141
   Safraz Khan

5. India 189
   Ashok Gulati

Index 235

Box
1.1   State Trading Enterprise Operations 34

Figures
1.1   Nominal Protection Rates in Sri Lanka, 1960–85 and 1993 15
3.1   Agriculture Labor Population, 1990–98 97

3.2	Paddy Production, Requirement Projections, 1999–2004	98
3.3	Tea and Rubber Production in Sri Lanka, 1990–98	99
3.4	Field Crop Production in Sri Lanka, 1994–98	101
3.5	Field Crop Imports in Sri Lanka, 1994–98	101
3.6	Wheat Imports, 1990–98	103
3.7	Volume of Milk Imports, 1990–97	106
3.8	Fish Production in Sri Lanka, 1994–98	107
3.9	Sectoral Composition of GDP, 1997	109

Tables

1.1	Bound and Post-UR Applied Tariff Rates for South Asia	3
1.2	Tariffs and Tariff Bindings by Percent Rates under the URAoA on Major Agricultural Imports, 1999–2000	4
1.3	Aggregate Measurement of Support to Indian Agriculture, 1986–98	10
1.4	Effective Rate of Protection in Agriculture in Bangladesh, 1992–2000	12
1.5	Nominal Protection Coefficients in Pakistan, Various Years, 1990–99	13
1.6	South Asia's Interests in Reform	23
A1.1	Nominal Protection Rates and Effective Protection Rates in South Asia, Various Years	33
2.1	Agriculture and GDP Growth Rates in Bangladesh, 1990–2000	39
2.2	Foodgrain Production and Food Security in Bangladesh, 1990–2000	40
2.3	Role of State Trading Agencies in Agricultural Trade in Bangladesh, 1991–99	44
2.4a	Bangladesh Tariff Structures, Average Measures, and Dispersions, 1991–2000: Unweighted Averages	46
2.4b	Bangladesh Tariff Structures, Average Measures, and Dispersions, 1991–2000: Import-Weighted Averages	46
2.4c	Bangladesh Tariff Structures, Average Measures, and Dispersions, 1990–2000: Average Tariffs and Dispersions	47
2.5	Nominal Tariff and Effective Protection Rates in Bangladesh, 1991–2000	48
2.6	Structure of HS Four-Digit Level Multiple Customs Duty Rates in Bangladesh, 1991–2000	49
2.7	Removal of Quantitative Restrictions, Various Years, 1989–2002	50
2.8	Estimates of Equilibrium (Shadow) Exchange Rates in Bangladesh During Base Period, Various Years, 1985–88 and 1994–97	51

2.9	Effective Exchange Rates on Import Substitutes, Various Years, 1991–99	52
2.10	Selective Features of Bangladesh's Trade in Agricultural Products, 1980–97	53
2.11	Average Growth Rates of Imports of Agricultural Products, 1980–97	54
2.12	Average Growth Rates of Exports of Agricultural Products, 1980–97	56
2.13	Trend Growth Rates of Agricultural Products: Results of Regression Analysis (Imports)	58
2.14	Trend Growth Rates of Agricultural Products: Results of Regression Analysis (Exports)	60
2.15	Trade Liberalization and Economic Performance in the 1990s, Annual Growth Rates	62
2.16	Export Subsidies and Other State Supports for Exports, 1991–2000	64
2.17	Bangladesh: Schedule of Commitments for Agricultural Products to WTO	65
2.18a	Domestic Supports to Bangladesh Agriculture, 1986–96: Support to Agricultural Outputs, Various Years	67
2.18b	Domestic Supports to Bangladesh Agriculture, 1986–96: Agricultural Input Subsidy and Price Supports, Various Years	67
2.18c	Domestic Supports to Bangladesh Agriculture, 1990–95: Support to the Seed Subsector	68
2.19	Market Access Opportunity of Imports in Bangladesh, Various Years, 1986–96	69
A2.1a	Agricultural Products of Bangladesh, Grouped into Harmonized System Codes: Primary Products	76
A2.1b	Agricultural Products of Bangladesh, Grouped into Harmonized System Codes: Processed Products	77
A2.2	Operative Tariff Rates and Value-Added Tax on Major Agricultural Products in Bangladesh, 1991–2000	78
A2.3	Effective Rates of Protection in Bangladesh, 1992–2000	83
A2.4	Effective Rates of Protection in Agriculture in Bangladesh, 1992–2000	85
3.1	Milk Collection and Utilization by Local Milk Industries, 1990–96	104
3.2	Dairy Product Imports by Major Source Countries and Market Share, 1995–97	105
3.3	U.N. World Food Program Operational Expenditures, 1993–97	108

3.4	Cooperative Wholesale Establishment's Percentage Share of Food Commodity Imports, 1995–98	110
3.5	Paddy Marketing Board Capacity Utilization, 1990–96	112
3.6	Replanting and New Planting Subsidies Granted to the Tea Sector, 1995–98	113
3.7	Subsidies Granted to the Coconut Sector, 1997–98	114
3.8	Major Changes to Import Tariffs in the Agriculture Sector, 1995–98	118
3.9	Export Subsidies Granted to the Agriculture Sector, 1995–97	122
3.10	Export Cesses and Surcharges, 1999	123
3.11	Total Availability of Selected Agricultural Commodities, 1994–98	129
3.12	Incentive Structure for Agriculture, 1993	130
A3.1	Total Population and Labor Force and Agriculture Sector Labor, 1990–98	132
A3.2	Agriculture Sector Share of GDP, 1990–97	132
A3.3	Crop Cultivation Land Extent, 1990–98	133
A3.4	Agricultural Commodity Production in Sri Lanka, 1990–98	134
A3.5	Major Dairy Product Imports, 1995–97	135
A3.6	Fish Production and Imports in Sri Lanka, 1994–98	135
A3.7	Quantity and Value of Food Imported by the Cooperative Wholesale Establishment, 1994–98	136
A3.8	Local Purchases of Agricultural Commodities by the Cooperative Wholesale Establishment, by Volume, 1994–98	136
A3.9	Total Agriculture Exports, by Volume, 1994–98	137
A3.10	Total Agriculture Commodity Imports, by Volume, 1994–98	137
4.1	Performance of Overall Economy, 1990–99	143
4.2	Basic Data on Agriculture, 1990–99	144
4.3	Agriculture Sector Performance, 1990-99	145
4.4	Agricultural and GDP Growth, 1960–98	146
4.5	Growth of Agriculture Sector, 1970s to 1990s	146
4.6	Tariff Range for Agricultural Commodities, 1996–2000	153
4.7	Quantitative Restrictions on Various Commodities, 1996–99	155
4.8	Average Tariff Rates for Various Commodities, 1996–2000	157
4.9	Number of Agricultural Commodities in Various Tariff Slabs, 1996–99	160
4.10	Nominal Protection Coefficients by Crops, 1990–99	161
4.11	Product-Specific and Nonproduct–Specific Aggregate Measurement of Support, 1986–98	163
4.12	Quantities of Major Primary Agricultural Exports and Their Total Value, 1990–99	170
4.13	Value of Major Primary Agricultural Exports, 1990–99	171

4.14	Quantities of Major Primary Agricultural Imports and Their Total Value, 1990–99	172
4.15	Value of Major Primary Agricultural Imports, 1990–99	174
4.16	Unit Value Indices and Terms of Trade, 1991–99	175
4.17	Unit Value of Major Agricultural Exports, 1990–99	176
4.18	Unit Value of Major Agricultural Imports, 1990–99	176
4.19	Exports of All Commodities, 1995–99	177
4.20	Imports of All Commodities, 1995–99	179
5.1	Tariff Commitment Made by India in the URAoA	191
5.2	Difference in UR Final Bound Rates and MFN Tariff Rates	193
5.3	Difference between MFN Tariff Rates for 1999–2000 and Corresponding UR Final Bound Rates	194
5.4	Different Types of Nontrade Barriers Imposed on India's Imports for Agriculture Sector (HS 1–24), 1999–2000	196
5.5	Different Quantitative Restrictions for Products, Still Maintained for Balance of Payment Reasons, 1999–2000	197
5.6	Different Types of Quantitative Restrictions for Products, Still Maintained for Balance of Payment Reasons, by Commodity Groups (HS Sections I–IV), 1999–2000	198
5.7	Aggregate Measurement of Support to Indian Agriculture, Selected Crops, 1986–98	206
5.8	Foodgrain Subsidy, 1991–99	219
5.9	Subsidy on Rice and Wheat: Food Corporation of India, 1991–99	220
5.10	Central Foodgrain Stocks and Minimum Buffer Stocks, 1994–99	221
5.11	Foodgrain Allocation and Offtake under the Public Distribution System and the Targeted Public Distribution System, 1991–99	222

Preface

Agriculture plays a crucial role in South Asian economies, accounting for close to 28 percent of gross domestic product. In most low- and middle-income developing countries in Sub-Saharan Africa, South Asia, East Asia, and the Pacific, a large proportion of the work force remains dependent on agriculture. In South Asia, of the 70 percent of the population that live and work in rural areas, the majority depends on the agricultural sector for its livelihood.

Furthermore, South Asia is home to approximately 1.3 billion people, which is the largest regional population in the world. In 1998, the population in South Asia ranged from 19 million in Sri Lanka to 980 million in India (1.016 billion in 2000). One of the major issues in South Asia is poverty. Approximately 522 million people live below $1 per day, representing 40 percent of the world's poor.

The inclusion of agriculture under the rules of the General Agreement on Tariffs and Trade (GATT)/World Trade Organization (WTO) is considered one of the major achievements of the Uruguay Round, which in 1986 established the WTO, the successor to the GATT. The Uruguay Round Agreement on Agriculture (URAoA) established a rules-based system for agricultural trade and set guidelines to reduce protection in agriculture and distortional policies in trade. However, more work needs to be done in order for countries to benefit from the liberalization process. A multilateral trading system that improves market access, creates opportunities for poor countries to increase exports, and promotes better agriculture and rural sector policies and institutions can enhance the livelihood of the poor, especially the poor in rural areas.

For major agricultural exports from South Asia, tariff rates in industrialized countries are still considered prohibitive. South Asia has the potential to gain from further progress in domestic policy reform and in the further opening of international markets to their exports. The new WTO round will help the region to advance in this process of trade liberalization. The World Bank will be instrumental in strengthening the capacity of developing countries to benefit from the liberalization process. Developing countries often lack the capacity to participate effectively and to negotiate forcibly.

Recognizing the important role of agriculture and trade liberalization in alleviating poverty in developing countries, the World Bank in May 1999 initiated an integrated program of research and capacity building with the goal of assisting developing countries in participating more effectively in multilateral trade negotiations. The program is financed by grants from the Department for International Development (DFID) in the United Kingdom, the government of the Netherlands, and the Research Advisory staff of the World Bank. The message behind this World Bank program is that despite the substantial unilateral trade reforms carried out by developing countries in the 1980s, and the limited progress by industrialized countries in liberalizing their own agricultural trade regimes, there is much room for further progress on both sides. Most developing countries missed the opportunity during the Uruguay Round to "lock in" their own liberalization policies. On the side of the industrialized countries, even though the Uruguay Round succeeded in making protection more transparent and limiting trade-distorting subsidies, protection was not substantially reduced.

This volume is part of the program's series of work under the "built-in" agenda, which is the continuation of the reform process begun in the Uruguay Round, as well as the new trade issues in the WTO that affect developing and industrialized countries. The studies in this volume were presented at a regional conference in New Delhi, India, in 1999. The conference was sponsored by the World Bank. The studies have been revised and updated. They are intended for policymakers, analysts, and other stakeholders from industrialized and developing countries. These studies provide valuable insights into various issues, perspectives, and interests of South Asia in the new WTO trade round.

We are grateful to the DFID–UK, the government of the Netherlands, and the World Bank for their financial support of this research. We also thank the staff of DFID–UK who provided suggestions that contributed to the program of research. We are indebted to Gary Pursell and John Nash for their helpful comments and suggestions. Special thanks go to Sanda Lay Chao, Joe Carroll, and Helen Freeman for their editorial support.

Contributors

C. A. F. Dowlah
The World Bank

Ashok Gulati
Institute of Economic Growth, Delhi, India
National Council of Applied Economic Research, Delhi, India

Merlinda D. Ingco
The World Bank

Tonia Kandiero
The World Bank

Saman Kelegama
Institute of Policy Studies, Colombo, Sri Lanka

Safraz Khan, Director
Mahbubul Haq Human Development Centre, Islamabad, Pakistan

Glossary of Abbreviations and Acronyms

ACD	Additional custom duty
AMS	Aggregate measurement of support
AoA	Agreement on Agriculture
BADC	Bangladesh Agricultural Development Corporation
BCD	Basic custom duty
CIS	Commonwealth of Independent States
CPI	Consumer price index
CWE	Cooperative Wholesale Establishment
EERm	Effective exchange rate for imports
EERx	Exchange rate for exports
EFTA	European Free Trade Association
EP	Effective protection
EPC	Effective protection coefficient
EPP	Export parity price
EPR	Effective protection rate
ESAP	Enhanced Structural Adjustment Program
FCI	Food Corporation of India
GATT	General Agreement on Tariffs and Trade
GSTP	Global System of Trade Preferences
HS	Harmonized System
HYVs	High yielding varieties
IMF	International Monetary Fund
IPP	Import parity price
IPRs	Intellectual property rights
ITC	Indian Trade Classification (HS)
MFN	Most favored nation
NP	Nominal protection
NPC	Nominal protection coefficient
NPR	Nominal protection rate
NTB	Nontrade barrier
OFC	Other field crop

OGL	Open General License
PMB	Paddy Marketing Board
PSE	Producer subsidy equivalent
%PSE	Percentage PSE
QR	Quantitative restriction
SAARC	South Asian Association for Regional Cooperation
SAP	Structural Adjustment Program
SAPTA	South Asian Preferential Trading Arrangement
S&D	Special and Differential (Treatment)
SIL	Special Import Licenses (India)
SLECIC	Sri Lanka Export Credit Insurance Corporation
SLEDB	Sri Lanka Export Development Board
SLSI	Sri Lanka Standards Institution
SPM	Phytosanitary measures
SPS	Sanitary and phytosanitary
STC	State Trading Corporation
STE	State trading enterprise
TRIPS	Trade-Related Aspects of Intellectual Property Rights
UNCTAD	United Nations Conference on Trade and Development
UR	Uruguay Round
URAoA	Uruguay Round Agreement on Agriculture
WES	Wage earner scheme
WTO	World Trade Organization
XPB	Export performance benefit

1
Introduction

Merlinda D. Ingco and Tonia Kandiero

Historically, industrialized countries dominated trade negotiations from the establishment of the General Agreement on Tariffs and Trade (GATT) through the lengthy Uruguay Round (UR) negotiations in the 1980s and 1990s. These negotiations established the World Trade Organization (WTO)—the GATT's successor organization—and formulated the UR Agreement on Agriculture (AoA). Even though developing countries possibly have the most to gain from a substantial reduction of existing export subsidies and removal of other trade impediments (Gorter, Ingco, and Ruiz 2000; Ingco 1995), these countries have been the most powerless, and the most ineffective. This is why it is imperative that developing countries, particularly those in South Asia, seize the moment to actively participate in this process of shaping a more globally integrated economic environment and to convey, for instance, their experience from implementing the reduction commitments and the effect of those commitments under the URAoA, the consequence of Special and Differential (S&D) Treatment, and their concerns regarding food security and the environment and the possible negative effects of the execution of the reform program. The new round, it is hoped, will cover broader issues, with established deadlines and room for tradeoffs.

Implementation of the Uruguay Round Agreement on Agriculture

The inclusion of agriculture in the UR marked a major turning point in trade negotiations. Even though this momentous development created a sense of euphoria among developing countries, challenges still lie ahead. There is a consensus that accomplishments of the URAoA were rather modest in removing some trade policy distortions by developed countries. Adhikari (2000) argues that the attempt to liberalize the agricultural sector through the URAoA to secure market access has had mixed outcomes. Developing countries did not gain as much as expected because of the ways in which rules have been implemented, and these countries have strongly argued that market access opportunities have been greatly affected by increased protection and subsidies in developed countries. In addition, with export subsidies an integral part of the agriculture policies of several industrialized countries, most industrialized countries would rather commit to reducing these subsidies rather than seek an outright ban (Murphy 1999).

South Asian trade has been dictated by inward-looking import substitution policies. Sri Lanka was the first to initiate liberalization policies in the late 1970s. Sri Lanka's efforts set an important precedent for the pace of trade reform, and provided lessons for the rest of South Asia, which sporadically adopted trade reforms in the early 1980s. Intense trade liberalization policies were initiated in the early 1990s. Even though general trade reforms have made headway, agriculture reforms were virtually untouched, especially in Bangladesh, India, and Pakistan. In comparison, agricultural trade reforms in Southeast Asia and Latin America were comparable with the reforms in other sectors, such as manufacturing (Valdés 1999).

The key provisions or pillars of the URAoA are market access, domestic support, and export subsidies. The implementation of the URAoA brought some progress in market access, but this is still an issue. South Asian countries do not have aggregate measurement of support (AMS) commitments and made no notifications on "blue-box" support measures pertaining to production-limiting programs (World Bank–FAO 1998), and their use of export subsidies were within the URAoA provisions. India, Pakistan, and Sri Lanka presented a standard list of exempted "green-box" measures and S&D Treatment.

Market Access

Tariffs (customs duties) are a component of market access and the URAoA addressed three key elements: (a) the "tariffication" of nontariff barriers, (b) reduction of tariffs to reasonable levels, and (c) maintenance of current access levels for each individual product. Under tariffication, member countries are required to convert nontariff barriers during the base period (1986–88) into tariff equivalents and to establish a base rate of duty for individual commodities covered by the URAoA. The average reduction of tariffs after tariffication of nontariff barriers should be 24 percent for developing countries and 36 percent for industrialized countries. Industrialized countries had a time frame of six years within which to decrease their tariff levels while developing countries had 10 years. Minimum access should be established at not less than 3–5 percent of domestic consumption during the base period (1986–88). As a result, imports, previously subject to nontariff barriers, now have minimal access at a lower tariff rate. From the URAoA commitments made by South Asia it is clear that market access has made the most progress with applied tariffs below the bound rates (tables 1.1 and 1.2). This indicates that the region has honored its URAoA commitments on bound rates.

Table 1.1 Bound and Post-UR Applied Tariff Rates for South Asia

Country	Sector	Bound rate (percent)	Applied rate (percent) post-UR
Bangladesh	Agriculture	200	29.9
India	Agriculture	100, 150, 300	—
Pakistan	Agriculture	100–150	71.5
Sri Lanka	Agriculture	50	35.5

Source: Adapted from Ingco and Winters (2001).

Sri Lanka made significant efforts in the liberalization process, instituting a progressive tariff regime. Tariffs on agricultural products were bound at 50 percent on average in the UR (table 1.1). The tariff regime was reformed from a 13-band structure in 1990 to a 3-band structure in 1995. Import duty rates in 1995 were at 10 percent, 20 percent, and 35 percent, and were subsequently revised to 5 percent, 10 percent, and 30 percent across the board (Kelegama 2001). Import duties on agricultural commodities, however, are not part of the three-band tariff structure and justify the need for the agricultural sector to lower tariff rates. Products such as sugar, tobacco, cigarettes, and liquor are subject to ad valorem tariffs. These commodities are also outside the three-band rates. Furthermore, Sri Lanka offers preferential tariffs to a number of countries. These are applied to more than 120 items (the largest category is for live animals and animal products). Sri Lanka also provides duty-free access on approximately 300 items under a bilateral trade arrangement with India. Ad hoc waivers and exemptions are still a part of the agricultural tariff regime with their negative impact on the commodity market and domestic production.

In the past many agricultural products were subject to import controls such as licensing, and imports of some commodities (for example, onions and potatoes) were not allowed into Sri Lanka. Since the URAoA most of the import controls have been relaxed. However, paddy rice and maize are still bound by import controls in order to protect domestic producers.

Pakistan greatly enhanced its market access opportunities to other nations for their exports committing to bind more than 90 percent of its agricultural tariff lines. However, 6 percent of agricultural tariff lines remain unbound, in particular cotton, tobacco, alcoholic beverages, and pig meat (Ingco and Winters 1996). Pakistan set its bound tariff rates in the range of 100 percent to 150 percent (table 1.1).

Over time tariffs have significantly declined and are expected to decline even further from an applied rate of about 72 percent in 1996; the average tariff rate in the agricultural sector was reduced to 35 percent in 1999. The average tariff rate on live animals was at 34 percent, and dropped to 16 percent in the period 1996–2000. The rate for coffee, tea, mate, and spices

Table 1.2 Tariffs and Tariff Bindings by Percent Rates under the URAoA on Major Agricultural Imports, 1999–2000

Product	Sri Lanka Applied (A)	Sri Lanka Bound (B)	Bangladesh Applied (A)	Bangladesh Bound (B)	India Applied (A)	India Bound (B)	Pakistan Applied (A)	Pakistan Bound (B)
Paddy rice	35	50	0	50	0	0	25	100
Common rice	35	50	0	200	0	0	25	100
Basmati rice	35	50	0	200	0	0	25	100
Soft wheat	0, 20	50	7.5	200	0	100	0	150
Hard wheat	0, 20	50	0	150	0	100	0	150
Wheat flour	0, 35	50	15	200	32	150	10	100
Oilseeds	35	50	7.5, 22.5	200	42	100	10, 25, 40	100
Edible oils	10, 20	50	30, 35	200	22, 32	45, 300	45, 5, 25	100
Oil cakes/meals	10	50	15	200	42	150	25	100
Nonedible oil from seeds	35	50	45	200	32	300, 100	0	100
Coarse grains	35	50	0	200	0	0, 100	25	100
Coarse grain flour	35	50	15	200	42	150	10	100
Pulses	35	50	45	200	7	100	0	100
Live animals	10, 0, 35	50	7.5, 30	200, 50	0, 22, 42	100	25, 10, 15, 45	100
Meat	30	50	30	200	12	55, 150	15, 45	100
Hides and skins	10	50	7.5	200	0	25	0, 10	100
Leather	10, 20	50	7.5	200	0	25	15, 10	100

Product						
Milk and cream	30, 20, 5	50	45	200	0, 32	100	0–45	100
Other dairy products	50	—	—	—	32	0, 40, 100, 150	100	—
Vegetables	35	50	0, 15, 45	200	12	100, 35	35, 0	100
Fruit	35	50	35	50	42, 32	100, 30, 55	45, 0	100
Sugar	Rs3.50kg	50	30	200	0	150	10	150
Cotton	10	50	0	200	0	150	10	100
Wood and wood products	10	50	7.5, 15, 30	200	0–32	25, 40	0–45	50
Fish and marine products	0, 10	50	0, 30	—	12	NB	35, 45	NB
Spices: cassia, cinnamon, cloves	35	50	30, 45	200	32	100, 150	35	100
Spices: all other	35	50	45	200	32	150, 100, 35	0–45	100
Tea	35	50	45	50, 200	12	150	45	150
Raw tobacco	75	—	15	200	42	100	45	100
Coffee beans, processed coffee	35	50	45	200	12	100, 150	45	100
Cocoa beans, processed cocoa	30	50	45, 22.5	200	42, 43	100, 150	25, 35, 45	100
Flax, hemp	10	50	30	200	22, 32	100	25, NB	—
Greasy wool	10	50	0	200	12	25	10	30
Raw silk	20	50	0	200	32	100	25	100

Note: Rs = Sri Lankan rupees; NB = not bound.
Source: Athukorala (2000).

also declined, from 42 percent in 1996–97 to 24 percent in 1999–2000 and for cotton fell from 51 percent in 1996–97 to 26 percent in 1999–2000 (Khan 2001).

Pakistan has eliminated almost all quantitative quotas in the area of nontariff barriers except for a few agricultural items. In 1993–94 import licenses were abolished. Most of the export restrictions such as export quotas, the necessity of requesting permission from ministerial departments, and the requirement to export rice and cotton through export corporations have been removed.

Market access reform in Bangladesh began in the early 1980s with a reduction in import duties and was followed by a reduction in quotas in 1985 and a simplification of tariffs in 1986. The most intense period for trade reforms occurred in the 1990s with a movement toward lower tariff rates.

Bangladesh has significantly reformed both tariff and nontariff barriers over the years. In 1995 Bangladesh elected to set ceilings rather than undertake tariffication. The latter approach would have resulted in low or in some cases negative tariffs (UN FAO 2000). Bound rates were set at a high level of 200 percent for most of the agricultural products (table 1.1). The bound rate of 200 percent could send a misleading signal about the state of trade reform in the country (Dowlah 2001). Bangladesh has the potential to substantially reduce its bound tariffs in the next round. In 1999–2000, the unweighted average tariffs for all agricultural products declined to 20 percent from 57 percent in 1991–92. In a similar way, the import-weighted average tariff fell to 14 percent from 57 percent in the same period (Dowlah 2001). Even though tariff rates have shown significant declines, there is still a concern regarding tariff dispersion (that is, widely varying tariff levels across commodities).

Under the minimum access level provision, the current access opportunity is above the threshold for all commodities, except for potatoes and sugar. Tariff equivalents for potatoes were negative in recent years as well as in the base year and imports are not likely to increase with the reduction of tariff rates. The tariff equivalent for sugar was positive in both the base and in the current years. Import duties on major agricultural products were reduced significantly. The highest custom duty rate was drastically reduced, from 350 percent in 1991–92 to 37.5 percent in 1999–2000. In addition, the import-weighted average custom duty rate, as a proportion of import values, declined from 42 percent in 1991–92 to 16 percent in 1999–2000 (Dowlah 2001).

Compared with the other three South Asian countries, India announced exceedingly high tariff bindings, as high as 300 percent for edible oils and 100 percent for raw products (table 1.2). The bound tariff rates are ad valorem, except for two commodities where bound rates are committed in the form of specific rupees per kilogram (Gulati 2001).

The Indian government has expressed a strong commitment to reduce tariffs and remove nontariff barriers on agriculture to meet WTO's market access commitments. However, India would like to ensure that it has access to the rest of the world as well given that some industrialized countries, such as countries in the European Union and East Asia, are still protectionist. India agreed to adjust tariff rates for 3,373 commodities at six-digit Harmonized System (HS) level or commodity subgroups of six-digit HS level, which include agricultural and nonagricultural products (Gulati 2001). These commodities account for approximately 65 percent of India's tariff lines. Agricultural commodities (including vegetables, animal or vegetable fats and oils, and meat) account for only 20 percent of the 3,373 lines. The Vajpayee government's budget proposal for 2002–03 would reduce tariffs to two levels by March 31, 2004. Raw materials and intermediate products and components would face a 10 percent tariff while the tariff on finished products would be set at 20 percent.

Until April 1, 2002, India maintained quantitative restrictions (QRs) on some agricultural products under the Balance of Payment provision of the WTO. Although the Balance of Payment restrictions were "eliminated," imports in three categories remain prohibited: animal fats, items that require import licenses, and products where importation is controlled by state trading enterprises. The last group includes "canalized" items such as grains (U.S. Trade Representative 2002). In total, there are 2,114 products subject to QR. Officially, India is committed to phasing out QRs on all products, except for 632 commodities because of security and religious reasons (Gulati 2001).

All countries in South Asia did not subject their pre-existing QR in the agricultural sector to tariffication. As a result, they did not offer minimum access levels to imports under tariff quotas. It is important to note that agricultural tariffs were not bound before the URAoA, and QRs were justified under GATT's Balance of Payment provision (World Bank–FAO 1998).

Overall, as a result of the URAoA, South Asia made a significant effort in market access. However, bound tariff rates and applied tariff rates are still considered high and need to be reduced further. In addition, there is still evidence of the use of QRs, particularly in India and Pakistan, and these restrictions should be re-evaluated and phased out in the next trade round.

Domestic Pricing Policies and Incentives

Export subsidies and domestic support in South Asia are within the URAoA provisions and do not require any adjustments. In general, domestic policies that South Asia has adopted have contributed significantly to the underperformance of the agricultural sector and have hindered efforts to reduce rural poverty.

Developing countries have long emphasized the importance of the agricultural sector, and yet it is evident that their policies are often biased against the sector. Sources of bias mainly arise from sector policies (such as export duties, subsidies, and the use of parastatal margins) that result in keeping farm prices below the world price and in failure to adjust exchange rates to external shocks. Sector polices have a more direct (explicit) impact, and failure to adjust exchange rates against shocks has an indirect (implicit) effect. A well-cited study by Krueger, Schiff, and Valdés (1991) on pricing policy in agriculture between 1960 and 1984 concludes that, in the case of South Asia, direct intervention was positive on importables and negative for exportables. The intervention was negative for total trade, concluding that the direct taxation on exports dominated the tax on imports. Indirect intervention was the highest in South Asia, amounting to –32 percent.

The long history of taxing agriculture in South Asia was a consequence of import substitution policies to promote the industrial sector, and substantial resources were transferred from agriculture to industry. From the mid-1980s to the 1990s South Asian exchange rates went through a series of devaluations, and these substantially reduced the level of indirect protection to agriculture. Currently, all the South Asian countries pursue more flexible exchange rate regimes.

Protection can be measured by using aggregate measurement of support (AMS), nominal protection (NP) and effective protection (EP) rates, decomposing prices to account for changes in the international prices, changes in the NP rate, and changes in real exchange rates (Valdés 1996).[1] The main objective of this section is to assess protection in terms of the level of taxation or subsidization of commodities. These indicators measure the extent to which protection affects incentives indicators (see Appendix 1).

Policies in India

Historically, India's agricultural sector has faced the heaviest rates of agricultural taxation. This bias contributed to a 4.5 percent decline in agricultural value added growth rate in the period 1980–90 to 2.8 percent in 1990–2000. In recent years India has made considerable effort to improve sector policies and incentives. To deal with the issue of implicit taxation, the Indian rupee was devalued by 130 percent between 1985 and 1992 (World Bank–FAO 1998), and from 1998–99 to 1999–2000 the rupee depreciated by 7 percent against the U.S. dollar (IMF 2000), providing more incentives to export agricultural products. India also exempts exporters from import duties on raw materials and intermediate inputs and income tax on export earnings.

In addition, India permits exporters outside the export processing zones to import inputs free of import duties through duty exemption schemes

INTRODUCTION

and duty drawback schemes. The duty exemption schemes are put in place to make sure that these imports are used for export processing. The advantage of duty drawback rates is that they are easy to administer and reduce rent seeking. Although India has attempted to use export processing zones, these zones have not been successful because the zones are subject to bureaucratic impediments and are poorly located (Venkatesan 1998). India still applies export taxes on several products for environmental and cultural reasons and restricts exports of some products (for example, seeds, onions, and minerals) to state trading enterprises.

India's Special Import Licenses (SIL) on restricted inputs include concessionary tariffs and duty exemptions on raw materials. Furthermore, no corporate taxes are levied on export income under SIL, a provision that some have argued allows India to price agrochemicals in particular at below market levels. Following a WTO panel report, SIL programs were terminated on April 1, 2001 (U.S. Trade Representative 2002).

The URAoA provided for the reduction of domestic support as measured by AMS. India, as in most of the South Asian countries (except for Bangladesh), did not make any commitments to reduce its AMS.

The total AMS is calculated by taking the sum of the product-specific support as a percent of value of agricultural output and the nonproduct-specific support as a percent of value of agricultural output.[2] AMS is calculated on the basis of fixed external reference prices, under the assumption that India is a net importer of nonproduct-specific imports. From the calculated estimates of AMS during the period 1986–98 the product-specific support was negative for most of the crops in a significant number of years. The support fluctuated from –32 percent of the value of agricultural products in 1987, declining to –69 percent in 1992, recovering to –32 percent in 1997, and dropping again slightly to –42 percent in 1998 (table 1.3).[3] The AMS for agricultural products is considered negative, because domestic prices of most of the products are less than the corresponding world market price. This could also mean that the products are in effect taxed. The nonproduct-specific support amounted to 2.25 percent of agricultural produce in 1986 and 4.12 percent in 1997 (table 1.3).

In the period 1995–96 the nominal protection coefficient (NPC) for nine major crops (wheat, cereals, pulses, groundnut, cotton, soybean, tobacco, jute, and sugar) in India was 0.6 (WTO 1998).[4] This indicates that domestic prices were maintained below international prices, and this could explain the reason why AMS was negative in the 1990s.

Even though the nonproduct-specific support figures in table 1.3 are positive, the total AMS is still negative. Given the negative AMS, India has no obligations to reduce support commitments. However, India must ensure that the AMS is not greater than the de minimis 10 percent level during the implementation phase until 2004. Recent studies have also reported negative AMS in Pakistan and Sri Lanka (World Bank 1996).

Table 1.3 Aggregate Measurement of Support to Indian Agriculture, 1986–98

Year	Product specific	Nonproduct specific	Total AMS
1986	−34.29	2.25	−32.04
1987	−32.08	3.20	−28.88
1988	−35.54	3.32	−32.22
1989	−36.97	3.39	−33.58
1990	−31.78	3.36	−28.42
1991	−62.23	3.60	−58.63
1992	−69.31	3.46	−65.85
1993	−54.75	3.14	−51.61
1994	−43.27	3.40	−39.87
1995	−44.09	3.90	−40.19
1996	−45.84	3.62	−42.22
1997	−32.16	4.12	−28.04
1998	−41.89	3.49	−38.40

Note: All figures are expressed as a percentage of total value of production of selected commodities in Indian agriculture.
Source: Gulati (2001).

Policies in Bangladesh

Bangladesh did not escape from the bias against the agricultural sector in favor of its industrial sector. For a long period the agricultural sector was taxed and negatively subsidized by the government through high protection to manufactured products and through an overvalued exchange rate. The combination of import substitution policies, exchange rate controls, and tariffs adversely affected the agricultural sector.

In 1992 Bangladesh replaced its multiple exchange rates by unifying official and secondary exchange rates, and pegged the taka with a weighted basket of currencies (Dowlah 2001).[5] Currently, the country has moved to a more flexible exchange rate regime, with no restrictions on payments and transfers for current account transactions. While the effective exchange rate for exports rose from 38.5 percent in 1992 to 46.3 percent in 1998, effective exchange rates for imports fell from 63.8 percent in 1992 to 51.9 percent in 1996 (World Bank 1999). The ratio of effective exchange rates for imports relative to exports is often used as an indicator of anti-export policies. The more the ratio is greater than 1, the more intense is the anti-export bias. The relative incentives for production of import substitutes declined from 1.7 in 1991–92 to 1.3 in 1996–97. However, traces of an anti-export bias have remained, and the structure of trade policy–induced incentives is still skewed in favor of import substitutes.

Table 1.4 presents protection through indirect taxes. In 1999–2000, cotton and rice were the least protected products, with effective protection rates of –1.40 percent and –4.70 percent, respectively. Low protection rates, in particular during the post-UR period, show a continued bias against agriculture toward the manufacturing sector (Dowlah 2001). This could be because the agricultural sector faced high taxes on its inputs and its outputs.[6] Despite the bias against agriculture, Bangladesh did not have price subsidies or export duties on agricultural exports. Furthermore, by 1995 Bangladesh had managed to abolish state trading in all agricultural products, with the exception of rice, wheat, coarse grain, and oilseeds (Athukorala 2000).

Internally, there is rising pressure to increase the level of support for agriculture within strictures imposed by the WTO. Since only rice and wheat benefit from support regimes, the general AMS levels are quite low. One proposal would be to provide sectorwide subsidies on electricity. The principal constraint on creating new subsidies or increasing existing ones is the lack of budgetary wherewithal, a condition that seems unlikely to change in the foreseeable future.

Policies in Pakistan

Pakistan also practiced domestic policies that led to a substantial transfer of resources from the agricultural sector to the industrial sector. Since independence in 1947, Pakistan's main source of government revenue has come from duties on tradable goods. As a tax policy, Pakistan imposed import taxes on manufactures and export taxes on unprocessed cotton and jute (Krueger, Schiff, and Valdés 1991). The foreign exchange earnings from exporting agriculture commodities were used to purchase investment goods for the manufacturing industry.

During the period between 1960 and 1986, total protection on agriculture was reported as –39.5 percent. Direct and indirect protection were –6.4 percent and –44.9 percent, respectively (Krueger, Schiff, and Valdés 1991). In the 1990s there were some crop-to-crop variations of NP rates.[7] With the exception of coarse rice, major crops—such as wheat, basmati rice, seed cotton, and sugarcane—had low protection rates between 1990–93 (table 1.5).

This indicates that minimum support for these products was below export-import prices and so was, in effect, taxed. Between 1993 and 1994 rice and sugarcane had positive support. However, in 1998–99, sugarcane was the only crop with high protection among the selected crops. The low protection rates during and post-UR were a consequence of a history of support price programs that had been in place for many years, with the objective to keep producer prices stable (Athukorala 2000).

Table 1.4 Effective Rate of Protection in Agriculture in Bangladesh, 1992–2000

Item	1992–93	1993–94	1994–95	1995–96	1996–97	1997–98	1998–99	1999–2000
1 Rice	-8.00	0.90	2.40	-5.80	-5.70	-5.40	-5.30	-4.70
2 Wheat	-3.90	8.50	11.00	2.00	2.20	2.60	2.80	0.20
3 Coarse grains	-4.90	-4.10	-0.80	-0.20	-0.20	0.10	0.10	0.40
4 Sugar cane	68.40	71.30	14.20	14.80	15.00	15.20	15.20	15.80
5 Cotton	4.80	5.40	-2.00	-1.70	-1.70	-1.50	-1.50	-1.40
6 Tobacco	12.50	-0.90	10.20	11.80	12.10	11.10	11.30	12.20
7 Potato	58.90	60.40	48.80	36.70	35.70	26.90	24.50	23.10
8 Other vegetables	71.70	43.60	44.50	32.10	32.20	32.10	32.10	26.90
9 Pulses	19.90	18.10	17.40	16.90	17.00	18.20	11.30	8.30
10 Oilseeds	53.80	42.70	35.60	24.60	24.70	22.80	22.80	19.70
11 Fruits	58.20	60.50	44.90	40.20	39.90	38.10	36.30	33.10
12 Tea	82.70	85.10	66.00	48.70	48.80	46.40	43.40	41.00
13 Other crops	64.90	40.40	41.50	28.30	28.60	28.10	27.20	22.50
14 Livestock	74.30	54.00	42.00	33.20	32.80	28.80	28.00	24.80
15 Forestry	38.80	32.70	23.90	22.70	22.90	19.70	19.20	16.90
16 Other fruits	489.20	327.40	88.50	88.30	86.00	76.70	68.30	66.90
17 Edible oil	74.80	46.50	39.60	55.60	53.70	41.40	35.30	35.00
18 Sugar and gur	96.30	42.30	52.30	51.10	51.40	40.00	38.50	31.10
Average EPR	69.58	51.93	32.22	27.74	27.52	24.52	22.75	20.66
Coefficient of variation	63.30	70.59	131.26	115.99	117.66	120.93	122.68	116.89

Note: Only URAoA commodities, 1992–93 to 1999–2000. EPR = effective protection rate.
Source: Calculated on the basis of data obtained from Bangladesh Tariff Commission and Dowlah (2001).

Table 1.5 Nominal Protection Coefficients in Pakistan, Various Years, 1990–99

Item	Unit	1990–91	1991–92	1992–93	1993–94	1994–95	1997–98	1993–94 to 1997–98	1998–99
Wheat									
1 Support price	Rs/ton	2,800	3,100	3,250	4,000	4,000	6,000	4,865	6,000
2 IPP by agricultural prices	Rs/ton	4,818	3,547	5,019	4,385	4,697	9,574	9,625	7,455
3 NPC (1/2)		0.58	0.87	0.65	0.91	0.85	0.63	0.51	0.85
Rice basmati									
1 Support price	Rs/ton	7,075	7,700	8,500	9,000	9,720	77,50	5,912	8,250
2 EPP by agricultural prices	Rs/ton	11,988	8,796	10,833	8,171	9,743	89,68	9,100	10,403
3 NPC (1/2)		0.59	0.88	0.78	1.1	1	0.86	0.65	0.79
Rice coarse									
1 Support price	Rs/ton	3,750	4,000	4,250	4,528	4,875	3,825	2,932	4,375
2 EPP by agricultural prices	Rs/ton	3,983	3,503	4,498	3,709	2,960	3,867	3,725	4,640
3 NPC (1/2)		0.94	1.14	0.94	1.22	1.65	0.99	0.79	0.94
Seed cotton									
1 Support price	Rs/ton	6,125	7,000	7,500	7,875	10,000	12,500	10,575	14,375
2 EPP by agricultural prices	Rs/ton	10,362	10,996	9,935	9,486	12,408	21,471	22,502	20,182
3 NPC (1/2)		0.59	0.64	0.75	0.83	0.81	0.58	0.47	0.71
Sugarcane								1992–93 to 1996–97	
1 Support price	Rs/ton	385	421	440	462	515	875	508	875
2 IPP by agricultural prices	Rs/ton	577	581	481	458	641	713	1,195	706
3 NPC (1/2)		0.67	0.72	0.91	1.01	0.8	1.23	0.43	1.24

Note: IPP = import parity price; EPP = export parity price; NPC = nominal protection coefficient; Rs = rupees.
Source: Khan (2001).

Pakistan also maintained subsidy programs on farm inputs, such as fertilizers, pesticides, fuel, and others. These subsidies rose from 1 percent of total value of agricultural output in 1961 to approximately 3 percent in the mid-1990s (Khan 1997). In support of this policy, product-specific AMS in the major crops was 12,335 million Pakistan rupees (1986–87), –4,200 million rupees (1993–94), and about –6,435 million rupees (1997–98) (Khan 2001). The negative AMS provided support for the argument that Pakistan heavily discriminated against its agricultural sector in the post-UR.

In addition to these direct intervention policies against agriculture, Pakistan maintained a fixed exchange rate regime for many decades. This resulted in overvalued exchange rates, which led to the crowding out of exports. The Pakistan rupee went through a series of devaluations from the 1980s until the mid-1990s. Currently, Pakistan maintains a flexible exchange rate regime, and this has contributed significantly to its better export performance. In support of its export performance, Pakistan experienced a depreciation in the nominal real exchange rate from an index of 71.1 in 1995–96 to 56.8 in 1998–99 (IMF 2001).

In the pre-UR period Pakistan's economy was characterized by import substitution policies and overvalued exchange rate regimes. These characteristics were unfavorable to the agricultural sector. The post-UR brought about some progress in policy reform, although the reforms were piecemeal, and there continues to be some evidence of taxation in the agricultural sector.

Policies in Sri Lanka

Sri Lanka undertook substantial unilateral trade liberalization after the change in government in 1977. However, the policies tended to favor the industrial sector, leaving agriculture virtually untouched. Nonetheless, efforts to improve agricultural sector policies were more evident in the early 1990s. Total protection during the period between 1960 and 1985 amounted to –40.1 percent (Krueger, Schiff, and Valdés 1991, figure 1). Of the total protection, –9 percent was due to direct protection and –31 percent was due to indirect protection. In terms of indirect intervention, agricultural products were affected considerably, especially between 1977 and 1987, owing to an overvalued exchange rate regime. The net indirect protection was –44.2 percent in 1977 and –27.6 percent in 1987 (World Bank 1994).

The export duty on tea was reduced significantly from 29.1 percent in 1981 to 1.46 percent in 1990. The export duty on rubber also declined from 55.3 percent in 1991 to 24 percent in 1990 (World Bank 1994). To show progress in policy reform, export taxes on both commodities were abolished in 1992. In addition, any ad valorem taxes that existed were also abolished in the same year. After the abolition of taxes on plantation crops

Figure 1.1 Nominal Protection Rates in Sri Lanka, 1960–85 and 1993

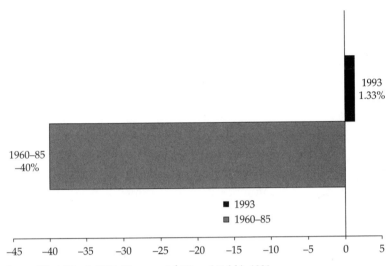

Source: World Bank 1996; Krueger, Schiff, and Valdés 1991.

in 1992, the only existing levy was used to finance activities such as subsidies to tea and rubber industries and smallholder farmers. These subsidies were seen as counteracting tax disincentives resulting from export duties and import taxes.

In 1993 the NP rate in agriculture was 1.33 percent (Kelegama 2001) (see figure 1.1), and the effective rate of protection in agriculture was 24 percent (World Bank 1996). In 1990 and 1993 there was zero protection in the plantation (tree) crops (appendix 2, table A1) while the nonplantation crops experienced positive effective protection of 35 percent. Compared with the manufacturing sector the overall agricultural sector was less protected. However, the gap narrowed in the 1990s. In 1993 the effective protection coefficient (EPC) for the manufacturing sector was 30 percent, compared with 24 percent in the agricultural sector.

To boost exports Sri Lanka put in place a fiscal incentive scheme to permit duty-free imports for investments of over 4 million Sri Lankan rupees (Rs) for new investors and over Rs 1 million for existing investors (Kelegama 2001). In 1999 the minimum investment requirement was revoked to grant smaller industries the same benefits. Further, items used in the agriculture sector, such as greenhouses, planting material, packaging material, and refrigerated trucks, were exempt from import duty. Sri Lanka established the Sri Lanka Export Development Board (SLEDB) and the Sri Lanka Export Credit Insurance Corporation (SLECIC) to provide institutional support for exporters. The SLEDB provides technical and skills development support to exporters and financial assistance under the agricultural products and rubber products rebate scheme. The SLECIC provides export insurance and guarantees services for the development of exports. Similarly, the development authorities for tea, rubber, and coconut also provide institutional support to the respective industries utilizing funds raised by export levies on each of the products.

In the UR, Sri Lanka committed to support its agriculture under the *de minimus* rule. For the most part these domestic support programs qualify as green box assistance for research and extension, plant quarantine inspections, and seed certification. The Food and Agriculture Organization notes that input subsidies for fertilizer purchases and irrigation services may total 3 percent of value added in the large paddy sector. In addition, plantation crops for export (mostly tea, rubber, and coconut) are assessed a small levy that funds a number of minor production incentive subsidies.

During the implementation of the URAoA, export subsidies and producer subsidies in the form of new planting and replanting subsidies were applied to a few agricultural commodities, including cloves, coffee, and nutmeg. Producer prices have also stabilized despite several currency devaluations. By 1998 the support was less than 1 percent of total value added for nontree crops (Athukorala 2000).

Issues of Interest for South Asia in the New Trade Negotiations

Apart from the traditional issues, South Asia is prepared to discuss other core issues in the new trade negotiations, such as state trading enterprises, food security, sanitary and phytosanitary measures (SPS), and trade-related aspects of intellectual property rights (TRIPS).

State Trading Enterprises

State trading enterprises that participate in agricultural trade are subject to discipline in the URAoA. Its provisions require that WTO member countries reduce market access restrictions, export subsidies, domestic support, and any other measures provided by state trading enterprises (Ingco and Ng 1998). The objectives of state trading enterprises include market regulation, price stabilization, and promotion of exports. State trading enterprises are government-sanctioned monopolies, with the authority to intervene in the purchase of domestic production, control output prices, influence distribution, conduct trade, and set producer and consumer prices (Ingco and Ng 1998).[8] These activities by state trading enterprises have the potential to create distortionary effects in the market (Appendix 3).

For South Asian countries, particularly India, state trading enterprises are an issue. For India there are several concerns about the Food Corporation of India (FCI). First, FCI holds a monopoly on imports of food grains, and does not allow equal opportunity to other competing agencies in imports and procurement (Gulati 2001). For example, FCI imposes levies on rice and sugar, which violate the principle of equal opportunity among competing parties. Second, FCI's economic losses are written off by the government and hence this represents a subsidy to FCI. In this context, under the WTO FCI could face some problems if its methods of operating were reviewed.

In Sri Lanka the Cooperative Wholesale Establishment (CWE) is the main state trading enterprise operating in the agricultural sector. The main goals of the CWE are price stabilization and food security issues (Kelegama 2001). Major imports by the CWE include rice, wheat flour, lentils, and onions. In addition to imports, CWE purchases local agricultural products under a guaranteed price scheme. Over the years the formal market intervention role of the CWE has declined, but it still has the potential to provide stocks of essential commodities in the event of food shortages. Another major state trading enterprise is the State Trading Corporation (STC). The STC, with its monopoly rights to import 90 products, currently competes with the private sector and is considered to play a significant interventionist role in the agricultural sector. Even though the formal market intervention role of state trading enterprises has been reduced, the STC has the potential to ensure that Sri Lanka has sufficient essential agricultural commodities in case of food shortages.

Pakistan has two export state trading enterprises: one for rice and another for cotton. The Trading Corporation of Pakistan is involved in the import of agricultural commodities. Pakistan did not volunteer to submit bindings to the GATT or WTO for import or export markups for the state trading enterprises (Khan 2001). The country claims that these state trading enterprises perform their activities on a commercial basis. However, subsidies for export of cotton were estimated at US$2 million in 2001 (U.S. Trade Representative 2002). Private entities have also been involved in the export of rice and cotton, as well as in the imports of other items.

Until 1992–93 the state trading enterprises in Bangladesh enjoyed a monopoly in importing food grains. However, in 1992 food grain imports by state trading enterprises fell to 3 percent from 94 percent in 1978 (Dowlah 2001). By 1995 most of the state trading enterprises' activities involved in agricultural commodities were abolished, except for their limited involvement in rice, wheat, coarse grain, and oilseeds (Chowdhury et al 1999). Even though state control is still visible in these commodities, private trading is also allowed. In the new trade round Bangladesh may have some difficulty in meeting the commitments made under the URAoA in limiting the role of state trading enterprises (Dowlah 2001).

Food Security

Food security is a sensitive issue for South Asia. For India, while this is seen as a distribution problem owing to the vastness of the country, there are several concerns. First, India believes that trade liberalization in agriculture has the potential to increase prices, inducing farmers to switch from cereals to cash crops, and thereby creating a shortage of food on a macroeconomic level. Second, to a certain extent fluctuations in the world price of basic food grains, such as rice and wheat, are likely to affect domestic markets, adversely affecting poor consumers and farmers. Finally, considering the size of the country, and the needs of its more than 1 billion people, if India were to enter the world market as a net food importer then world prices would increase, and if India entered as an exporter world prices would decrease.

In the new WTO round India advocates that countries should not rely on getting food from the world market. South Asian and other developing countries are encouraged to keep large stocks. India proposes that developing countries need to be allowed to provide domestic support to meet the challenges of domestic demand. These recommendations are likely to meet difficulties, since public stockholding of grains for food security would be subject to WTO discipline, and the application of domestic support is already subject to discipline in the URAoA.

In February 2001 India offered a proposal on food security at the WTO's Fifth Special Session on Agriculture. The proposal also focused on increasing flexibility with regard to domestic policy measures that govern food security, as well as poverty alleviation, rural development, and rural employment. India tabled nine specific ideas:

- Additional flexibility for providing subsidies to key farm inputs for agricultural and rural development
- Clarifications on certain implementation issues such as offsetting of positive nonproduct-specific support with negative product-specific support and suitable methodology of notifying domestic support in stable currency to take care of inflation and depreciation
- Maintenance of appropriate level of tariff bindings on agricultural products in developing countries, keeping in mind developmental needs and higher distortions prevalent in the international markets with a view to protect the livelihood of the farming population, and also linking the appropriate levels of tariffs in developing countries with trade distortions in the areas of market access, domestic support, and export competition
- Rationalization of low tariff bindings in developing countries, which could not be rationalized in the earlier negotiations

- Separate safeguard mechanisms on the lines of the Special Safeguards provision, including a provision for imposition of QRs in the event of a surge in imports or a decline in international process, as an S&D measure
- Measures taken by developing country members for alleviation of poverty and for rural development, rural employment, and diversification of agriculture should be exempt from any reduction commitments
- Rationalization of product coverage of the AoA by inclusion of certain primary agricultural commodities, such as rubber, jute, and coir
- Product-specific support given to low income and resource-poor farmers should be excluded from AMS calculations
- Flexibility enjoyed by developing countries in taking certain measures in accordance with other WTO-covered agreements should not be constrained by the provisions of the AoA

Food security in Bangladesh is also of serious concern because approximately half of the population in Bangladesh lives below the food-based poverty line (Dowlah 2001). As a result, the government continues to focus on food security and other related objectives, such as food self-sufficiency, stabilization of food prices in the domestic market, and improving food access for the poor. The government maintains a national food stock under the Public Foodgrain Distribution System in order to ensure enough foodgrains for the poor. In addition, food production and hence food security remain vulnerable to frequent natural disasters, such as droughts, floods, cyclones, and land erosion next to rivers and along the coastal areas. Emergency food aid is needed to deal with the consequences of these disasters.

As a net food importer, Bangladesh is concerned that WTO measures may lead to an increase in its import bill, because the reduction of export subsidies and production-enhancing policies may reduce supplies in the world market. Further, Bangladesh is worried that expected price increases in food and other agricultural commodities in the international market may call for adjustment in national food-security policies, such as in the public food distribution system or in consumer price policies, which could have serious political implications.

The key food security objective in Pakistan is to provide food products at prices that the majority of the population can afford. Therefore, the impact of liberalization on domestic price stability, mainly in sensitive food products, is of concern. In this context Pakistan recognized that it is important to monitor world market prices. Opening domestic agricultural markets to international trade may increase stabilization of the national market. In world markets production may shift from some countries with high protection to countries with relatively low protection. This may limit the negative impact of price variability on the purchasing power of the poor. A concern is that with production variability and with reduced government intervention in public stockholding, private stocks may not be able to meet the food deficit (Khan 2001). Another crucial area for Pakistan, as a net food importer, is the possibility of the rise in its food import bill due to trade liberalization if this results in increased prices for agricultural commodities.

In Sri Lanka the issue of food security is also important. Liberalization in agriculture has resulted in increased imports of major commodities in recent years, causing an increased availability of low-priced food items. Any shortages in production have been met by imports, so there is less risk of external supply shocks. Food imports, which have risen steadily since the mid-1980s, account for 90 percent of agricultural imports. However, food represents less than 20 percent of agricultural exports (UN FAO 2000). With the exception of tea, paddy rice, fisheries, and milk production, agricultural production has been declining over the last 10 years in almost all agricultural sectors. Some factors contributing to this decline include the rising cost of production, declining profit margins, inability to access high-yielding varieties of crops, population increases, and decreasing land availability. In the judgment of the Food and Agriculture Organization the surge in imports of food products is a direct consequence of policy changes made in Sri Lanka and in major food exporting countries. Moreover, the impact has been adverse enough to make food security a major issue for Sri Lanka in the Doha Round.

Sanitary and Phytosanitary Measures

Another area of concern for the South Asian countries in the new trade round relate to the implications of the WTO Sanitary and Phytosanitary Measures Agreement. The SPS Agreement recognizes that protection of health must be a priority. In general, the objective of these measures is to protect human, animal, and plant life, but unnecessary health and safety regulations should not be used as a mechanism for protecting domestic producers from competition.

Compliance with SPS provisions in India has been slow owing to the lack of infrastructure in food processing and related industries, the presence of weak legal and regulatory institutions that fail to ensure that products meet international SPS measures, and the inability to safeguard against the misuse of the SPS Agreement by importing countries (Gulati 2001). The issue of standards is of serious concern in horticultural products. India, which accounts for 60 percent of the world's mango production, has had problems meeting U.S. sanitary requirements. High pesticide residues have limited the export potential for India's grape and egg-powder exports. In 1999 exports of peanuts were restricted by the European Union owing to concerns of high levels of aflatoxin.

Bangladesh is concerned that SPS measures may have a negative impact on the export of raw jute, frozen food, dried fish, tea, vegetables, and other traditional products. Bangladesh has experienced problems meeting European Union standards for fish and fish products. Like most of the developing countries, Bangladesh lacks the required scientific equipment and personnel to carry out the provisions of the SPS Agreement.

Sri Lanka is still in the process of adopting measures to comply with the SPS provisions. Several issues have affected the ability of exporters and importers to thoroughly assess the legitimacy of national and international standards. One important issue is lack of information on prevailing SPS measures and their degree of consistency with the SPS Agreement. As a result, the estimates of the impact of SPS measures are often not reliable (Kelegama 2001). Like Bangladesh, Sri Lanka has limited accredited scientific equipment and significant financial constraints to acquire expertise to assess SPS measures. Further, the application of the S&D provision governing developing countries such as Sri Lanka has not been clear to the local exporters, and has only complicated the issue. To date, the volume of exports covered by SPS requirements imposed by trading partners has been comparatively low. As a result, Sri Lanka's still-developing SPS capabilities have not been a drag on exports. However, in the longer run, exports of fruits, vegetables, nuts, and spices will almost certainly be constrained if SPS measures cannot be more rigorously enforced.

Pakistan has few regulations and standards that meet international hygienic and quality standards. The concerns for Pakistan are both in the areas of imports and exports. It has been observed that exporting countries have taken advantage of the poor domestic and physical infrastructure to enforce standards. Consumers have directly suffered because of the poor quality of some imported foodstuffs. On the export side, Pakistan's vegetables and fruit have faced the issue of standards in the international market, specifically in the European Union, Japan, Canada, and the United States. By improving its ability to comply with standards in this area Pakistan has considerable potential to take advantage of the global market (Khan 2001).

Trade-Related Aspects of Intellectual Property Rights

The UR Trade-Related Aspects of Intellectual Property Rights Agreement came into effect in 1995. The TRIPS Agreement grants minimum standards for levels of protection to innovators of intellectual property in numerous fields. The fields that it covers are copyrights and related rights, trademarks, geographical indicators, industrial designs, patents and plant variety protection, layout designs of integrated circuits, protection of undisclosed information, and control of anticompetitive practices in contractual licenses.

India and Bangladesh are the only two countries in South Asia that have expressed a strong interest in addressing the issue of TRIPS in the new trade negotiations. Developing countries are considered disadvantaged in this area owing to "patent illiteracy" in comparison with industrialized countries. In addition, putting in place laws to protect plant varieties has been a challenging task for developing countries, and the implementation time has not been long enough for them. India would like to ensure that efforts by developing countries are not adversely affected by lack of knowledge and preparation to deal with these issues. India is ready to enact legislation relating to its indigenous plant knowledge to ensure that indigenous producers are adequately protected and no one preempts India in patenting what it produces. India is also interested in keeping track of the violators of provisions (for example, geographical indicators) to avoid undermining India's export potential. Furthermore, India has taken major steps toward a *sui generis* system to protect plant varieties and the rights of farmers, communities, and breeders. This system is expected to give incentives to breeders and private companies to conduct research. Pakistan has drafted a new law on plant breeders' rights that is currently awaiting legislative approval (U.S. Trade Representative 2002).

Bangladesh is concerned with the complexities and uncertainties associated with TRIPS. In particular, Bangladesh is keen to address the issues regarding the impact of TRIPS on plants and animals, plant variety protection systems, and food security and agricultural biodiversity (Dowlah 2001). The observed trend is that intellectual property rights seem to favor producers of knowledge and technology in industrialized countries. These producers acquire strong intellectual property rights involving important research tools and marketable products, leaving developing countries behind in terms of catching up with the knowledge gap, as well as with the adoption of technology (World Bank 1998). In this context, Bangladesh is concerned that by adopting the patent protection of plant varieties and seeds, producers would have to purchase seeds from industrialized countries at a high price thus affecting the local seed industry and raising the cost of agricultural production. This would translate into higher prices for agricultural commodities.

South Asia's Policy Options in the New World Trade Organization Round

In the new trade round the main policies for South Asia include the traditional issues as well as the new issues on the agenda. Table 1.6 focuses on the pillars of the URAoA: market access, domestic support, and export competition. Sri Lanka has plans to reform its tariff structure to a two-

Table 1.6 South Asia's Interests in Reform

Unilateral reforms

Market access
  Sri Lanka
  - Reform the tariff structure to a two-band structure.
  - Remove the remaining nontariff barriers (for example, the import controls on paddy rice, maize, and wheat).

  Bangladesh
  - Expand exports of nontraditional and processed agricultural products by improving market access in both industrialized and developing countries.
  - Reduce its bound tariff rates significantly below the current level of 200 percent, and eliminate QRs.
  - Liberalize its tariff structure further since the unilateral tariff liberalization did not achieve greater export income.

  India
  - Abolish all quotas and QRs on imports and exports around the world, with an exception for those member countries with balance of payment problems.

Domestic support
  Sri Lanka
  - Reduce production subsidies and credit concessions to the agriculture sector.
  - Address the need to recalculate AMS with reference to the base period of 1986–88, since the cost of production continues to change.

  Pakistan
  - Clarify definitions of eligible production and methods of measuring AMS.

  Bangladesh
  - Obtain subsidy exemptions for important agricultural inputs from domestic support commitments.

  India
  - Reduce the ceiling for total AMS to 40 percent, 30 percent for product-specific domestic support, and 10 percent for nonproduct-specific domestic support.
  - Change the commitments of domestic support for both total AMS and individual product-specific support.
  - Add both product-specific and nonproduct-specific support in the estimation of total AMS. Even if the product-specific support is negative, this must be done.

(Table continues on the following page.)

Table 1.6 South Asia's Interests in Reform   *(continued)*

Export competition
   Sri Lanka
   • Reduce the remaining export subsidies.
   India
   • Push for line-by-line reduction commitment on export subsidies if India is unsuccessful in getting all export subsidies removed.

Reforms by other countries

Market access
   Sri Lanka
   • Discuss the issue of tariff escalation and the use of nontariff barriers by industrialized countries.
   Pakistan
   • Enforce discipline of the calculation of tariff equivalents. The calculation of tariff equivalents and nontariff barriers were left to the members, so there is a need to monitor member countries' adherence to the guidelines and to reduce tariff peaks.
   • Press for uniform tariff rates. Since the tariff base levels are different across countries, the required implementation would leave a large dispersion of tariff rates and peaks among the member countries.
   Bangladesh
   • Increase liberalization commitments in the case of industrialized countries in the new round.
   • Monitor commitments on expansion of market access, such as tariffication of nontariff barriers in industrialized countries.
   India
   • Abolish all quotas and QRs on imports and exports around the world, with an exception for those member countries with balance of payment problems.
   • Substantial reduction in tariff bindings, including elimination of peak tariffs and tariff escalations in industrialized countries.

Domestic support
   Pakistan
   • Improve transparency and investigate the misuse of green box measures by industrialized countries.
   • Address the need to recalculate AMS with reference to the base period of 1986–88, since the cost of production continues to change.
   India
   • Blue box and de-coupled and direct payments in the green box to be included in the amber box to be subjected to reduction commitments.
   • Accelerated reduction in AMS so as to bring it below de minimis by the industrialized countries in three years and by the developing countries in five years.

Table 1.6 South Asia's Interests in Reform *(continued)*

Export competition
  Pakistan
  - Address shortcomings of the reduction commitments.

  Bangladesh
  - Monitor the reduction in export subsidies in industrialized countries.

  India
  - Propose that industrialized countries, in particular those in the European Union, completely remove export subsidies.
  - Prohibit savings in export subsidies in monetary terms or quantities to be carried over to the next year.

band structure, as well as to remove the remaining nontariff barriers. Sri Lanka is interested in raising with industrialized countries the issues associated with tariff escalation and the use of nontariff barriers. For Pakistan, interests in the new round include enforcing discipline of calculation of tariff equivalents, and the need for uniform tariffs in order to deal with the issue of tariff peaks. Since adoption of the AoA, several countries have raised questions about Pakistan's support notifications—in particular, the shift to calculating AMS in U.S. dollars rather than in rupees, the definition of what constitutes eligible production, and the system for arriving at the total AMS. Resolving these administrative issues will be important for Pakistan's participation in the new round of negotiations. The key issues for Bangladesh and India are further reduction of bound tariff rates, as well as elimination of QRs.

India has several interests in the area of domestic support. First, it wants to reduce the ceiling for total AMS to 40 percent, 30 percent for product-specific domestic support, and 10 percent for nonproduct-specific domestic support. Second, India wants to change the commitments of domestic support for both total AMS and individual product-specific support. Third, India wants to add both product-specific and nonproduct-specific support in the estimation of total AMS, even if the product-specific support is negative.

Also, the negative AMS has meant that the South Asian countries did not have to make reduction commitments in the new round. Sri Lanka is committed to reducing production subsidies and credit concessions to the agricultural sector. So far, the fertilizer subsidy is the most common subsidy. Pakistan's interests are centered on the transparency and misuse of the green box by industrialized countries. In addition, Pakistan recognizes that there is a need to recalculate AMS with reference to the base period of 1986–88, given that the cost of production continues to change. Bangladesh suggests that South Asian countries should obtain subsidy exemptions for important agricultural inputs from domestic support commitments.

Among the South Asian countries only India has made any notifications for export competition. Sri Lanka is committed to further reducing the remaining export subsidies. The Indian position is that disciplines in market access, domestic support, and export competition should be negotiated in the context of broad food security concerns and will require differential treatment for developing countries. Pakistan's focus is on the shortcomings of the reduction commitments. For instance, the European Union allows subsidies to cheese production through an inward-processing program, which involves exporting of a subsidized product and then exporting to another country. Bangladesh considers that the reduction in export subsidies in industrialized countries needs to be monitored. India strongly suggests that industrialized countries, specifically those in the European Union, should completely remove remaining export subsidies. Furthermore, India recommends that savings in export subsidies in monetary terms or quantities should not be allowed to be carried over to the next year.

MARKET ACCESS. It is clear that South Asia is committed to high bound rates and still maintains high applied rates, perhaps as an instrument to deal with balance of payment adjustments. In the new WTO round, South Asia is strongly encouraged to reduce the applied and the exceedingly high bound rates, reducing bound rates to the same level or close to applied rates.

South Asia has phased out most of its QRs. However, mainly in India and to a lesser degree in Pakistan, there are QRs on a number imports based on reasons of national security, among others. South Asia is encouraged to phase out the remaining QRs.

DOMESTIC PRICING POLICIES. There is a strong need for South Asia (India, Bangladesh, and Pakistan in particular) to change policies that are biased against the agricultural sector. Some measures include indirect measures, such as managing exchange rates in order to avoid real exchange rate appreciation. Some direct measures that should be reformed include duties on exports, taxes on imports, export subsidies, and parastatal margins. Although Sri Lanka has made substantial progress, it is still important for the country to discipline its level of subsidization.

STATE TRADING ENTERPRISES. The issue of state trading enterprises is a more serious one for India. For the FCI to adhere to WTO disciplines, India needs to come up with a new strategy to deal with the problem of food insecurity. One way is to introduce food stamps in urban areas and use the provision of food for work programs such as construction of infrastructure as a safety net in rural areas. India should also consider reforming other state trading enterprises, such as the STC and commodity boards.

INTRODUCTION   27

FOOD SECURITY. Food security is of considerable concern. However, suggesting trade-distorting measures such as the use of domestic support is not seen as the appropriate way to deal with this issue. In the new round, India, in particular, should focus on well-defined income policies, whether employment-generation programs, restructuring the current public distribution system in rural areas, or introducing inflation-indexed food stamps to deal with food security. On the trade side, South Asia may consider looking into establishing a futures market. Government intervention should be through tariffs, although they should be minimal tariffs, and not through direct purchase and stockpiling by government or state trading enterprises. To be cautious, South Asian countries should ensure that domestic policies do not clash with rules governed by the multilateral trading system.

SANITARY AND PHYTOSANITARY MEASURES. South Asian countries need to consider several options on SPS standards. First, countries need to have a better knowledge of the role of institutions such as Codex to help understand harmonized international procedures for evaluating consumer and environmental concerns. The Harmonized System with international standards, guidelines, and recommendations has the potential to eliminate barriers and promote trade. Second, large investments in infrastructure, and development of the expertise needed to carry out SPS provisions, are critical. Finally, South Asian countries may be encouraged to request a longer period for the implementation of SPS provisions, although they should take into consideration that a possible outcome of the negotiations is that industrialized countries will not accept lower standards.

TRADE-RELATED ASPECTS OF INTELLECTUAL PROPERTY RIGHTS. The policy options in the area of TRIPS are associated with geographical indications, capacity building, and protection of traditional knowledge. South Asia and other developing countries should request extra protection for geographical indications in products where they have a comparative advantage. Some developing countries have also shown a keen interest to accord similar protection in special products such as basmati rice, Blue Mountain coffee, and Darjeeling tea. Even though the benefits from this instrument may not be clear, this item should be discussed in the new trade agenda.

Most developing countries have implemented much of the legislation required by the TRIPS Agreement. However, there is a need to improve the capacity to implement services, such as patent and trademark offices, administrative and judicial courts, and customs procedures. In order to effectively implement TRIPS, considerable technical assistance is necessary for developing countries.

South Asia should propose legislative changes in the TRIPS Agreement to strengthen their right to protect indigenous, or traditional, knowledge. Braga, Fink, and Sepúlveda (1998) suggest two alternatives. One is for developing countries to form "community intellectual rights" that would set conditions to protect indigenous knowledge. However, community intellectual rights advocates have not come up with procedures to receive financial benefits from the use of indigenous knowledge. The second way is to establish "farmers' rights," giving farmers the legal right to have control over knowledge of plant varieties and to benefit from any profits from commercial use. These suggestions can be incorporated into internationally recognized legal instruments.

Conclusion

Efforts to reform the agriculture sector have been piecemeal. In the pre-UR era, all four countries of South Asia followed sector policies that were biased against the agricultural sector and favored the industrial sector. There was still some evidence of continued bias against agriculture in Bangladesh, India, and Pakistan during the implementation of the UR. Countries in South Asia, like most developing countries, were exempted from WTO reduction commitments on domestic support and export subsidies for development and balance of payment reasons. As a result, they were not required to act on the domestic support and export subsidy pillars. In the area of market access, South Asia committed to exceedingly high bound tariff rates and still maintains relatively high applied rates.

Sri Lanka has an impressive record in the area of trade reform when compared with Bangladesh, India, and Pakistan. Sri Lanka's trade liberalization efforts began in the late 1970s, although reforms in agriculture lagged. Nevertheless, in terms of market access, Sri Lanka's applied tariff rates are well below the 50 percent bound rate for all agricultural products it committed to in the URAoA. Although most QRs have been removed, a number of restrictions still apply to a selected number of products, still subject to restriction for reasons of national security. Sri Lanka believes that the implementation of the URAoA did not increase market access for its exports and the impact of the URAoA was minimal.

India has exceedingly high bound tariffs and QRs on imports. The justification for imposing QRs is based on balance of payment grounds. In the case of AMS, India's numbers are negative, which means that the sector could, in effect, be taxed, although India has no obligation to reduce its support commitments. Nevertheless, India appears better prepared for the next round of negotiations compared with the URAoA negotiations. Like India, Pakistan's efforts to liberalize have been greatly affected by high bound rates, several QRs, and domestic support for exports. With

Introduction

the exception of sugarcane and one or two other major products, most of the agricultural products are taxed.

In Bangladesh agriculture covers only crops and livestock. Fisheries and forestry are not fully captured by agriculture as defined by the URAoA. Nonetheless, Bangladesh has also fulfilled most of its URAoA commitments. However, bound and applied tariff rates need to be reduced further. In addition, there is still evidence of negative protection in agriculture (for example, in the cotton and rice sectors).

Although there is some indication of progress in the area of market access, the overall implementation scorecard for South Asia indicates that as developing countries, they were not required to take action on export subsidies and domestic support. As a result, it is likely that they did not fully capture the benefits from the implementation of the URAoA. In the new trade round, apart from the traditional implementation issues, South Asia is also interested in discussing issues such as state trading enterprises, food security, SPS, and TRIPS.

Appendix 1. Indicators of Protection

Nominal Protection

NP is regarded as the simplest measure of protection. This measure of protection is a simple estimate of the extent to which the price of the particular product has been affected by government intervention. One of the notable flaws with this measure is that it does not control for variations in input prices. NP is generally measured as the NPC of a product. This measure is defined as the ratio of the product's domestic price to its international price (Pursell and Gupta 1998). In simple notations, NPC can be expressed as

$$(1.1) \qquad \text{NPC} = P_d / P_r$$

where P_d is the domestic price of the commodity at the farm gate and P_r is the world reference price of what the producer would fetch under free trade at the same exchange rate.

If NPC > 1, then the product is protected. If NPC < 1, then the product is disprotected or in effect taxed.

For large countries like India, the weighted averages for each Indian state's NPCs are calculated to represent averages for all of India's NPCs. The average NPC is expressed as

$$(1.2) \qquad \text{NPC}_w = \Sigma_s \, \text{NPC}_s \, \psi_s$$

where

(1.3) $$\psi_s = P_{rs}Q_s / \Sigma_s P_{rs}Q_s$$

(1.4) $$\Sigma_s \psi_s = 1$$

and P_{rs} is the world reference price for the state, Q_s is the crop production of the state, NPC_s is the nominal protection coefficient of the state for the crop, NPC_w is the weighted average nominal protection coefficient for the crop, and s represents the states included in the average.

Effective Protection

EP of a product measures the extent to which the margin between the selling price and the cost of tradable inputs on the international market has widened or narrowed. This is achieved by combining the effective protection of the commodity and the protection of tradable inputs. In this discussion, EP is measured by EPC, which is defined as the ratio of value added at domestic prices to the estimated value added at world reference prices (Pursell and Gupta 1998). In simple terms, EPC is expressed as

(1.5) $$EPC = VA_d / VA_r$$

where VA_d is the value added at domestic prices and VA_r is the world reference price.

EPC is a more superior indicator of incentives to producers than NPC since it takes into account the effects of the protection of the inputs traded internationally as well as the protection of a product itself.

If EPC > 1, then the protection is positive. If EPC < 1, then protection is negative. If EPC = 1, then effective protection is zero.

As in the case of NPC, the weighted average of the state level indicators can be measured by using total value added at world reference prices in each state as weights.

Producer Subsidy Equivalents

Producer subsidy equivalents (PSEs) are part of AMS. They capture the overall effects of different types of governmental programs and interventions in a single number. This method is better compared to other tools like nominal or effective rates of protection since these often account for only a small proportion of the transfers between the government and the producers of agricultural commodities.

PSEs can be represented in different ways depending on the analysis they desire to undertake. There are two in particular, which are appropri-

Introduction

ate and suitable for cross-country comparisons (Gulati 2001). The first measure divides the PSE by the value to the producers and is multiplied by 100 to get the percentage PSEs. It presents the PSEs relative to the size of the farmers' gross revenue. The other is PSE per unit of output of a commodity where the PSE is divided by the level of production. This measure captures the subsidies provided by the government for the production of a unit of output. For simplicity purposes, percentage PSEs (%PSE) are considered rather than PSE per unit of output.

%PSE can be expressed as:

(1.6)
$$\% \text{ PSE} = \text{total transfers} / \text{value to producers} = \{Q * (P_d - P_w * X) + G + I\} / (Q * P_d + G)$$

where

Q = the quantity produced
P_d = the producer price in domestic currency units
P_w = the world price in world currency units
X = an exchange rate conversion factor
G = direct government payments
I = indirect transfers

Equation 1.6 means that %PSE could be negative if domestic price is less than the world reference price or positive if domestic price is greater than the world reference price. In addition, %PSE can be higher or lower depending upon the level of distortion created by increased price support. Trade distorting support contributes to lower world prices and inflicts a cost on producers in countries not protecting their domestic markets. Furthermore, even if government policies remain unchanged, changes in exchange rates and domestic production can alter %PSE. Also, all transfers do not have the same weight in the %PSE measurement. Transfers from price support programs and direct payments (G) appear in both the numerator and the denominator. However, indirect transfers (I) appear only in the numerator. The implication is that a country can lower or increase the %PSE without changing total transfers to producers merely by shifting transfers from indirect programs to direct payments or price support programs.

Decomposing Agricultural Prices

A common approach taken to assess the level of taxation or subsidization on a commodity is to decompose prices into changes in the international price for that commodity, changes in the nominal protection rate, and changes in the real exchange rate (Valdés 1996). Most of these studies focus on the evolution of agricultural prices.

(1.7)
$$P_{it} = \frac{P_{it}}{CPI_t}$$

where P_{it} is the nominal price of agricultural good i at time t, measured in domestic currency and CPI_t is the consumer price index at time t. P_{it} can be further expressed as

(1.8)
$$P_{it} = P^*_{it} E_t (1 + \gamma_{it})(1 + t_{it})$$

where P^*_{it} is the corresponding border price the country faces (for importables and for exportables) measured in foreign currency (US$). E_t is the nominal exchange rate (measured in units of domestic currency per US$) at time t. γ_{it} is meant to be a markup factor including transport costs and competitive profit margins to make the border price comparable to the domestic price. t_{it} is the residual after the markup and is meant to be the nominal protection rate.

Alternatively from equation (1.7) P_{it} can be expressed as

(1.9)
$$P_{it} = \left(\frac{P_{it}}{P^*_{it} E_t}\right)\left(\frac{P^*_{it}}{CPI^*_t}\right)\left(\frac{CPI^*_t E_t}{CPI_t}\right)$$

where CPI^*_t is the general level of the foreign prices at time t (U.S. consumer price index). The first expression in brackets is the NPC. It is a measure of direct price incentives resulting from sector policies. The second expression in brackets is the international terms of trade of the product. The final expression in brackets is the real exchange rate (RER) and captures the effect of economy-wide policies on agricultural prices. The direct and indirect incentives (NPC) is given by (NPC). It measures the effect of both the sector and economywide policies. The total effect on price incentives is the combination of the policy-induced incentives and the terms of trade movements.

Using equation (1.7) and (1.8) this can be expressed as

(1.10)
$$P_{it} = (1 + \gamma_{it})(1 + t_{it}) P^*_{it} RER_t$$

where RER is defined as the ratio of international domestic prices. Equation (1.10) can be rearranged as

(1.11)
$$\frac{P_{it}}{P^*_{it} RER_t} = (1 + \gamma_{it})(1 + t_{it})$$

The right side of this expression corresponds to a hypothetical transport cost and competitive margin profit, explicit export and import tariffs, and implicit import and export tariffs resulting from inefficiencies arising from the operations of the different parastatals involved in marketing.

Appendix 2

Table A1.1 Nominal Protection Rates and Effective Protection Rates in South Asia, Various Years (percent)

Category		Percent	Source
Bangladesh			
Nominal protection rate			
1991	Total agriculture	76.0	Dowlah (2001)
2000	Total agriculture	31.0	Dowlah (2001)
Effective protection rate			
1992–93	Total agriculture	69.6	Dowlah (2001)
1999–2000	Total agriculture	20.7	Dowlah (2001)
Sri Lanka			
Nominal protection rate			
1960–85	Total agriculture	–40.1	Krueger, Schiff, and Valdés (1991)
1993	Total agriculture	1.33	Kelegama (2001)
Effective protection rate			
1990	Plantation tree crops	0.00	World Bank (1996)
1993	Plantation tree crops	0.00	World Bank (1996)
1993	Total agriculture	24.0	World Bank (1996)
1990	Manufacturing	80.0	World Bank (1996)
1993	Manufacturing	30.0	World Bank (1996)
India			
Nominal protection rate			
1995–96	Wheat, cereals, pulses, groundnut, cotton, jute, and sugar	–40.0	WTO (1998)
Pakistan			
Nominal protection rate			
1960–86	Total agriculture	–39.5	Krueger, Schiff, and Valdés (1991)
Nominal protection rate			
1990–91	Wheat (import)	–42.0	Khan (2001)
	Basmati rice (export)	–41.0	Khan (2001)
	Rice—coarse (export)	–6.0	Khan (2001)
	Seed cotton (export)	–41.0	Khan (2001)
	Sugarcane (import)	–33.0	Khan (2001)
1998–99	Wheat (import)	–15.0	Khan (2001)
	Basmati rice (export)	–21.0	Khan (2001)
	Rice—coarse (export)	–6.0	Khan (2001)
	Seed cotton (export)	–29.0	Khan (2001)
	Sugarcane (import)	24.0	Khan (2001)

Appendix 3

Box 1.1 State Trading Enterprise Operations

Most Trade Distorting Operations

- Administration of price support schemes for domestic production through different price schemes
- Determination of the purchase price and/or sales prices of domestic production and imports
- Authorization or management of production and processing of domestic goods
- Purchases and sales of all or a significant percentage of domestic production based on the predetermined floor and ceiling prices; administration of marketing arrangements
- Monopoly on imports and/or exports
- Maintenance and administration of QRs and licenses on imports and/or exports
- Maintenance of global or bilateral agreed quotas, phytosanitary regulations, and restraints arrangements
- Restriction on export licenses

Least Trade-Distorting Operations

- Quality control of domestic production
- Provision of export-related support services such as storage, shipping, handling, processing, and packaging
- Promotion and advertising activities for both exports and national consumption
- Maintenance of emergency stocks of key staples

Source: Ingco and Ng (1998).

Endnotes

1. AMS captures the impact of different types of government programs and intervention in one figure. AMS is considered to be better than NPR or EPR, since the latter only captures a small part of the transfers between the government and the producers of agriculture commodities.

2. According to Gulati (2001), nonproduct-specific support is composed of subsidies on inputs (for example, power, irrigation, fertilizer, and credit). Product-specific support is computed as the difference between the applied administered price and a fixed external reference price of the base period 1986–88. The selected commodities include rice, wheat, maize, sorghum, bajra, gram, arhar, soybean, rape-

seed and mustard, groundnut, sunflower, and cotton. These commodities account for 60 percent of the value of output in the Indian crops. The value of production is calculated by multiplying quantity of production by applied administered price. The prices could be procurement prices or minimum support.

3. Such estimates assume that India is a net importer. If it is assumed that India is a net exporter of some commodities, in particular rice, the product-specific support would give different results. Regardless, AMS is still negative.

4. NPR = –40 percent.

5. Multiple exchange rates are one form of exchange controls. The idea is to enforce different exchange rates for each class of imports depending on the importance of various imports as determined by the government. In this context, multiple exchange rates restrict trade as well as distort price signals.

6. This measure of protection implicitly takes into account tariffs on each input.

7. Although this is not a realistic assumption to calculate NPCs, the study assumes that support prices are equal to market prices. The study is aware that market prices in Pakistan often differ substantially from support prices.

8. For details on the negative impact of state trading enterprises see Ingco and Ng (1998).

Bibliography

Adhikari, R. 2000. "Agreement on Agriculture and Food Security: South Asian Perspective." *Journal of Asian Economics* 11: 43–64.

Athukorala P. 1999. "Agriculture Trade Agenda in the WTO 2000 Negotiations: Interests and Policy Options for South Asia." Paper for the conference on Agriculture and New Trade Agenda from a Development Perspective: Interests and Options in the Next WTO Negotiations, Geneva, October 1–2.

———. 2000. "Agricultural Trade Policy Reform in South Asia: The Role of the Uruguay Round and Policy Options for the Future WTO Agenda." *Journal of Asian Economics* 11: 169–73.

Athukorala P., and S. Kelegama. 1998. "The Political Economy of Agricultural Trade Policy: Sri Lanka in the Uruguay Round." *Contemporary South Asia* 7: 7–26.

Bhagwati, J. 1993. *India in Transition: Freeing the Economy*. Oxford, U.K.: Clarendon Press.

Braga, C., C. Fink, and C. P. Sepúlveda. 1998. "Intellectual Property Rights and Economic Development." TechNet Working Paper. World Bank, Washington, D.C.

Chowdhury, N., H. Rahman, and S. Zohir. 1999. "Bangladesh Agriculture and the Uruguay Round: Policies, Commitments, and Prospects." In B. Blarel, G. Pursell, and A. Valdés, *Implications of the Uruguay Rounds Agreement for South Asia: The Case of Agriculture*. Washington, D.C.: World Bank.

Dowlah, C. A. F. 2001. "Agriculture Trade Agenda in the WTO 2000 Negotiations: Interests and Policy Options for Bangladesh." Paper for the Conference on The South Asia Workshop on Agriculture and New Trade Agenda in WTO Negotiations, Delhi, January 11–13.

Gorter H., M. Ingco, and L. Ruiz. 2000. *Export Subsidies and Domestic Support Measures: Issues and Suggestions for the New Multilateral Rules for the Next WTO Round.* Washington, D.C.: World Bank.

Gulati, A. 2001. "Agriculture Trade Agenda in the WTO 2000 Negotiations: Interests and Policy Options for India." Paper for the Conference on The South Asia Workshop on Agriculture and New Trade Agenda in WTO Negotiations, Delhi, January 11–13.

IMF (International Monetary Fund). 2000. "India: Recent Economic Developments." IMF Country Report 00/155. Washington, D.C.

———. 2001. "Pakistan: Recent Economic Developments." IMF Country Report 01/11. Washington, D.C.

Ingco, M. 1995. "Agricultural Trade Liberalization in the Uruguay Round: One Step Forward One Step Back?" Supplementary Paper for the Conference on Uruguay Round and Developing Countries. World Bank, Washington, D.C.

Ingco, M., and F. Ng. 1998. "Distortionary Effects of State Trading in Agriculture: Issues for the Next Round of Multilateral Trade Negotiation." Policy Working Paper 1915. World Bank, Washington, D.C.

Ingco, M., and A. Winters. 1996. "Pakistan and the Uruguay Round: Impact and Opportunities, A Quantitative Assessment." South Asia Regional Internal Discussion Paper. World Bank, Washington, D.C.

———. 2001. "Agricultural Trade Liberalization in New Trade Round: Perspectives of Developing Countries and Transitional Economies." Discussion Paper 418. World Bank, Washington, D.C.

Kelegama, S. 2001. "Agriculture Trade Agenda in the WTO 2000 Negotiations: Interests and Policy Options for Sri Lanka." Paper for the Conference on The South Asia Workshop on Agriculture and New Trade Agenda in WTO Negotiations, Delhi, January 11–13.

Khan, S. 1997. "Agricultural Crisis in Pakistan: Some Expectations and Policy Options." *Pakistan Development Review* 36: 419–66.

———. 2001. "Agriculture Trade Agenda in the WTO 2000 Negotiations: Interests and Policy Options for Pakistan." Paper for the Conference on The South Asia Workshop on Agriculture and New Trade Agenda in WTO Negotiations, Delhi, January 11–13.

Krueger, A. O., A. Schiff, and A. Valdés. 1991. *The Political Economy of Agricultural Pricing Policies. Vol. 2: Asia.* Baltimore: Johns Hopkins University Press.

Murphy, S. 1999. "Trade and Food Security: An Assessment of the Uruguay Round Agreement on Agriculture." Catholic Institute for International Relations, London.

Pursell, G., and A. Gupta. 1998. "Trade Policies and Incentives in Indian Agriculture: Methodology, Background Statistics and Protection and Incentive Indicators, 1965–95." World Bank, Washington, D.C. Processed.

Roy, D. K. 1991. "Export Performance of Bangladesh: A Constant Market Share Analysis." *Bangladesh Development Studies* 3: 64–81.

UN FAO (Food and Agriculture Organization). 2000a. *Agriculture, Trade, and Food Security Issues and Options in the WTO Negotiations from the Perspective of Developing Countries: Report and Papers of an FAO Symposium Held at Geneva on 23–24 September 1999.* Vol. 1: *Issues and Options.* Rome.

———. 2000b. *Agriculture, Trade, and Food Security Issues and Options in the WTO Negotiations from the Perspective of Developing Countries: Report and Papers of an FAO Symposium Held at Geneva on 23–24 September 1999.* Vol. 2: *Country Case Studies.* Rome.

U.S. Trade Representative. 2002. "2002 National Trade Estimate Report on Foreign Trade Barriers." Washington, D.C.

Valdés, A. 1996. "Surveillance of Agricultural Price and Trade Policy in Latin America." Discussion Paper 349. World Bank, Washington, D.C.

———. 1999. "Measures of Agricultural Support Policies in Transitional Economies: 1994–1997." *American Economic Review, Papers and Proceedings* 89:265–70.

Valdés, A., and A. F. McCalla. 1999. "Issues, Interests and Options of Developing Countries." Paper for the Conference on Agriculture and New Trade Agenda from a Development Perspective: Interests and Options in the Next WTO Negotiations, Geneva, October 1–2.

Venkatesan, R. 1998. "Policy Competition Among States in India for Attracting Foreign Direct Investment." National Council of Applied Economic Research, New Delhi. Processed.

World Bank. 1994. *Sri Lanka: Three Crops Strategy.* Washington, D.C.

———. 1996. *Sri Lanka: Non-plantation Crop Sector Policy Alternatives.* Washington, D.C.

———. 1999. *Bangladesh: Trade Liberalization.* Washington, D.C.

———. 2001. *World Development Indicators 2001.* Washington, D.C.

World Bank–FAO (Food and Agriculture Organization). 1998. *Implications of the Uruguay Round Agreement for South Asia: The Case of Agriculture.* Washington, D.C.: World Bank.

2
Bangladesh

C. A. F. Dowlah

Overview on Agriculture and the Food Sector

The agricultural sector employs more than 60 percent of Bangladesh's labor force and contributes approximately one third to the country's gross domestic product (GDP).[1] In addition, about 80 percent of Bangladesh's 128 million people live in rural areas, and nearly 90 percent of them are directly or indirectly involved in agriculture or agriculture-related occupations. Historically, agricultural growth has lagged behind the country's GDP growth, and the performance of the sector has been poor in comparison with many other Asian countries.[2] After an initial spurt in the late 1970s and 1980s, largely owing to a conversion to high yielding varieties of seeds and fertilizer-irrigation technology, agricultural growth stagnated in the early 1990s.[3] The crop subsector accounts for more than 70 percent of agricultural value. In the late 1990s, however, agriculture bounced back with better growth rates (table 2.1).

With a record production of almost 25 million tons in 1999–2000, Bangladesh currently enjoys near self-sufficiency in foodgrains (see table 2.2). Rice accounts for more than 60 percent of the agricultural value added and covers 70–75 percent of the total planted crop area in the country. Production of rice was steady in the 1970s and 1980s when it grew annually at 2.8 and 4.0 percent, respectively.

During 1990–97 rice production nearly stagnated as the average annual growth rate plummeted to less than 1 percent.[4] However, several successive bumper harvests in the late 1990s helped to raise the growth rate of rice production to around 2 percent annually in the 1990s. Wheat, another major crop of the country, and which currently accounts for almost 10 percent of total foodgrain production, also slowed to an average annual growth rate of 1.3 percent in the early 1990s.[5] Overall, annual foodgrain production in Bangladesh averaged 2.4 percent in the 1990s (table 2.2).

Domestic Agricultural Policies

Owing to the Structural Adjustment Program (SAP) and the subsequent Enhanced Structural Adjustment Program (ESAP), carried out during the

Table 2.1 Agriculture and GDP Growth Rates in Bangladesh, 1990–2000 (old and new series)

Category	1990–91	1991–92	1992–93	1993–94	1994–95	1995–96	1996–97	1997–98	1998–99	1999–2000	Average
With base year 1984–85											
Agriculture's share (percent of GDP)	37.6	36.9	35.9	34.6	32.8	32.2	32.4	31.6	31.6	26.1	33.2
GDP growth rates (percent)	3.4	4.2	4.5	4.2	4.4	5.3	5.9	5.7	5.2	6.0	4.9
Agricultural growth rates (percent)	1.6	2.2	1.8	0.3	−1.0	3.7	6.4	2.9	5.1	7.2	3.0
Crop sector growth rates (percent)	1.2	1.7	9.8	−1.6	−3.8	2.8	6.2	1.4	4.4	7.2	2.9
With base year 1995–96											
Agriculture's share (percent of GDP)	24.66	23.96	23.28	22.2	20.81	20.32	20.39	19.67	19.35	19.32	21.4
GDP growth rates (percent)	3.3	5.0	4.6	4.1	4.9	4.6	5.4	5.2	4.9	5.5	4.8
Agricultural growth rates (percent)	1.2	1.4	1.4	−0.7	−1.9	2.0	5.6	1.6	3.3	5.5	1.9
Crop sector growth rates (percent)	0.8	1.1	1.0	−1.7	−3.4	1.7	6.4	1.1	3.2	6.1	1.6

Source: Author's calculation from Bangladesh Ministry of Finance (2000).

Table 2.2 Foodgrain Production and Food Security in Bangladesh, 1990–2000 (million metric tons)

Category	1990–91	1991–92	1992–93	1993–94	1994–95	1995–96	1996–97	1997–98	1998–99	1999–2000
Gross domestic production	18.86	19.32	19.52	19.18	18.08	19.06	20.34	20.66	21.81	24.34
Annual growth rate (in percent)	0.60	2.40	1.00	−1.80	−5.70	5.40	6.70	1.60	5.60	8.30
Total imports	1.58	1.56	1.18	0.96	2.57	2.43	1.03	1.93	5.50	2.10
Closing stock on June 30	5.72	6.02	5.90	5.29	5.21	5.60	5.84	5.62	6.40	6.90
Foodgrain available for consumption	18.60	18.61	18.85	18.80	18.84	19.11	19.07	20.69	24.10	23.45
Total foodgrain requirement	18.84	18.17	19.51	19.85	20.19	20.54	20.87	21.21	21.09	21.89
Shortfall in foodgrain availability	0.23	0.58	0.67	1.05	1.35	1.42	1.81	0.52	2.55	1.46
Average per capita daily foodgrain available (gm)	459	451	449	440	434	433	425	454	520	—

Sources: Compiled by the author from several issues of the *Bangladesh Foodgrain Digest*, 1999; United Nations World Food Program, Dhaka; and the Bangladesh Ministry of Finance (2000).

mid-1980s through the mid-1990s, agricultural input markets in Bangladesh are now substantially liberalized. Reforms have been quite extensive in the areas of fertilizer marketing, privatization and deregulation of minor irrigation, and seed development and marketing. There is no denying, however, that with the famine of 1974 still in the public memory and the availability of food being a major determinant of political support, the government closely monitors developments in the sector.

The fertilizer sector, which played a crucial role along with modern high-yielding varieties in doubling rice production in Bangladesh, went through some fundamental reforms. Up to the early 1980s fertilizer production, pricing, marketing, and distribution were all extensively controlled by state enterprises. Fertilizer marketing was controlled by the Bangladesh Agricultural Development Corporation (BADC), which enjoyed a monopoly on imports and purchases of fertilizer from domestic factories. However, by the late 1980s, BADC withdrew its control, and an elaborate network of private sector companies took over the fertilizer marketing operation. But following the so-called "Urea Crisis of 1995,"[6] a major policy reversal took place. The government now administers the fertilizer pricing, marketing, and distribution system throughout the country. Production of fertilizer, however, is still a state-monopoly in Bangladesh[7] whereby six state-owned enterprises produce fertilizer from abundantly available and highly subsidized natural gas.[8] These six state-owned enterprises—all of which function at a loss—produce around 1.8 million tons annually, while domestic demand stands at around 2.2 million tons. The gap is met by imports.[9]

Sweeping policy reforms were also carried out in the area of minor irrigation since the late 1980s. The ban on imports of small engines was lifted, and all import duties on irrigation equipment were removed. Regulations on engine standardization as well as spacing of wells were also withdrawn. As a result a robust private economy now operates in the minor irrigation sector, which has not only brought down prices for irrigation equipment but also contributed to a substantial increase in irrigated area. The overall average growth rate of irrigated areas in Bangladesh was 4.3 percent during 1972–95, with 4.3 percent in the 1970s, 4.0 percent in the 1980s, and 2.6 percent in the early 1990s (Shahabuddin 1999). The total irrigated area of the country increased from 3.7 million hectares in 1996 to 4.1 million hectares in 2000 (Bangladesh Ministry of Finance 2000). Minor irrigation played a crucial role in the expansion of irrigation area as more than 90 percent of irrigation now takes place through this mode.

The seed sector, however, has experienced more cautious reform measures. Currently, a dual marketing structure operates in this sector. Major crops—such as rice, wheat, jute, potato, and sugarcane—are classified as notified crops, and their varietal development, evaluation, multiplication, quality control, and distribution are still largely handled by public institutions. The private sector's role in these areas is still negligible. In recent years, some legislation, such as the Seed Amendment Act of 1997 (passed in March 1998) and the Seed Rules of 1998, has widened the scope for private sector participation in seed production, imports, and marketing. The private sector can now import seeds of any crop other than the five notified crops, and seeds of notified crops can now be imported for trials. Also, subject to the seeds' adjudged suitability, the variety can be multiplied and the seeds sold. Furthermore, state-owned agricultural research institutes, which previously provided breeder seeds only to the BADC, are now allowed to provide them to the private sector as well.[10] Still, the private sector's participation in the seed sector remains limited mostly to non-notified crops, especially vegetables and fruits, because they cannot compete with the heavily subsidized operation of the public sector in notified seeds (World Bank 1997).

Liberalization of agricultural inputs has paid great dividends.[11] Much of the expansion in rice output came from a shift from traditional varieties to modern varieties and the expansion of area under boro rice.[12] Higher application of agricultural inputs, such as irrigation and fertilizer, also had a significant role in expanding rice production. Wheat also owes its expansion to similar factors. Production of other crops, such as vegetables and nonrice winter crops, have grown considerably slower, owing to many factors, including land constraints, problems of transport, marketing, and the availability of improved seeds. For details see World Bank (1999a, pp. 11–13) and Mitchell (1998).

Food Security Policies

About half of Bangladesh's population lives below the food-based poverty line and cannot afford a minimum dietary daily intake standard of 2,100 kilocalories. About one quarter of the population is ultra-poor, classified as those who cannot even afford 1,800 kilocalories, which is the bare minimum for human survival. Therefore, food, or lack of it, plays a crucial role in the agriculture-led political economy of Bangladesh. As a result, all governments in Bangladesh have emphasized food self-sufficiency, along with stabilizing food prices in the domestic market and improving food access to the poor. The lack of purchasing power of the poor, even in years of normal market foodgrain supply and prices, spurs the government to operate various direct distribution and employment programs, often with substantial assistance from both bilateral and multilateral donors. The government regularly maintains a national food stock, which is called the Public Foodgrain Distribution System, to ensure sufficient foodgrain at prices within reach of the poor.[13]

At the same time, a robust private sector marketing mechanism has also evolved over the years. The share of food production that is marketed rose from 10 to 14 percent in the 1960s to nearly 50 percent in the 1990s, and the market volume also increased sixfold (Ahmed, Haggblade, and Chowdhury 2000). Private foodgrain markets are found to be highly competitive, although collusion of a small number of traders in some geographically isolated regions cannot be ruled out.

Domestic procurement of foodgrain by the government is done mainly through purchases from traders at prices set in advance of the foodgrain harvests. The need for grain by the Public Foodgrain Distribution System, along with a desire to maintain farmer price incentives and a general mistrust of private traders, are commonly cited reasons by the government for the domestic procurement.[14] The estimated average cost of production, world prices, market conditions, and foodgrain needs for distribution channels determine the procurement amount and prices. The government, however, only procures several hundred thousand tons every year.[15] The public share of the rice market fell from 30 percent in the 1960s to 15 percent in the 1970s, 11 percent in the 1980s, and 7 percent in the 1990s. Procurement prices have normally been above market price levels that have benefited grain sellers to the government more but had little effect on the market price received by other sellers (Ninno and Dorosh 1998).[16] Also, the gradual cutbacks in the subsidized food-rationing system and public food procurement helped in removing impediments to market-determined rice prices.[17]

The Bangladesh government also procures grain internationally on a commercial basis. Prior to the rolling back of the role of parastatals in import trade in 1991–92, the government enjoyed a de facto monopoly in importing foodgrain (such as the Trading Corporation of Bangladesh, the Directorate of Food, and other statutory importers, such as the Bangladesh Food and Allied Corporation). Since then, the trade regime in agriculture has changed so much that the share of state trading agencies in foodgrain imports fell to 3 percent in 1992 from 94 percent in 1978. However, if all agricultural imports handled by government and semi-government bodies are taken into consideration, the share would range between 5 and 24 percent even in the 1990s (table 2.3). In addition, the government routinely procures foodgrain through food aid, which has, however, declined in recent years. Bangladesh received 1.07 million tons of food aid annually during 1992–97, which was 45 percent below the average amount received during 1987–92.[18] Also, the need for food aid has been declining as domestic production of foodgrain has been increasing.

Bangladesh's annual foodgrain imports ranged between 1.58 and 5.5 million tons in the 1990s, while its overall production ranged between 18.8 and 24.3 million tons (table 2.2). Although food production almost

Table 2.3 Role of State Trading Agencies in Agricultural Trade in Bangladesh, 1991–99 (import value, in US$ millions)

Fiscal year	Total agricultural imports	Government imports	Semi-government	Total government and semi-government	Percent of total agricultural imports
1991–92	516.03	36.84	20.63	57.46	11.14
1992–93	636.52	42.13	0.18	42.32	6.65
1993–94	613.58	35.30	0.18	35.48	5.78
1994–95	1,020.92	145.77	4.91	150.68	14.76
1995–96	1,220.38	294.25	3.04	297.30	24.36
1996–97	997.32	169.70	—	169.70	17.02
1997–98	1,253.08	125.42	0.12	125.54	10.02
1998–99[a]	1,432.86	182.91	—	182.91	12.77

a. Up to March 1999.

Source: Calculated by the author on the basis of data from the National Board of Revenue and the World Bank.

doubled in the last two decades, the country's food import bills still remain significant. In recent years, foodgrain imports constituted about 18 percent of its total import bills and 34 percent of its total export earnings, compared to around 26–30 percent of import bills and about 50–70 percent of export earnings in the 1980s (USAID 1999). Fiscal pressures in the 1990s fell in relative terms, but it remains formidable for the economy as resources cannot be diverted to alternative uses. Food subsidy in the 1990s ranged between Tk1.6 billion to Tk3.8 billion, excluding the Food-For-Education Program, one of the largest food-subsidized programs in the country.[19] In addition, the food security of the country remains vulnerable to frequent natural disasters, such as droughts, floods, cyclones, and land erosion by rivers along the coastal areas, which often result in emergency food shortages.[20]

Agricultural Trade Regime

Overall Trade Liberalization

As was already outlined, Bangladesh significantly reformed its economic policy environment, including the agricultural trade regime, during the mid-1980s through the mid-1990s. Extensive trade reforms were carried out to liberalize external trade and foreign exchange regimes, to promote the private sector, and to improve export competitiveness. The tariff reforms were wide-ranging, covering both tariff and nontariff barriers. Quantitative restrictions (QRs) on imports were significantly dismantled, and import procedures were deregulated. Tariff structures were rationalized by reducing average tariff rates and the number of duty slabs, by bringing down the statutory nominal protection level closer to the observed level, and by narrowing the dispersion of tariffs among similar commodities. The control list of banned and restricted items also was brought down to a minimum level (World Bank 1999c).

TARIFF REFORMS. Currently, Bangladesh has a cascading tariff structure in which tariff rates gradually increase with higher stages of fabrication, and final consumer goods are generally subject to the highest tariff rates, followed by intermediate and capital goods. Also, with continued reforms, the highest rates of both weighted and unweighted tariffs fell significantly. As table 2.4a shows, in fiscal year 1999–2000, unweighted average tariffs for all commodities fell to 20.2 percent from 57.3 percent in 1991–92. Similarly, import-weighted average tariffs fell from 24.1 percent to 14.1 percent during the same period (table 2.4b). In table 2.4c, the top customs duty rate was cut drastically from a level of 350 percent in 1991–92 to 40.0 percent in 1998–99, while duty rate slabs were lowered from 18 percent to only 7 percent. Table 2.4c also indicates how import-weighted average customs duty collection, as a proportion of import values, declined from 42 percent in 1990–91 to 14.1 percent in 1998–99. The top rate for average unweighted customs duty also declined from more than 88 percent to 20 percent during the same period.[21] Table 2.5 shows that the import-weighted average nominal protection rate also declined from 28.7 percent in 1991–92 to 20.3 percent in 1998–99, while the average import unweighted nominal protection rate fell from more than 67 percent to 27 percent during the same period (table 2.5). Table 2.5 also shows how the average effective protection rate (EPR) across all sectors declined from 75.7 percent in 1992–93 to 24.5 percent in 1999–2000.

The structure of customs duty was also simplified by reducing multiple customs duty rates of the same Harmonized System (HS) codes into fewer rates, and thus economywide the share of a single customs duty rate for the same HS four-digit code increased from 63 percent in 1991 to almost 75 percent in 1999–2000, and the multiple customs duty rates declined from more than 36 percent to 26 percent during the same period (table 2.6). At the same time, the number of QRs for the HS four-digit codes banned and/or restricted owing to trade or nontrade reasons was lowered to 124 by 1999 from 315 in 1989–90 (table 2.7). In the meantime, the procedures of import valuation have also been reformed, and from fiscal year 1999–2000 preshipment inspection for imports has been made mandatory.[22]

Table 2.4a Bangladesh Tariff Structures, Average Measures, and Dispersions, 1991–2000: Unweighted Averages

Commodity categories	FY92	FY93	FY94	FY95	FY96	FY97	FY98	FY99
Primary commodity	55.22	47.74	34.89	31.61	24.55	22.28	21.89	21.34
Capital goods	45.00	38.68	26.16	13.87	12.30	12.48	12.10	12.26
Intermediate inputs	49.51	41.63	31.80	23.23	20.15	19.61	19.15	18.93
Final consumer goods	80.29	63.56	49.89	38.62	33.69	32.30	30.63	29.02
Total	57.30	47.37	36.02	25.92	22.32	21.47	20.69	20.20

Table 2.4b Bangladesh Tariff Structures, Average Measures, and Dispersions, 1991–2000: Import-Weighted Averages

Commodity categories	FY92	FY93	FY94	FY95	FY96	FY97	FY98	FY99
Primary commodity	23.37	23.21	27.15	17.26	13.17	16.34	13.57	10.36
Capital goods	18.71	18.46	16.15	12.51	9.54	10.43	8.23	8.57
Intermediate inputs	24.14	23.65	22.87	26.26	22.65	22.16	21.28	20.36
Final consumer goods	47.27	36.47	36.68	26.45	24.09	23.13	20.14	18.02
Total	24.14	23.56	24.09	20.79	17.01	17.99	16.05	14.13

Table 2.4c Bangladesh Tariff Structures, Average Measures, and Dispersions, 1990–2000: Average Tariffs and Dispersions

Descriptions	FY91	FY92	FY93	FY94	FY95	FY96	FY97	FY98	FY99
Average customs duty (unweighted)	88.60	56.68	46.82	35.83	25.44	22.15	21.49	20.69	20.20
Average customs duty (collection)	42.10	24.14	23.56	24.09	20.79	17.01	17.99	16.05	14.13
Dispersion (coefficient of variation)	72.00	71.88	65.57	68.22	75.63	74.40	75.74	74.40	72.40
IDSC	—	—	—	—	—	—	—	2.50	2.50
Average license fee (collection)	—	1.20	1.44	1.48	1.46	1.22	1.28	1.25	1.08
Top customs duty rate	350	350	300	300	60	50	45	42.5	40
Number of tariff slabs	18	18	15	12	6	7	7	7	7

Note: IDSC = infrastructure development surcharge.
Sources: National Board of Revenue and the World Bank (1999c).

Table 2.5 Nominal Tariff and Effective Protection Rates in Bangladesh, 1991–2000

Fiscal year	Unweighted protection rate (all sectors)	Weighted protection rate (all sectors)	Unweighted protection rate in agriculture	Weighted protection rate in agriculture	Average effective rate of protection (all sectors)[a]	Average effective rate of protection (agricultural sector)[a]
1991–92	67.35	28.67	76.45	33.57	—	—
1992–93	55.37	28.23	61.87	31.55	75.71	69.58
1993–94	42.43	29.28	45.75	33.49	56.65	51.93
1994–95	31.32	26.12	40.98	19.20	40.57	32.22
1995–96	27.11	22.34	35.07	15.32	33.02	27.74
1996–97	26.85	24.02	34.22	20.39	32.43	27.52
1997–98	28.23	23.89	36.22	18.03	28.55	24.52
1998–99	27.20	20.31	33.94	12.38	26.77	22.75
1999–00	24.10	—	30.93		24.47	20.66

— Not available.

a. See appendix tables A2.2 and A2.3 for commodities included in effective exchange rate calculation for agricultural and all other sectors and for their standard deviation as well as dispersion rates.

Note: See appendix table A2.2 for operative tariff rates of agricultural products.

Source: Compiled from World Bank estimates based on National Board of Revenue data.

Table 2.6 Structure of HS Four-Digit Level Multiple Customs Duty Rates in Bangladesh, 1991–2000

Customs duty rates	Fiscal year									
	1991–92	1992–93	1993–94	1994–95	1995–96	1996–97	1997–98	1998–99	1999–2000
Single	785	801	933	934	900	877	868	873	925
	(63.2)	(64.5)	(75.1)	(75.2)	(72.5)	(70.6)	(69.9)	(70.3)	(74.5)
Multiple	457	441	309	308	342	365	374	369	317
	(36.8)	(35.5)	(24.9)	(24.8)	(27.5)	(29.4)	(30.1)	(29.7)	(25.5)
Total	1,242	1,242	1,242	1,242	1,242	1,242	1,242	1,242	1,242
Structure of HS four-digit level multiple customs duty rates (agricultural goods)									
Single	101	106	114	121	122	118	118	118	117
	(70.1)	(73.6)	(79.2)	(84.0)	(84.7)	(81.9)	(81.9)	(81.9)	(81.2)
Multiple	43	38	30	23	22	26	26	26	27
	(29.9)	(26.4)	(20.8)	(15.9)	(15.3)	(18.1)	(18.1)	(18.1)	(18.7)
Total	144	144	144	144	144	144	144	144	144

Note: HS = Harmonized System. All sectors, parentheses show percent of total HS four-digit code.
Source: Compiled from the National Board of Revenue and World Bank data sources.

Table 2.7 Removal of Quantitative Restrictions, Various Years, 1989–2002

Fiscal year	Total	Trade reasons		Nontrade	
		Banned	Restricted	Mixed	Reasons
1989–90	315	135	66	52	62
1990–91	239	93	47	39	60
1995–97	120	5	6	17	92
1997–2002	124	5	6	17	96

Note: Number of Harmonized System four-digit codes.
Source: Bangladesh Ministry of Commerce, import policy orders for various years.

Although Bangladesh has reduced tariff rates steadily, there is still evidence of "water in the tariff." First of all, the dispersion of tariff rates remains very high relative to the average rate, and the reduction in the EPR is not significant. As table 2.5 indicates, average EPR declined from 75.7 percent in 1992–93 to 24.5 percent in 1999–2000, which is still high. Second, reduction in the top rates of customs duty for final consumer goods was not followed by simultaneous and proportional adjustment in intermediate and capital goods (table 2.4c). Third, the tariff schedule was simplified by reducing the number of tariff rates applied to a particular product, while the proportion of tariff lines with multiple rates at the HS-4 digit level remained substantial (table 2.6). Fourth, the divergence between unweighted average tariffs and collection rates remains high, indicating a continuation of end-user concessions (table 2.4c).[23] And finally, trade reforms have not eradicated the strong incentives for smuggling, especially across the long porous Indian border.[24]

EXCHANGE RATE REFORMS. Bangladesh also carried out far-reaching reforms in its exchange rate regime beginning in the early 1990s. In 1992, multiple exchange rates were replaced by unifying official and secondary exchange rates and pegging the taka with a weighted currency basket. Currently, Bangladesh pursues a relatively flexible exchange rate policy and maintains no restrictions on payments and transfers for current account international transactions. Although the taka has been devalued several times in recent years, the real effective exchange rate continues to appreciate.[25] Moreover, despite the basic flexibility in the exchange rate determination, rigidities stemming from trade control measures lead to some misalignment in the official exchange rate. Table 2.8 shows the extent of distortions in the exchange rate by comparing the official exchange rate with the estimated free-trade equilibrium exchange rate, and table 2.9 indicates the effective exchange rate on import substitutes during the 1990s.[26]

Table 2.8 Estimates of Equilibrium (Shadow) Exchange Rates in Bangladesh During Base Period, Various Years, 1985–88 and 1994–97

Period	Official exchange rate	Equilibrium (shadow) exchange rate	
		Tax approach	Elasticity approach
Base			
1985–86	29.89	36.50 (0.819)	35.12 (0.851)
1986–87	30.63	37.35 (0.820)	33.95 (0.902)
1987–88	31.24	38.10 (0.820)	35.91 (0.870)
Average	30.58	37.32 (0.820)	34.99 (0.876)
Current			
1994–95	40.20	46.05 (0.873)	46.21 (0.870)
1995–96	40.90	45.95 (0.890)	48.69 (0.840)
1996–97	42.70	47.39 (0.901)	46.98 (0.909)
Average	41.27	46.46 (0.808)	47.29 (0.873)

Note: The figures in parentheses represent the implicit standard conversion factors used to convert official exchange rates into equilibrium (shadow) exchange rates.
Source: Shahabuddin (1999).

Agricultural Trade Liberalization

Viewed from the standpoint of the Uruguay Round (UR) Agreement on Agriculture (AoA), the share of agriculture in the overall trade volume of Bangladesh has been declining (table 2.10).[27] While in the 1980s agriculture constituted around 21 percent of the total trade of Bangladesh, during 1995–97 that share dropped to around 12 percent. The share of agricultural imports and exports, in the overall trade of the country, also fell from 18.6 percent for agricultural imports and 8.6 percent for exports during 1980–84 and to 11.9 percent for imports and 1.5 percent for exports during 1995–97. But as a part of agricultural trade alone, agricultural imports increased from 90 percent in the early 1980s to more than 94 percent in the late 1990s. Agricultural trade, in terms of both exports and imports, is dominated by primary products (more than 61 percent of imports and more than 97 percent of exports). Tables 2.11 and 2.12 show average annual growth rates of imports and exports of agricultural products in the 1980s through the 1990s, reflecting a sluggish growth of imports and an absolute decline in exports in the 1990s. Tables 2.13 and 2.14 show statistical trend growth rates of agricultural products—both primary and processed products—covering the same period, along with R^2 and the standard errors of the growth coefficients.

In the 1990s, as table 2.6 indicates, the share of a single customs duty rate for agricultural goods increased from 70 percent to 81 percent. At the

Table 2.9 Effective Exchange Rates on Import Substitutes, Various Years, 1991–99

Fiscal year	Imports in million Tk (1)	Weighted protective rates			Overall protective rate (percent) (5)	Nominal exchange rate in Tk (6)	EERm (7)	EERm/ EERx (8)	EERx/ EERm (8)
		CD + LF + IDS (percent) (2)	SD (percent) (3)	VAT (percent) (4)					
1991–92	100,812.9	25.34	0.00	3.32	28.67	38.15	49.09	1.274	0.785
1992–93	107,231.3	25.00	0.00	3.23	28.23	39.14	50.19	1.263	0.791
1993–94	112,675.4	25.57	0.00	3.71	29.28	40.00	51.71	1.278	0.783
1994–95	161,236.2	22.25	0.72	3.15	26.12	40.20	50.70	1.251	0.799
1995–96	201,046.0	18.24	1.40	2.70	22.34	40.84	49.96	1.211	0.826
1996–97	204,852.5	19.32	1.72	2.98	24.02	42.70	52.96	1.225	0.816
1997–98	233,013.8	19.34	1.80	2.75	23.89	45.46	56.32	1.221	0.819
1998–99	260,708.7	17.06	1.14	2.11	20.31	48.50	58.35	1.186	0.843

Notes: CD = customs duty; EERm = effective exchange rate for imports; EERx = exchange rate for exports; IDS = infrastructure development surcharge; LF = license fees; SD = special duty; Tk = taka; VAT = value-added tax.

Source: Based on World Bank estimates.

Table 2.10 Selective Features of Bangladesh's Trade in Agricultural Products, 1980–97

Category	1980–84	1985–89	1990–94	1995–97
Total agricultural trade (as percent of total trade)	20.88	22.77	12.81	12.54
Agricultural imports (as percent of total trade)	18.64	20.87	11.83	11.92
Agricultural imports (as percent of total agricultural trade)	90.23	91.66	92.35	94.26
Agricultural imports (as percent of total imports)	25.16	29.48	18.88	19.52
Agricultural exports (as percent total exports)	8.65	6.49	2.64	1.59
Imports of primary agricultural products (as percent of agricultural imports)	66.16	53.34	60.23	61.55
Exports of primary agricultural products (as percent of agricultural exports)	93.16	97.21	95.80	97.50

Note: See appendix table A2.1 for the classification of products. The division of the agricultural products into primary and processed products has been made on the basis of OECD classification guidelines as provided in the Standard International Trade Classification (SITC), Revision 2, and Bangladesh's trade statistics that follow the Bangladesh Standard Trade Classification Code System, which is essentially based on the SITC codes.

same time, both weighted and unweighted tariff rates fell for agricultural products. As table 2.5 indicates, the average unweighted nominal protection level in agriculture fell from more than 76 percent in 1991–92 to 31 percent in 1999–2000, and the average weighted protection rate fell from more than 33 percent in 1991–92 to 12 percent in 1998–99. Also, average effective protection rates for the URAoA-defined agricultural commodities fell from 69.6 percent in 1992–93 to 20.7 percent in 1999–2000. The existing exchange rate regime, however, appears to have created negative incentives for a few agricultural products.[28]

The Export Regime

Bangladesh is officially committed to an export-oriented growth strategy. Several export promotion schemes provide Bangladesh exporters with

Table 2.11 Average Growth Rates of Imports of Agricultural Products, 1980–97

Product group	Year and period annual average (million US$)				Average annual growth (percent)				Percent of total			
	1980–84	1985–89	1990–94	1995–97	1985–89 over 1980–84	1990–94 over 1985–89	1990–94 over 1980–84	1995–97 over 1990–94	1980–84	1985–89	1990–94	1995–97
Primary Agricultural Products												
Live animals	0.004	0.123	0.119	1.651	100.32	–0.61	41.10	92.86	0.000	0.005	0.004	0.045
Meat	0.001	1.870	1.390	1.164	375.72	–5.75	111.75	–4.35	0.000	0.072	0.041	0.032
Milk and cream, fresh	0.000	0.009	0.000	0.036	n.e.	–78.06	n.e.	n.e.	0.000	0.000	0.000	0.001
Eggs in shell	0.000	0.004	0.939	0.348	n.e.	197.41	n.e.	–21.99	0.000	0.000	0.028	0.009
Plants, flowers, bulbs, tubers	0.000	0.001	0.001	0.007	n.e.	7.55	n.e.	59.89	0.000	0.000	0.000	0.000
Vegetables, fresh, chilled, etc.	1.844	11.957	45.299	21.632	45.34	30.52	37.73	–16.87	0.091	0.461	1.330	0.586
Fruits and nuts, fresh/chilled/dried	7.924	12.871	14.560	15.296	10.19	2.50	6.27	1.24	0.391	0.496	0.428	0.414
Coffee, tea, mate, and spices	4.700	10.461	24.222	10.163	17.35	18.28	17.82	–19.52	0.232	0.403	0.711	0.275
Cereal, cereal products, unmilled	233.375	305.272	179.586	226.367	5.52	–10.07	–2.59	5.96	11.513	11.773	5.274	6.129
Oilseeds and oleaginous fruits	7.861	14.572	38.005	46.411	13.14	21.13	17.07	5.12	0.388	0.562	1.116	1.257
Raw sugar and honey	0.006	0.339	5.659	22.856	126.62	75.63	99.51	41.76	0.000	0.013	0.166	0.619
Tobacco, unmanufactured	0.939	1.787	5.709	7.684	13.74	26.15	19.78	7.71	0.046	0.069	0.168	0.208
Raw cotton	80.763	48.565	71.640	90.170	–9.67	8.09	–1.19	5.92	3.984	1.873	2.104	2.441
Total imports, primary products	337.41	407.83	387.13	443.78	3.86	–1.04	1.38	3.47	16.645	15.728	11.368	12.015
Processed Agricultural Products												
Meat, processed	0.024	0.001	0.000	0.011	–42.75	–30.03	–36.71	155.36	0.001	0.000	0.000	0.000
Dairy products, other than fresh milk	32.347	74.660	72.327	34.125	18.21	–0.63	8.38	–17.12	1.596	2.879	2.124	0.924

Eggs not in shell and egg yolks	0.001	0.204	0.023	0.002	222.07	-35.27	44.38	-45.27	0.000	0.008	0.001	0.000
Vegetables, preserved or prepared	0.380	0.430	0.152	0.188	2.47	-18.79	-8.78	5.47	0.019	0.017	0.004	0.005
Fruits and nuts, preserved/prepared	0.032	1.862	14.850	16.452	125.28	51.48	84.73	2.59	0.002	0.072	0.436	0.445
Cereal products, other	1.856	4.250	0.574	1.309	18.02	-33.00	-11.07	22.88	0.092	0.164	0.017	0.035
Animal or vegetable fats or oils excluding	117.825	175.773	146.138	212.273	8.33	-3.63	2.18	9.78	5.813	6.779	4.291	5.747
Sugar and sugar preparations	16.346	96.648	13.634	2.823	42.68	-32.51	-1.87	-32.42	0.806	3.727	0.397	0.076
Coffee, tea, and mate preparations	0.036	0.052	0.020	0.087	7.72	-16.92	-5.40	43.76	0.002	0.002	0.001	0.002
Food products, n.e.s.	0.660	1.676	4.085	4.131	20.47	19.51	19.99	0.28	0.033	0.065	0.120	0.112
Animal feed, excluding unmilled cereals	1.241	1.250	2.251	4.837	0.16	12.48	6.14	21.07	0.061	0.048	0.066	0.131
Tobacco, manufactured	1.804	1.299	1.718	0.934	-6.36	5.75	-0.49	-14.14	0.089	0.050	0.050	0.025
Cotton, carded or combed	0.020	0.015	0.113	0.086	-5.26	49.03	18.82	-6.57	0.001	0.001	0.003	0.002
Total imports, processed products	172.572	358.120	255.786	277.259	15.72	-6.51	4.01	2.04	8.513	13.811	7.511	7.506
Total imports of primary and processed products	509.987	764.559	642.793	721.042	8.44	-3.41	2.34	2.91	25.159	29.484	18.876	19.521
Total imports of Bangladesh	2,027.074	2,593.047	3,405.322	3,693.615	5.05	5.60	5.32	2.05	100	100	100	100

n.e. Not estimated.
n.e.s. Not elsewhere specified.

Table 2.12 Average Growth Rates of Exports of Agricultural Products, 1980–97

Product group	Year and period annual average (million US$)				Average annual growth (percent)				Percent of total			
	1980–84	1985–89	1990–94	1995–97	1985–89 over 1980–84	1990–94 over 1985–89	1990–94 over 1980–84	1995–97 over 1990–94	1980–84	1985–89	1990–94	1995–97
Primary Agricultural Products												
Meat	5.244	12.016	1.727	0.014	18.04	−32.16	−10.51	−70.14	0.740	1.123	0.085	0.001
Milk and cream, fresh	0.000	0.009	0.000	0.036	n.e.	n.e.	n.e.	n.e.	0.000	0.000	0.000	0.000
Eggs in shell	0.000	0.001	0.000	0.000	n.e.	−63.44	n.e.	n.e.	0.000	0.000	0.000	0.000
Plants, flowers, bulbs, tubers	0.000	0.026	0.015	0.017	n.e.	−10.46	n.e.	3.32	0.000	0.002	0.001	0.001
Vegetables, fresh, chilled, etc.	1.756	12.413	6.806	16.013	47.87	−11.32	14.51	23.85	0.248	1.160	0.335	0.680
Fruits and nuts, fresh/chilled/dried	0.234	0.624	0.951	0.026	21.72	8.78	15.07	−59.47	0.033	0.058	0.047	0.001
Coffee, tea, mate, and spices	46.882	40.637	39.509	19.241	−2.82	−0.56	−1.70	−16.46	6.616	3.798	1.946	0.817
Cereal, cereal products, unmilled	1.364	0.001	0.026	0.013	−77.28	99.75	−32.64	−16.89	0.192	0.000	0.001	0.001
Oilseeds and oleaginous fruits	0.083	0.002	0.117	0.002	−52.43	125.54	3.58	−64.09	0.012	0.000	0.006	0.000
Raw sugar and honey	0.045	0.000	0.000	0.000	−73.42	n.e.	−50.94	n.e.	0.005	0.000	0.000	0.000
Tobacco, unmanufactured	0.955	1.363	2.192	0.999	7.36	9.97	8.66	−17.83	0.135	0.127	0.108	0.042
Raw cotton	0.553	0.388	0.080	0.131	−6.85	−27.04	−17.56	12.95	0.078	0.036	0.004	0.006
Total exports, primary products	57.105	67.470	51.424	36.455	3.39	−5.29	−1.04	−8.24	8.058	6.305	2.533	1.548

Processed Agricultural Products												
Meat, processed	0.000	0.002	0.000	0.006	n.e.	−69.05	n.e.	n.e.	0.000	0.000	0.000	0.000
Dairy products, other than fresh milk	0.000	0.121	0.069	0.021	n.e.	−10.69	n.e.	−25.33	0.000	0.011	0.003	0.001
Eggs not in shell and egg yolks	0.000	0.035	0.000	0.003	n.e.	−74.05	n.e.	n.e.	0.000	0.003	0.000	0.000
Vegetables, preserved or prepared	0.000	0.008	0.000	0.052	169.88	−66.31	−4.65	527.57	0.000	0.001	0.000	0.002
Fruits and nuts, preserved/prepared	0.000	0.110	0.960	0.030	220.42	54.13	122.23	−57.80	0.000	0.010	0.047	0.001
Cereal products, other	0.156	0.174	0.060	0.077	2.14	−19.28	−9.20	6.69	0.022	0.016	0.003	0.003
Animal or vegetable fats or oils excluded	0.069	0.120	0.502	0.266	11.80	33.04	21.96	−14.64	0.010	0.011	0.025	0.011
Sugar and sugar preparations	0.531	0.428	0.303	0.000	−4.20	−6.67	−5.45	−93.90	0.075	0.040	0.015	0.000
Coffee, tea, and mate preparations	0.000	0.000	0.000	0.000	−62.56	n.e.	−22.97	n.e.	0.000	0.000	0.000	0.000
Food products, n.e.s.	0.005	0.064	0.088	0.032	65.28	6.45	32.64	−22.17	0.001	0.006	0.004	0.001
Animal feed, excluding unmilled cereals	3.264	0.727	0.204	0.011	−25.94	−22.44	−24.21	−51.80	0.461	0.068	0.010	0.000
Tobacco, manufactured	0.169	0.150	0.071	0.436	−2.43	−13.97	−8.36	57.62	0.024	0.014	0.003	0.019
Cotton, carded or combed	0.000	0.000	0.000	0.000	n.e.	n.e.	n.e.	n.e.	0.000	0.000	0.000	0.000
Total exports, processed products	4.195	1.938	2.256	0.935	−14.31	3.08	−6.02	−19.76	0.592	0.181	0.111	0.040
Total exports of primary and processed products	61.300	69.409	53.679	37.390	2.52	−5.01	−1.32	−8.64	8.650	6.487	2.644	1.588
Total exports of Bangladesh	708.650	1070.03	2030.39	2354.653	8.59	13.67	11.10	3.77	100	100	100	100

n.e. Not estimated.
n.e.s. Not elsewhere specified.

Table 2.13 Trend Growth Rates of Agricultural Products: Results of Regression Analysis (Imports)

Product group	Trend growth rate (percent) (1979–80 to 1996–97)	Standard error of coefficient of dependent variable	R^2	Percent of total 1994–95 to 1996–97
Primary Products				
Live animals	11.60	0.0284	0.51090	0.040
Meat	10.60	0.0215	0.60200	0.030
Milk and cream, fresh	7.60	0.0429	0.16460	0.000
Eggs in shell	10.70	0.0259	0.51520	0.010
Plants, flowers, bulbs, tubers	12.40	0.0451	0.32270	0.000
Vegetables, fresh, chilled, etc.	30.30	0.0759	0.49920	0.590
Fruits and nuts, fresh/chilled/dried	102.50	0.3290	0.37770	0.410
Coffee, tea, mate, and spices	96.60	0.1367	0.75740	0.280
Cereals, cereal products, unmilled	8.90	0.5059	0.00190	6.130
Oilseeds and oleaginous fruits	0.06	0.0381	0.00002	1.260
Raw sugar and honey	12.40	0.0202	0.70230	0.620
Tobacco, unmanufactured	0.86	0.0435	0.00240	0.210
Raw cotton	−1.60	0.0336	0.01530	2.440
Total imports of primary products	111.00	0.5105	0.22900	12.010

Processed Agricultural Products

Meat, processed	0.60	0.0518	0.00099	0.000
Sugar and sugar preparations	139.00	0.3308	0.52600	0.920
Eggs, not in shell and egg yolks	7.60	0.0448	0.15570	0.000
Vegetables, preserved or prepared	−18.00	0.195	0.05500	0.010
Fruits and nuts, preserved or prepared	19.00	0.0385	0.61570	0.450
Cereal products, other	−14.00	0.2087	0.02940	0.040
Animal or vegetable fats or oils excluding fish oils	120.00	0.3804	0.38560	5.750
Sugar and sugar preparations	−13.00	0.1322	0.06280	0.080
Coffee, tea, and mate preparations	−3.30	0.0615	0.01790	0.000
Food products, n.e.s.	78.70	0.0835	0.84740	0.110
Animal feed, excluding unmilled cereals	24.00	0.1883	0.09230	0.130
Tobacco, manufactured	3.40	0.4189	0.00040	0.030
Cotton, carded or combed	5.21	0.0372	0.10920	0.000
Total imports of processed products	20.80	0.0428	0.59760	7.510
Total imports of primary and processed products	126.00	0.3548	0.44310	19.520
Total imports of Bangladesh	158.00	0.3186	0.60720	100.00

n.e.s. Not elsewhere specified.

Table 2.14 Trend Growth Rates of Agricultural Products: Results of Regression Analysis (Exports)

Product group	Trend growth rate (percent) (1979–80 to 1996–97)	Standard error of coefficient of dependent variable	R^2	Percent of total 1994–95 to 1996–97
Primary Products				
Meat	−7.90	0.0342	0.2514	0.000
Milk and cream, fresh	−5.50	0.1223	0.0125	0.000
Eggs in shell	−3.60	0.0912	0.0096	0.000
Plants, flowers, bulbs, tubers	8.70	0.0408	0.2216	0.000
Vegetables, fresh, chilled, etc.	66.50	0.1030	0.7224	0.680
Fruits and nuts, fresh/chilled/dried	−1.60	0.1304	0.0009	0.000
Coffee, tea, mate, and spices	−111.00	0.8721	0.0931	0.820
Cereals, cereal products, unmilled	1.80	0.0413	0.0124	0.000
Oilseeds and oleaginous fruits	−2.90	0.0430	0.0288	0.000
Raw sugar and honey	−17.50	0.0670	0.2994	0.000
Tobacco, unmanufactured	19.80	0.0451	0.5479	0.040
Raw cotton	−11.40	0.0575	0.1982	0.010
Total exports of primary products	19.70	1.0260	0.0023	1.280

Processed Agricultural Products				
Meat, processed	−0.60	0.0617	0.0006	0.000
Dairy products, other than fresh milk	5.40	0.0412	0.0988	0.000
Eggs, not in shell, and egg yolks	4.30	0.0617	0.0297	0.000
Vegetables, preserved or prepared	3.10	0.0596	0.0170	0.000
Fruits and nuts, preserved or prepared	9.80	0.0267	0.4581	0.000
Cereal products, other	2.10	0.0354	0.0215	0.000
Animal or vegetable fats or oils excluding fish oils	2.40	0.0385	0.0245	0.010
Sugar and sugar preparations	−5.80	0.0287	0.2074	0.000
Coffee, tea, and mate preparations	−9.10	0.0899	0.0605	0.000
Food products, n.e.s.	17.10	0.0388	0.5485	0.000
Animal feed, excluding unmilled cereals	−12.60	0.0383	0.4046	0.000
Tobacco, manufactured	16.20	0.0309	0.6341	0.020
Cotton, carded or combed	−1.10	0.1155	0.0006	0.000
Total exports of processed products	−32.00	0.2471	0.0990	0.040
Total exports of primary and processed products	−7.41	1.036	0.0003	1.320
Total exports of Bangladesh (XPB since 1980–81)	106.00	0.1689	0.7111	100.000

n.e.s. Not elsewhere specified.

access to world-priced inputs. Some of these schemes, which contributed significantly to the rapid increase in export earnings in recent years, include (a) special bonded warehouse facilities, (b) export-processing zones, and (c) duty drawback schemes. Special bonded warehouses, numbers of which now exceed 2,000, allow firms producing exclusively for export to import and stock duty-free inputs. The scheme is monitored through the use of passbooks and preset input-output coefficients, such as the fabric-garment conversion factor to check inventory of fabric.[29] The export processing zones provide a secure foothold for direct foreign investment. The firms—both local and foreign—in export processing zones import raw materials, supplies, and capital goods free of duty, retain foreign currency earnings, operate in a labor market free of trade unions, and are exempt from income tax for 10 years. They also enjoy better infrastructure facilities, including uninterrupted power and efficient telephone connections.[30] The duty drawback schemes, extensively used by leather exporters, provide rebates of duties and taxes for exports. The use of such schemes increased in recent years as a result of the application of standard rates to a growing number of products and streamlining of procedures.

Overall, the export promotion schemes helped the country in boosting exports in recent years. As table 2.15 indicates, average annual export growth jumped to 16 percent in the 1990s from a mere 7 percent in the 1980s. But the export regime is still plagued with some serious inconsistencies. Although the structure of relative incentives for production of import substitutes declined from 1.66 in 1992 to 1.26 in 1996, it has remained essentially unchanged since then. While the effective exchange rate for exports (EERx) rose from 38.5 in 1992 to 46 in 1998, the effective exchange rate for imports (EERm) fell from 63.8 in 1992 to 51.9 in 1996. Therefore, an antiexport bias remains, and the structure of trade policy–induced incentives still remains skewed in favor of import-substitutes (World Bank 1999b). Moreover, the overall amount of subsidy

Table 2.15 Trade Liberalization and Economic Performance in the 1990s, Annual Growth Rates (percent)

Category	Before liberalization 1980s averages	FY90	FY92	FY94	FY96	FY98	Post liberalization 1990s averages
Real GDP	4.0	7.0	5.0	3.8	5.0	5.6	5.0
Manufacturing	3.0	1.0	10.0	5.0	6.0	9.0	7.0
Agriculture	2.0	10.0	2.5	0.8	3.4	3.0	3.3
Exports (in nominal US$)	7.0	37.0	25.0	4.0	8.0	12.0	16.0

Source: World Bank.

to exports, in terms of cash, export credit,[31] bank credit at lower interest rates,[32] and export performance benefit (XPB)[33] through foreign exchange regimes, does not seem to be considerable (table 2.16).

In sharp contrast to such a robust growth in overall exports, agricultural exports, however, did not increase much. None of the export facilities, such as bonded warehouses, duty drawbacks, or export processing zones, seems to have played a considerable role in promoting agricultural exports. As a result, in sharp contrast to the double-digit growth rates of overall exports, agricultural exports demonstrated a marked decline. As table 2.10 indicates, the share of agricultural exports in total exports fell from 8.65 percent in 1980–84 to 6.49 percent in 1985–89, to 2.64 percent in 1990–94, and then to 1.59 percent in 1995–97.[34] Exports of processed agricultural products, which were already relatively negligible, showed a much steeper decline in the 1990s than those of primary agricultural products.[35] This was because agriculture was taxed and negatively subsidized by the government through higher protection to manufactured products as well as through exchange rate distortions in the form of overvaluation of the domestic currency. It is believed that the relative high protection of import substitution activities along with extensive import and exchange controls and high import tariffs significantly disadvantaged the export sector in general and agricultural exports in particular.[36]

Bangladesh's Commitments to the Uruguay Round Agreement on Agriculture

The URAoA required all member countries to submit a country schedule, providing quantitative commitments on a commodity-by-commodity basis on market access (tariffs and nontariff barriers), domestic support, and export subsidies. As a developing country Bangladesh is exempted from reduction commitments on tariffs, export subsidies, and domestic support to agriculture, but it is obligated to freeze domestic support to agriculture at the 1986–88 level and bind all tariffs. Bangladesh reported no import quota, export subsidy, or domestic support to agriculture for the base period of 1986–88, but reported bound tariff rates at 200 percent for all but two of the seven product groups reported to the World Trade Organization (WTO). Bangladesh also declared a 200 percent bound rate of tariff for all agricultural goods except 13 (six-digit HS code) items for which the bound rate was 50 percent and it set bound tariffs at 50 percent (plus a 30 percent additional charge) (table 2.17) for all nonagricultural products. The actual tariff rates in all product groups, except fertilizers and agricultural machinery, were, however, far lower than the reported bound tariff in both the periods 1986–88 and 1995–97. Actual tariffs were higher than bound tariffs for agricultural machinery only, for which the bound tariff was reported at 0 percent, although during the base period

Table 2.16 Export Subsidies and Other State Supports for Exports, 1991–2000

Fiscal year	Export (mil. Tk) (1)	Cash subsidy (mil. Tk) (2)	Export credit (mil. Tk) (3)	Export (percent) (4)	Interest rates (percent)		Interest subsidy (mil. Tk) (7)	Cash-interest subsidy (percent of exports) (8)	Nominal exchange rate (Tk) (9)	EERx (10)
					General (5)	Difference (6)				
1991–92	75,220.0	25.1	11,774.0	9.6	15.8	−6.2	0.0097	0.0100	38.15	38.53
1992–93	88,000.0	21.8	15,802.0	9.0	17.2	−8.2	0.0147	0.0149	39.14	39.72
1993–94	98,000.0	77.9	18,047.0	9.0	15.1	−6.1	0.0112	0.0120	40.00	40.48
1994–95	131,310.0	289.5	19,524.0	9.0	13.1	−4.1	0.0060	0.0082	40.20	40.53
1995–96	138,460.0	450.0	19,325.0	9.0	13.9	−4.9	0.0069	0.0102	40.84	41.25
1996–97	165,710.0	800.0	22,643.0	9.0	14.3	−5.3	0.0072	0.0121	42.70	43.22
1997–98	203,970.0	2,000.0	22,749.1	9.0	13.5	−4.5	0.0050	0.0148	45.46	46.14
1998–99	206,500.0	3,000.0	—	9.0	13.5	−4.5	0.0000	0.0145	48.50	49.20
1999–2000	—	—	—	9.0	13.5	−4.5			49.50	

— Not available.
Note: EERx = exchange rate for exports; Tk = taka.
Source: World Bank.

Table 2.17 Bangladesh: Schedule of Commitments for Agricultural Products to WTO

HS code	Brief description of products	Pre-UR applied rate of duty (percent)	Post-UR applied rate of duty (percent)	UR bound rate of "other duties and charges" (percent)	Implementation period
101.11	Live horses	7.5	50	30	1995
104.1	Live sheep	7.5	50	30	1995
105.11	Live fowl	30	50	30	1995
208.2	Frog legs	45	50	30	2004
501	Human hair	30	50	30	1995
701.1	Sweet potatoes	7.5	50	30	2004
902.1	Green tea (nonfermented)	60	50	30	2004
902.3	Black tea	60	50	30	2004
1006.1	Rice in the husk	7.5	50	30	1995
1008.3	Canary seeds	15	50	30	1995
1201	Soybean seeds	15	50	30	1995
1207.2	Cotton seeds	15	50	30	1995
1703.1	Molasses	45	50	30	2004

Source: WTO.

the actual tariff for agricultural machinery was 60 percent. In the aftermath of the Uruguay Round, operating tariffs were even much lower than that which prevailed in the base period and significantly lower than bound tariffs.[37]

Export Regimes

Bangladesh did not declare any export subsidies in its schedule of UR commitments. As was noted, some subsidy elements may be traced to measures such as (a) XPB as practiced up to 1992, (b) interest rate discounts, (c) special tariff concessions on imports of capital machinery, and (d) export credit guarantee schemes.[38] With the erosion of differences between the official exchange rate and the wage earner scheme exchange rate and abolition of the multiple exchange system, the benefits of XPB eroded by 1992.[39] Export subsidies in the form of bank credit at lower than market interest rates, especially for nontraditional export products[40] still continues (see table 2.16). Duty concession on imported machinery has been substantial, ranging between 50 percent and 100 percent in 1986–88. But it was not available for firms partially selling in the export market and it may not qualify as an export subsidy. Export credit guarantees against possible losses at preshipment, postshipment, or comprehensive levels do not appear to have involved any subsidies. Therefore, as far as the three conditions of the URAoA are concerned, it can be concluded that Bangladesh did not provide any direct or indirect price-distorting subsidies on its agricultural products in 1986–90. Moreover as a developing country, Bangladesh has no obligation to reduce whatever subsidies are being continued. Bangladesh has to only freeze those at the base year level.

Domestic Supports

As far as domestic support to agriculture is concerned, Bangladesh declared aggregate measurement of support (AMS) to agriculture in its schedule to WTO in November 1994. Bangladesh recognized that it provided exempted support, as provided in Annex 2 of the URAoA, for food security stocks, food aid, and natural disaster relief. The declaration also included investment aid or input subsidies to resource poor farmers and administrative costs of distributing seeds such as rice, potato, and wheat at government-fixed prices. The total AMS, nevertheless, remained zero because these were included in the nontrade-distorting green box measures.[41] A review of the related data for 1986–88 reveals that Bangladesh did not provide any direct price support to any of the agricultural commodities/products.

Bangladesh's supports to agriculture are mostly in the green box area, that is, nondistortionary in character. The government provides substantial support to research both on a product specific and on a general basis to pest and disease control, training, marketing, infrastructure, and extension services. As table 2.18a indicates, in 1995–96 such supports totaled about Tk9.8 billion, only about 3.3 percent of the value of agricultural product in the year.[42] Government budgetary supports to agricultural inputs are also insignificant. Although previously heavily subsidized, fertilizer received no budgetary subsidy in the years 1993–96 (table 2.18b).[43]

Table 2.18a Domestic Supports to Bangladesh Agriculture, 1986–96: Support to Agricultural Outputs, Various Years
(million taka)

Fiscal year	Support services, crop specific	Support services, nonspecific	Water resource development (irrigation)	All measures	Percent of total agricultural output
1986–87	421	2,731	776	3,928	1.8
1987–88	307	2,606	1,369	4,282	2.0
1988–89	539	3,972	2,412	6,924	3.1
1993–94	776	5,304	2,195	8,275	3.4
1994–95	756	5,420	2,150	8,326	2.9
1995–96	714	5,709	3,387	9,810	3.3

Source: Asaduzzaman (1999).

Table 2.18b Domestic Supports to Bangladesh Agriculture, 1986–96: Agricultural Input Subsidy and Price Supports, Various Years

Fiscal year	Fertilizer (percent of output)	Net irrigation (percent of output)	Price support to Rice (mil. Tk)	Price support to Wheat (mil. Tk)
1986–87	0.33	1.01	11.1	—
1987–88	0.60	1.34	170.4	—
1988–89	1.25	1.28	125.1	—
1993–94	0	0.81	–12.6	–0.5
1994–95	0	1.06	–198.3	–1.9
1995–96	0	0.83	31.9	0

Source: Bakth (1999).

Table 2.18c Domestic Supports to Bangladesh Agriculture, 1990–95: Support to the Seed Subsector
(AMS as percent of value of output)

	Paddy	Wheat	Maize	Veg.	Potato	Jute	Pulses	Oilseed
1990–91	0.05	2.27	6.91	0.40	0.84	0.42	0.005	0.05
1991–92	0.05	2.32	9.51	0.31	0.82	0.62	0.01	0.05
1992–93	0.06	1.99	13.63	0.32	0.72	0.79	0.03	0.07
1993–94	0.07	2.42	19.98	0.37	0.79	1.051	0.04	0.08
1994–95	0.05	1.92	15.49	0.44	0.58	0.87	0.03	0.07

Note: AMS = aggregate measurement of support.
Source: Bakth (1999).

Currently, however, fertilizer production, marketing, and distribution is highly subsidized. Still, subsidies were much higher in the mid-1980s than in the late 1990s. Support to irrigation equipment, owing to liberalization of this sector since the late 1980s, is now small. The whole operation of underground water irrigation is currently in the private sector, and only a few deep tubewells are being subsidized, and major irrigation projects, mainly involving surface water irrigation, are subsidized. Budgetary supports to such activities are not substantial (World Bank 1997). Government subsidy to seed production and distribution, calculated as budgetary outlay, is also minimal, and exceeds the de minimis limit only in the case of maize (table 2.18c).

Market Access

The minimum market access provision of the URAoA—defined in terms of imports of the current year as a percentage of the consumption in 1986–88—requires that market access should be at least 3 percent in the first year of implementation and raised 4 percent per year to reach 5 percent in the sixth year of implementation.[44] As table 2.19 shows, the current market access opportunity is considerably above the threshold level for all commodities except potato and sugar. In the case of potatoes, the tariff equivalent has been observed to be negative in both base and current years. Therefore, imports of potatoes are not likely to increase with the lowering of tariffs. For sugar, on the other hand, the tariff equivalent has been observed to be positive in both the base and current years. It is a restricted item, and its import is regulated through the state trading agency, the Trading Corporation of Bangladesh.[45] As was mentioned, Bangladesh has drastically rolled back the role of parastatals in import trade, especially since 1991–92.

Table 2.19 Market Access Opportunity of Imports in Bangladesh, Various Years, 1986–96

Item	Consumption in 1986–87 (million tons)	Access opportunities based on 1986–87 consumption (percent)	
		1986–87	1995–96
Rice	1066.9	2.4	9.7
Wheat	1045.3	57.5	40.8
Oilseed	58.7	17.8	11.0
Edible oil	539.5	74.9	625.2
Lentils	29.3	1.3	13.0
Onion	41.4	0.0	31.8
Potato	1.0	0.0	0.1
Sugar	0.8	39.1	0.3
Milk powder	93.4	27.7	9.1
Cotton	45.3	43.8	650.1

Source: Bakth (1999).

Changes Made to Meet UR Commitments and Challenges for the Future

From the viewpoint of the three key pillars of the URAoA—market access, domestic support, and export subsidies—Bangladesh's only obligation was "tariffication" of nontrade barriers (NTBs) and the binding of tariffs. Bangladesh met these requirements easily without any challenges or problems. The reason is simple: Bangladesh had liberalized its trade regime in excess of what was required by the WTO, and it did most of this before the emergence of the WTO itself.[46] Currently, the trading environment in Bangladesh is generally distortion free, and agriculture receives minimal domestic support. Whatever price-distorting or indirect supports given to agriculture are not substantial or untenable. The tariff bindings at the 200 percent level for some selected commodities gives a wrong signal about the country's actual trade regime. Bangladesh could easily reduce its bound tariff rates to around 50 percent or less, which would be not only more realistic, but also more appropriate for reflecting the actual state of trade liberalization in the country.

The only area in which Bangladesh might have experienced some difficulty in meeting the commitments made to the URAoA would be in limiting the role of the state trading agencies. In 1995, following the signing of the URAoA, state trading was removed from all the important agricultural products except rice, wheat, coarse grains, and oilseeds. While state control still remains on many of these products, private trading is also allowed in these products. Until 1992–93, the government enjoyed a de facto monopoly in importing foodgrain. Since then, the trade regime in agriculture has changed so much that the share of the private trade in agriculture had increased to 97 percent in 1992.[47]

As far as the so-called "built-in agenda of WTO" is concerned, the biggest challenge for Bangladesh appears to be gaining greater access to industrialized countries' markets because industrialized countries are reducing import restrictions and phasing out export subsidies. Bangladesh seems to have a comparative advantage in import substitution of edible oils, dairy products, and exports of agro-processed products, such as fruits and vegetables (Shahabuddin 1999). One main reason for the failure of the 1999 Seattle Ministerial Conference was that the developing countries believed that they were not obtaining the benefits from trade that more industrialized countries were achieving. Many policymakers as well as opinion leaders in Bangladesh shared this viewpoint.[48]

The challenges from the so-called "second generation" or the "new trade agenda"—involving the issues of intellectual property rights, trade-related environment and labor issues, food safety, investment, and competition policies—will, however, remain formidable for a poor country like Bangladesh. As in other parts of the world, these issues have generated considerable concern in Bangladesh as well. Some of the major concerns about these issues are enumerated below.

First, Bangladesh appears to be concerned with the complexities and uncertainties involved with the Trade-Related Aspects of Intellectual Property Rights, especially in respect to the impact of the Intellectual Property Rights regime on agricultural trade-related issues pertaining to plants and animals, plant variety protection systems, and food security and agricultural bio-diversity. The Intellectual Property Rights regime apparently tends to shift bargaining power toward the producers of knowledge and technology in the industrial countries, and many industrialized countries' firms are acquiring strong intellectual property rights, often involving fundamental research tools as well as marketable products, which put the developing countries and their firms and researchers in a disadvantageous position of catching up to the knowledge gap as well as adoption of technologies (World Bank 1998). Bangladesh is particularly worried that following patent protection of plant varieties and seeds farmers would have to procure seeds from industrialized countries' seed producers at an exorbitant cost, which would badly affect the local seed industry and increase the cost of agricultural production, and thereby increase the price of agricultural goods.[49]

Second, Bangladesh is also concerned with trade-related environmental issues. In particular, policymakers are worried about the implications of the Sanitary and Phytosanitary (SPS) measures, which might adversely affect its exports of raw jute, frozen food, dried fish, tea, vegetables, and other traditional products. Bangladesh has experienced severe setbacks in recent years in its export of fish and fish products to European countries owing to sanitary and phytosanitary standards imposed by the European Union. Also, Bangladesh now lacks the required scientific equipment and technologies to meet SPS requirements. Bangladesh is also concerned with trade-related labor and eco-labeling issues. It is apprehensive that these measures might create NTBs to its export potential.[50]

Third, as a net importer of food, Bangladesh suspects that WTO measures might increase its import bills, endangering its already precarious balance of payments situation. As was noted, the food-import bills of the country have risen in recent years, despite considerable progress made in increasing domestic production of foodgrain. As a net food importing country, Bangladesh may be eligible for increased food and financial aid to maintain food security, technical assistance to increase agricultural productivity, and export credits at favorable terms. Government officials believe that the promised assistance from the WTO or other donor agencies will not be forthcoming to help the country in dealing with balance of payment problems stemming from increased food import bills. Also, officials are worried that unexpected price increases in food and other agricultural products in international markets may call for modifications in national food security policies and strategies, such as a public food distribution system or consumer price policies. Both would be difficult and politically controversial. (See Bangladesh Ministry of Agriculture 1999a.)

Fourth, Bangladesh is concerned that it has been receiving conflicting signals on trade policy reform from multilateral bodies, such as the World Bank, the International Monetary Fund (IMF), and the WTO. Bangladesh has liberalized its trade regime much faster than what is required for conforming to the requirements of the WTO, but its officials claim that the World Bank/IMF has still been pushing for further reforms and liberalization. Government officials believe Bangladesh can further expand subsidized operations in agriculture, especially in the green box or the amber box areas without violating the WTO rules, but the World Bank/IMF would have strong objections to such measures. Bangladesh believes the activities of the WTO and the World Bank/IMF should be coordinated more closely to avoid sending conflicting signals to developing countries, including Bangladesh. (See Bangladesh Ministry of Agriculture 1999b.)

Another important concern for Bangladesh is that the government lacks the institutional capability to handle WTO-related matters, whether it relates to built-in issues or second generation issues. The Bangladesh Ministry of Commerce is now officially responsible for handling the matters on behalf of the government, but it lacks institutional capacity, proper staffing, as well as the logistical ability to perform effectively. Careful investigations into government agencies and trade policy resources have led many researchers to conclude that currently the government is not able to handle the challenges stemming from the WTO, as well as the task of preparing the nation to confront those challenges. (See Bangladesh Ministry of Agriculture 1997, 1998, 1999a.)

Policy Options and Recommendations for Bangladesh

The Bangladesh economy is more open now than at any other time in terms of size of trade, removal of quantitative restrictions, lowering of tariffs, deregulation of import procedures, and foreign exchange reforms. Trade liberalization also appears to have contributed to an impressive performance of the economy. As table 2.15 indicates, annual GDP growth rates averaged 5 percent in the 1990s, compared with 4 percent in the 1980s; manufacturing growth rates averaged 7 percent in the 1990s, compared with 3 percent in the 1980s; average agricultural growth increased to 3.3 percent in the 1990s, compared with 2 percent in the 1980s; average growth rates of exports increased to 16 percent in the 1990s, compared with 7 percent in the 1980s; and current account deficits as a percentage of GDP averaged 2.7 percent in the 1990s, compared with 4 percent in the 1980s.[51]

Agriculture, as defined by the URAoA, does not cover most activities that are commonly covered under the agricultural sector in Bangladesh.[52] While agriculture, as defined in Bangladesh, constitutes 25 percent of the country's international trade, the URAoA-defined agriculture constitutes only about half of that. Moreover, the entire URAoA-defined agriculture is unimportant for Bangladesh as far as export trade is concerned.[53] For Bangladesh, agricultural imports appear to be more important as imports soared under a liberalized trade regime in recent years. Domestic producers are coming under increasing pressures from cheap imports from abroad. Also a long porous border with India enables illegal imports of many agricultural commodities to pour into Bangladesh all year round.

Over the years Bangladesh has fulfilled most of the commitments or requirements of the WTO. The agricultural trade regime was liberalized much further under the auspices of the SAP and ESAP than what was required under the WTO. Major amber box support measures in fertilizer, irrigation, and seed production were eliminated. Existing price supports and trade distortionary subsidies are well within the limits of the WTO. In some cases they may well be increased without violating the provisions of the WTO. Export subsidies/support is minimal. Only a few quantitative restrictions still exist, but their role is not substantial. The role of the state trading organizations has been trimmed down to bare minimum. Bangladesh, however, needs to put a tariff on the remaining quantitative restrictions in agricultural trade, because tariffication would presumably benefit more than harm the economy.[54]

Bangladesh's concern in respect to new generation issues, such as trade-related environment and labor issues, food safety, and investment and competition policy, are largely similar to those of other developing countries. Bangladesh joins other developing countries in asserting that the multilateral trading system under WTO should protect the interests of the developing countries, which are dependent on the industrialized world for knowledge and technology. Bangladesh argues that the bargaining power should be shifted away from producers of knowledge toward the developing countries to bridge the gap in knowledge and promote transfer of technology. Moreover, Bangladesh is also concerned, as are other developing countries, that the industrialized world, especially the United States and the European Union countries, still maintain high government support for their farmers while pushing for further lowering of tariffs and subsidies in the developing countries.[55]

Viewed from these perspectives, Bangladesh's response to the challenges of the WTO can be analyzed both domestically and internationally. From the international perspective, as a leader among the least industrialized countries, Bangladesh is in a position to be a more active and informed participant in the multilateral trade negotiations under the auspices of the WTO, United Nations Conference on Trade and Development (UNCTAD), and other such forums. The exercise could be geared at securing a reasonable and acceptable share for the developing countries in the growth of trade in agricultural goods, commensurate with the needs of their economic development, as agreed to at the Marrakesh Agreement in 1994. Bangladesh could bargain for (a) raising liberalization commitments of the developing countries in the next rounds of multilateral negotiations under the WTO; (b) obtaining exemption of subsidies on key agricultural inputs from domestic support reduction commitments for the developing countries; (c) monitoring commitments of market access increase, reduction in export subsidies, and tarrification of NTBs in the industrialized countries; and (d) playing a stronger role in formulation/evaluation of the so-called "new generation issues" in the context of the developing countries.

From the domestic perspective, Bangladesh should concentrate on a four-prong strategy:

- Bangladesh should concentrate on building an institutional framework to analyze, prescribe, and monitor policy actions to face the challenges and to capitalize the opportunities stemming from the global trade regime under the WTO. Given the track record of the responsible government agencies and officials in terms of skill and performance levels, perhaps an effort should be directed at building up such capacities in the private sector. A nonprofit think tank/foundation could be established for handling the WTO matters and other issues pertaining to international trade. Also, Bangladesh should actively consider a politically appointed and accountable technocrat for representing the country at the WTO.

- Bangladesh should increase its efforts in capturing the opportunities opened by the URAoA by expanding exports of nontraditional and processed agricultural products and by improving market access in both industrialized and other developing countries. Bangladesh should undertake appropriate institutional measures to promote agricultural technology transfer, market research, infrastructure development, and a policy environment to facilitate its agro-processing industries. It should also reassess its policies regarding the imports of agro-processed products. Moreover, concessionary import facilities granted to neighboring countries—such as Bhutan—might discourage Bangladeshi entrepreneurs from getting into this business. This again would need a strengthened role of the private sector and almost commensurately a smaller role of the government. Government can launch an aggressive drive for increasing export opportunities by emphasizing what is called economic diplomacy by creating a more business-like operation of its embassies. Thus, at least the key embassies (that is, those that are important from a business perspective) should be manned by private sector individuals, who, unlike government officials, will be responsible and accountable for their assigned missions.
- Bangladesh should proceed in liberalizing its tariff structures further. There is still some "water" in the tariffs, and it has been found that unilateral tariff liberalization does contribute to greater GDP growth, export income, industrial production, and consumer benefits over the years. Also, Bangladesh should bring its bound tariff rates substantially below the current level of 200 percent and should eliminate its existing quantitative restrictions. As was explained, this will only reflect the truer picture of the trade liberalization in the country. Moreover, the cascading nature of the tariff structure now allows higher tariffs on finished products and lower tariffs on intermediate goods. As many of the finished products—such as paper, cotton, plastic—end up as inputs, the cost of domestically produced finished products becomes uncompetitive when compared with imported finished products. Further minimization of tariff dispersion and a faster movement toward a uniform tariff structure could remove such anomalies.
- Bangladesh should pursue a more appropriate foreign exchange and international trade regime, taking into consideration its neighboring countries and the role of illegal border trade. Domestic production of

many agricultural products is now badly affected by considerable smuggling across Bangladesh's long porous border with India. Historically, one major reason for this has been a more competitive exchange rate policy in India and relatively less liberalization of the Indian economy for imports of consumer goods vis-à-vis Bangladesh (World Bank 1999c). Bangladesh can effectively discourage such massive illegal trade with India by pursuing a more competitive exchange rate and trade liberalization policies.

Table A2.1a Agricultural Products of Bangladesh, Grouped into Harmonized System Codes: Primary Products

Product group	HS code	SITC (Rev. 2)/BSTC code
Live animals	01	00
Meat, fresh/chilled/frozen	02.01–02.09	011
Dairy products: milk and cream, fresh	04.01	0223
Eggs in shell, fresh/preserved/cooked	04.07	0251
Plants, flowers, bulbs, tubers	06	2926; 2927
Vegetables, fresh/chilled/dried/whole/cut, not further processed	07.01–07.09; 03.13	0541; 0542; 0544; 0545
Fruits and nuts, fresh/chilled/dried	08.01–08.10	057
Coffee, tea, mate, and spices	09.01–09.10	07111; 0721; 074; 075
Cereals, cereal products unmilled	10	041 – 045
Oilseeds and oleaginous fruits	12.01–12.08	22
Raw sugar and honey	04.09; 1701; 110–1701.120	0611; 0616
Tobacco, unmanufactured	24.01	121
Raw cotton	52.01	263 excluding 26340

Table A2.1b Agricultural Products of Bangladesh, Grouped into Harmonized System Codes: Processed Products

Product group	HS code	SITC (Rev. 2)/BSTC code
Meat, processed	02.10; 16.01; 16.02	012; 0142; 0149
Dairy products, other than fresh milk and cream	04 excluding (04.01, 04.07–04.09)	0224; 023; 024
Eggs, not in shell and egg yolks	04.08	0252
Vegetables, preserved or prepared	07.10–07.12; 20.01–20.06	0546; 0548 excluding 05481; 056
Fruits and nuts, preserved or prepared	08.01–08.14; 20.07–20.09	058
Cereal products	11.01–11.04; 19.04–19.05	046–048
Animal or vegetable fats or oils excluding fish oils	15 excluding 15.04	4 excluding 4111
Sugar and sugar preparations	17.01 excluding (1701.110, 1701.120); 17.02–17.04	0612; 0615; 0619; 062
Coffee, tea, and mate preparations	21.01	07112; 07113; 0712; 0722; 0723; 073
Food products, n.e.s.	21 excluding 21.01	098
Animal feed, not including unmilled cereals	23 excluding 23.07; 07.14	08 excluding 0814; 05481
Tobacco, manufactured	24 excluding 24.01	122
Cotton, carded or combed	52.03	26340

n.e.s. Not elsewhere specified.

Note: The division of agricultural products into primary and processed products has been made on the basis of OECD classification guidelines as provided in SITC, Revision 2, and Bangladesh's trade statistics follows the Bangladesh Standard Trade Classification Code System, which is essentially based on the SITC codes.

Table A2.2 Operative Tariff Rates and Value-Added Tax on Major Agricultural Products in Bangladesh, 1991–2000

Group	Unweighted				Weighted		
	CD + LF + IDS	VAT	SD	Total	CD + LF + IDS	VAT	SD	Total
			1991–92					
Rice	16.44	14.81	0.00	31.25	14.68	4.61	0.00	19.29
S1 Wheat	16.44	0.00	0.00	16.44	0.00	0.00	0.00	0.00
03 Sugar	81.44	12.25	0.00	93.69	97.33	14.47	0.00	111.80
04 Oilseed	41.44	0.00	0.00	41.44	22.45	0.00	0.00	22.45
05 Edible oil: crude	58.94	8.88	0.00	67.82	44.30	6.38	0.00	50.69
06 Edible oil: refined	93.44	14.05	0.00	107.49	99.45	15.13	0.00	114.57
07 Onion	31.44	0.00	0.00	31.44	32.41	0.00	0.00	32.41
08 Chilies (dry)	1.44	5.08	0.00	6.52	2.61	0.03	0.00	2.63
09 Potato	101.44	0.00	0.00	101.44	2.50	0.00	0.00	2.50
10 Milk	44.77	8.08	0.00	52.86	32.22	4.35	0.00	36.57
11 Pulses	21.44	0.00	0.00	21.44	12.98	0.08	0.00	13.06
			1992–93					
01 Rice	8.98	12.38	0.00	21.36	9.80	0.26	0.00	10.05
02 Wheat	8.98	0.00	0.00	8.98	4.93	0.00	0.00	4.93
03 Sugar	81.48	12.25	0.00	93.73	62.60	9.27	0.00	71.87
04 Oilseed	27.73	0.00	0.00	27.73	17.38	0.00	0.00	17.38
05 Edible oil: crude	50.23	6.72	0.00	56.95	44.30	6.58	0.00	50.88
06 Edible oil: refined	83.48	12.55	0.00	96.03	68.49	10.32	0.00	78.81
07 Onion	31.48	0.00	0.00	31.48	32.35	0.00	0.00	32.35

08	Chilies (dry)	12.73	8.63	0.00	21.36	19.23	0.00	19.23
09	Potato	76.48	0.00	0.00	76.48	70.14	0.00	70.14
10	Milk	45.41	4.86	0.00	50.27	34.43	5.04	39.47
11	Pulses	16.48	0.00	0.00	16.48	6.50	0.02	6.52

1993–94

01	Rice	8.98	0.00	0.00	8.98	10.00	0.00	10.00
02	Wheat	16.48	0.00	0.00	16.48	15.20	0.00	15.20
03	Sugar	61.48	9.25	0.00	70.73	62.25	9.21	71.47
04	Oilseed	27.73	0.00	0.00	27.73	17.48	0.00	17.48
05	Edible oil: crude	48.62	6.59	0.00	55.22	42.96	7.17	50.14
06	Edible oil: refined	64.48	9.70	0.00	74.18	48.48	7.45	55.94
07	Onion	31.48	0.00	0.00	31.48	32.48	0.00	32.48
08	Chilies (dry)	26.48	2.38	0.00	28.86	32.48	0.00	32.48
09	Potato	76.48	0.00	0.00	76.48	77.36	0.00	77.36
10	Milk	49.69	5.50	0.00	55.19	41.19	6.06	47.25
11	Pulses	16.48	0.00	0.00	16.48	17.50	0.00	17.50

1994–95

01	Rice	1.46	0.05	0.00	1.51	2.48	0.00	2.48
02	Wheat	8.96	0.69	0.00	9.65	10.97	0.00	10.97
03	Sugar	31.46	4.75	0.00	36.21	32.31	4.72	37.03
04	Oilseed	23.96	1.81	0.00	25.77	17.33	0.01	17.34
05	Edible oil: crude	38.96	5.88	0.00	44.84	33.75	4.96	38.70
06	Edible oil: refined	49.46	7.45	0.00	56.91	46.10	6.80	52.89
07	Onion	31.46	2.38	0.00	33.84	32.40	0.00	32.40
08	Chilies (dry)	27.71	0.00	0.00	27.71	32.49	0.01	32.50

(Table continues on the following page.)

Table A2.2 Operative Tariff Rates and Value-Added Tax on Major Agricultural Products in Bangladesh, 1991–2000 (continued)

Group		Unweighted				Weighted			
		CD + LF + IDS	VAT	SD	Total	CD + LF + IDS	VAT	SD	Total
09	Potato	61.46	4.63	0.00	66.09	52.17	0.03	0.00	52.19
10	Milk	46.46	5.76	0.00	52.22	45.36	6.69	0.00	52.06
11	Pulses	16.46	1.25	0.00	17.71	9.79	0.00	0.00	9.79
				1995–96					
01	Rice	1.22	0.04	0.00	1.26	0.62	0.00	0.00	0.62
02	Wheat	8.72	0.67	0.00	9.39	7.18	0.00	0.00	7.18
03	Sugar	31.22	4.71	0.00	35.93	32.50	4.71	0.00	37.21
04	Oilseed	18.10	1.37	0.00	19.47	10.00	0.00	0.00	10.00
05	Edible oil: crude	31.22	5.46	0.00	36.68	32.49	4.71	0.00	37.20
06	Edible oil: refined	38.72	5.84	0.00	44.56	28.72	4.23	0.00	32.94
07	Onion	31.22	2.36	0.00	33.58	32.38	0.00	0.00	32.38
08	Chilies (dry)	23.72	0.00	0.00	23.72	32.49	0.00	0.00	32.49
09	Potato	46.22	3.48	0.00	49.70	45.00	0.00	0.00	45.00
10	Milk	46.22	5.73	0.00	51.95	45.95	6.73	0.00	52.69
11	Pulses	12.47	0.95	0.00	13.42	9.42	0.00	0.00	9.42
				1996–97					
01	Rice	1.28	0.00	0.00	1.28	1.22	0.00	0.00	1.22
02	Wheat	8.78	0.68	0.00	9.46	7.47	0.00	0.00	7.47
03	Sugar	31.28	4.74	0.00	36.02	32.44	4.73	0.00	37.17
04	Oilseed	16.13	1.39	0.00	17.52	10.00	0.00	0.00	10.00

05	Edible oil: crude	31.28	4.06	0.00	35.34	32.66	4.74	0.00	37.40
06	Edible oil: refined	38.78	4.99	0.00	43.77	46.98	6.88	0.00	53.86
07	Onion	31.28	2.37	0.00	33.65	32.51	0.00	0.00	32.52
08	Chilies (dry)	23.78	0.00	0.00	23.78	32.50	0.16	0.00	32.66
09	Potato	46.28	3.50	0.00	49.78	10.39	0.00	0.00	10.39
10	Milk	46.28	10.10	0.00	56.38	46.49	6.85	0.00	53.34
11	Pulses	12.53	0.96	0.00	13.49	10.34	0.00	0.00	10.34

1997–98

01	Rice	1.25	0.00	0.00	1.25	0.36	0.00	0.00	0.36
02	Wheat	11.25	0.71	0.00	11.96	8.66	0.00	0.00	8.66
03	Sugar	33.75	4.80	0.00	38.55	34.98	4.80	0.00	39.77
04	Oilseed	18.10	1.37	0.00	19.47	12.43	0.00	0.00	12.43
05	Edible oil: crude	27.50	3.31	0.00	30.81	32.68	4.52	0.00	37.20
06	Edible oil: refined	39.17	4.77	0.00	43.93	47.29	6.64	0.00	53.94
07	Onion	33.75	2.40	0.00	36.15	31.25	0.00	0.00	31.25
08	Chilies (dry)	26.25	0.00	0.00	26.25	35.00	0.00	0.00	35.00
09	Potato	46.25	3.34	0.00	49.59	31.23	2.46	0.00	33.68
10	Milk	46.25	9.82	0.00	56.07	45.49	6.43	0.00	51.92
11	Pulses	15.00	0.99	0.00	15.99	13.16	0.00	0.00	13.16

1998–99

01	Rice	1.08	0.00	0.00	1.08	0.02	0.00	0.00	0.02
02	Wheat	7.08	0.57	0.00	7.65	9.76	0.00	0.00	9.76
03	Sugar	33.58	4.74	0.00	38.32	33.54	4.49	0.00	38.04
04	Oilseed	14.71	1.18	0.00	15.88	11.08	0.00	0.00	11.09
05	Edible oil: crude	21.08	2.46	0.00	23.54	22.80	2.88	0.00	25.69

(Table continues on the following page.)

Table A2.2 Operative Tariff Rates and Value-Added Tax on Major Agricultural Products in Bangladesh, 1991–2000 *(continued)*

Group	Unweighted				Weighted			
	CD + LF + IDS	VAT	SD	Total	CD + LF + IDS	VAT	SD	Total
06 Edible oil: refined	36.91	4.46	0.00	41.37	43.58	6.00	0.00	49.58
07 Onion	33.58	2.37	0.00	35.95	20.03	0.00	0.00	20.03
08 Chilies (dry)	22.33	0.00	0.00	22.33	19.76	0.00	0.00	19.76
09 Potato	43.58	3.12	0.00	46.70	12.86	0.02	0.00	12.88
10 Milk	43.58	9.48	0.00	53.06	42.93	6.05	0.91	49.89
11 Pulses	6.08	0.54	0.00	6.62	11.08	0.04	0.00	11.12
				1999–2000				
01 Rice	1.00	0.00	0.00	1.00	—	—	—	—
02 Wheat	5.50	0.50	0.00	6.00	—	—	—	—
03 Sugar	28.50	3.99	0.00	32.49	—	—	—	—
04 Oilseed	12.58	1.01	0.00	13.59	—	—	—	—
05 Edible oil: crude	18.50	2.49	0.00	20.99	—	—	—	—
06 Edible oil: refined	33.86	4.16	0.00	38.02	—	—	—	—
07 Onion	28.50	2.00	0.00	30.50	—	—	—	—
08 Chilies (dry)	22.25	0.00	0.00	22.25	—	—	—	—
09 Potato	41.00	2.93	0.00	43.93	—	—	—	—
10 Milk	41.00	9.50	2.70	53.21	—	—	—	—
11 Pulses	4.75	0.41	0.00	5.16	—	—	—	—

Note: CD = customs duties; LF = license fees; IDS = infrastructure development surcharge; VAT = value-added tax.
Sources: National Board of Revenue and World Bank estimates.

Table A2.3 Effective Rates of Protection in Bangladesh, 1992–2000

		Effective rate of protection							
	Sector name	1992–93	1993–94	1994–95	1995–96	1996–97	1997–98	1998–99	1999–00
1	Rice	−8.00	0.90	2.40	−5.80	−5.70	−5.40	−5.30	−4.70
2	Wheat	−3.90	8.50	11.00	2.00	2.20	2.60	2.80	0.20
3	Coarse grains	−4.90	−4.10	−0.80	−0.20	−0.20	0.10	0.10	0.40
4	Jute	64.40	67.20	30.60	31.80	32.00	32.40	32.50	26.80
5	Sugarcane	68.40	71.30	14.20	14.80	15.00	15.20	15.20	15.80
6	Cotton	4.80	5.40	−2.00	−1.70	−1.70	−1.50	−1.50	−1.40
7	Tobacco	12.50	−0.90	10.20	11.80	12.10	11.10	11.30	12.20
8	Potato	58.90	60.40	48.80	36.70	35.70	26.90	24.50	23.10
9	Other vegetables	71.70	43.60	44.50	32.10	32.20	32.10	32.10	26.90
10	Pulses	19.90	18.10	17.40	16.90	17.00	18.20	11.30	8.30
11	Oilseed	53.80	42.70	35.60	24.60	24.70	22.80	22.80	19.70
12	Fruits	58.20	60.50	44.90	40.20	39.90	38.10	36.30	33.10
13	Tea	82.70	85.10	66.00	48.70	48.80	46.40	43.40	41.00
14	Other crops	64.90	40.40	41.50	28.30	28.60	28.10	27.20	22.50
15	Livestock	74.30	54.00	42.00	33.20	32.80	28.80	28.00	24.80
16	Fish	78.40	45.30	45.10	28.40	28.50	27.90	28.00	23.20
17	Forestry	38.80	32.70	23.90	22.70	22.90	19.70	19.20	16.90
18	Other fruits	489.20	327.40	88.50	88.30	86.00	76.70	68.30	66.90
19	Edible oil	74.80	46.50	39.60	55.60	53.70	41.40	35.30	35.00
20	Sugar and gur	96.30	42.30	52.30	51.10	51.40	40.00	38.50	31.10
21	Salt	51.40	61.60	43.50	37.20	34.60	30.70	29.10	29.60
22	Yarn	68.00	57.40	60.90	51.70	35.00	34.20	33.70	30.50

(Table continues on the following page.)

Table A2.3 Effective Rates of Protection in Bangladesh, 1992–2000 *(continued)*

	Sector name	Effective rate of protection							
		1992–93	1993–94	1994–95	1995–96	1996–97	1997–98	1998–99	1999–00
23	Cloth: milled	189.70	147.50	131.60	98.00	110.20	86.20	78.20	72.70
24	Cloth: handloomed	157.70	128.50	114.60	87.60	94.90	75.50	68.80	64.60
25	Ready made garments	237.20	130.00	84.10	53.70	57.40	65.40	60.50	58.90
26	Jute textile	98.20	93.50	81.00	55.70	56.00	48.40	44.10	43.50
27	Paper	68.30	74.10	48.80	25.40	22.70	12.70	11.30	15.50
28	Leather and leather products	98.60	87.30	42.30	20.70	15.80	8.80	5.90	6.50
29	Chemical fertilizer	−5.60	−2.20	−5.00	−3.60	−3.00	0.40	0.50	0.60
30	Pharmaceutical	1.50	−2.20	−2.50	−2.60	−1.40	0.70	0.60	−1.70
31	Chemical	30.30	15.40	14.90	12.50	13.80	15.20	16.10	9.70
32	Petroleum products	40.20	32.80	45.70	35.50	35.70	32.30	31.20	27.30
33	Cement	56.00	30.60	21.40	18.50	19.10	19.00	20.30	21.20
34	Steel and basic metal	40.90	27.20	27.40	25.10	24.60	25.00	25.10	19.50
35	Metal products	52.70	43.30	25.10	25.80	27.00	18.20	17.30	15.40
36	Machinery	47.50	28.90	15.10	12.60	12.30	9.30	9.60	5.20
37	Transport equipment	69.90	49.10	41.90	38.00	22.80	21.80	19.80	17.90
38	Wood and wood products	124.30	81.00	48.10	47.30	47.30	32.90	32.90	31.80
39	Tobacco products	133.60	69.90	89.70	85.00	86.70	81.90	74.70	68.50
40	Other industries	72.70	65.10	38.50	37.30	29.60	21.90	21.00	19.90
	Average effective rate of protection	75.71	56.65	40.57	33.02	32.43	28.55	26.77	24.47
	Standard deviation	84.40	56.99	31.19	25.67	26.78	22.95	20.94	19.97
	Coefficient of variation	111.49	100.60	76.87	77.73	82.58	80.39	78.24	81.60

Note: Based on 40 major items across all sectors.

Table A2.4 Effective Rates of Protection in Agriculture in Bangladesh, 1992–2000

Items		1992–93	1993–94	1994–95	1995–96	1996–97	1997–98	1998–99	1999–00
1	Rice	−8.00	0.90	2.40	−5.80	−5.70	−5.40	−5.30	−4.70
2	Wheat	−3.90	8.50	11.00	2.00	2.20	2.60	2.80	0.20
3	Coarse grains	−4.90	−4.10	−0.80	−0.20	−0.20	0.10	0.10	0.40
4	Sugarcane	68.40	71.30	14.20	14.80	15.00	15.20	15.20	15.80
5	Cotton	4.80	5.40	−2.00	−1.70	−1.70	−1.50	−1.50	−1.40
6	Tobacco	12.50	−0.90	10.20	11.80	12.10	11.10	11.30	12.20
7	Potato	58.90	60.40	48.80	36.70	35.70	26.90	24.50	23.10
8	Other vegetables	71.70	43.60	44.50	32.10	32.20	32.10	32.10	26.90
9	Pulses	19.90	18.10	17.40	16.90	17.00	18.20	11.30	8.30
10	Oilseed	53.80	42.70	35.60	24.60	24.70	22.80	22.80	19.70
11	Fruits	58.20	60.50	44.90	40.20	39.90	38.10	36.30	33.10
12	Tea	82.70	85.10	66.00	48.70	48.80	46.40	43.40	41.00
13	Other crops	64.90	40.40	41.50	28.30	28.60	28.10	27.20	22.50
14	Livestock	74.30	54.00	42.00	33.20	32.80	28.80	28.00	24.80
15	Forestry	38.80	32.70	23.90	22.70	22.90	19.70	19.20	16.90
16	Other fruits	489.20	327.40	88.50	88.30	86.00	76.70	68.30	66.90
17	Edible oil	74.80	46.50	39.60	55.60	53.70	41.40	35.30	35.00
18	Sugar and gur	96.30	42.30	52.30	51.10	51.40	40.00	38.50	31.10
	Average effective rate of protection	69.58	51.93	32.22	27.74	27.52	24.52	22.75	20.66
	Coefficient of variation	63.30	70.59	131.26	115.99	117.66	120.93	122.68	116.89

Note: Only URAoA commodities, 1992–93 to 1999–2000.
Source: Calculated on the basis of data obtained from Bangladesh Tariff Commission.

Endnotes

1. Agriculture's share in GDP, however, has been declining. It fell from 38 percent in 1990–91 to 26 percent in 1999–2000, according to the old national accounts series with the base year 1984–85. Under the newly introduced series, with the base year 1995–96, agriculture's share in GDP fell from 24.7 percent to 19 percent during the same period (table 2.1). The Labor Force Survey of 1995–96—the latest official statistics available—shows agriculture as employing 74 percent of the rural labor force and 64 percent of the country's total labor force in 1995–96.

2. Owing to several successive bumper harvests in the late 1990s, annual agricultural growth rate averaged at 3.0 percent in the 1990s, while the overall GDP of the country grew by 4.9 percent (old series, with base year 1984–85). According to the new series, agriculture grew annually by only 1.9 percent in the 1990s, while the GDP grew by 4.8 percent during the same period (table 2.1). Growth performance of some Asian countries, such as Pakistan, China, Thailand, and Malaysia, had been a great deal superior to Bangladesh during the period (World Bank 1999a).

3. On average, agriculture grew by 1.9 percent in the 1970s, 2.7 percent in the 1980s, and 1.7 percent during 1990–97, with a negative growth rate in 1994–95 and less than 2 percent growth rates in 1990–91, 1992–93, and 1993–94 (table 2.1).

4. The near stagnation of foodgrain production in the early 1990s sparked quite a debate centering around declining soil productivity in Bangladesh, but with the recent upsurge in agricultural production the debate appears to have subsided now. However, some researchers claimed that rice production did not stagnate at all and rather grew by 3–4 percent annually in the early 1990s, and that the official statistical agencies had consistently underreported the actual production (Mitchell 1998).

5. Wheat production, however, almost doubled in the 1990s, from about 1.0 million tons in 1991–92, to 1.9 millions tons in 1998–99.

6. The so-called "Urea Crisis" refers to an unfortunate situation from December 1994 to March 1995 when several farmers were killed as they demonstrated against a seasonal shortage of fertilizer. There are varying perceptions of the causes of the crisis. A World Bank (1997) report suggests that a favorable international price led the government to export excessive amounts of urea, depleting domestic stock to 73,000 tons on October 31, 1994, 69 percent less than the 235,000 tons of stock on October 31, 1993. The government did so at a time when domestic demand for fertilizer increased to 2 million tons when farmers received better prices for good harvests in 1994.

7. There is, however, a joint venture fertilizer factory in Chittagong—named KAFCO—in which the government also has a substantial share. Reportedly some private sector single super phosphate production facilities are now at various stages of development. A Bangladesh-China joint venture diammonium phosphate project in the state sector is also in progress now.

8. Urea production is highly subsidized, and the production cost of urea routinely exceeds the sales price. Domestic production is subsidized with a direct subsidy amounting to about 10 percent and an indirect subsidy to natural gas pricing amounting to about 34 percent. The total economic subsidy on urea, including domestic production and imports, was estimated at US$196 millon in 1996–97 (World Bank 1997).

9. Application of chemical fertilizers in Bangladesh has gradually increased from 2.3 million tons in 1991–92 to 2.8 million tons in 1998–99. Urea constitutes almost 90 percent of the usage. In 1998–99, the country used 1.9 million tons of urea, while the shares of the triple super phosphate, murate of phosphate, and single super phosphate were 0.17, 0.21, and 0.36 million tons, respectively. The share of diammonium phosphate, which was introduced in 1997–98, is on the rise. Its application jumped from 6,000 tons in 1997–98 to 38,000 tons in 1989–99. Bangladesh depends on imports of phosphate and potash supplies because domestic phosphate production is very limited and there are no known potash reserves in the country. About 50 percent of its urea imports, however, come from KAFCO at significantly lower prices than those purchased from the international market.

10. The country's seed rules classify seeds into three categories: breeder seed, also called basic seed; foundation seed, which is the progeny of breeder seed; and certified seed, which is the progeny of foundation seed.

11. Ahmed, et. al (2000) claims that reforms in agricultural input markets increased rice production by 20–32 percent in 1992–93, in comparison with what production would have been in the absence of reforms.

12. Output and area under modern varieties increased by 9.24 percent and 7.71 percent, respectively, and areas and output of modern varieties increased by 9.3 percent and 9.8 percent, respectively, during this period, while the total area under rice cultivation declined by 0.8 percent per annum (Shilpi 1998).

13. Although getting foodgrains to the poor at a relatively subsidized price remains a professed objective of the Public Foodgrain Distribution System, a substantial part of the money distributed through the system ends up as salary and budget supports to government employees, especially members of armed and paramilitary services, fire and civilian defense personnel, and other segments of the nonpoor. For details see Dowlah (2000).

14. In the late 1980s, when large-scale rationing programs were in place, total foodgrain stocks ranged from 0.85 million tons to 1.5 million tons. Since 1993–94, however, foodgrain stocks have been significantly lower, ranging from 0.44 million tons to 1.1 million tons. Currently, owing to several successive bumper harvests, government's foodgrain stock again exceeds 1.5 million tons. Maintenance of such a large stock is, however, questionable, especially at a time when food shortages can be met by imports in a few weeks.

15. Total domestic procurement of foodgrain—from farmers and private traders—ranged between 166,000 and 955,000 tons in the 1990s, and the amount exceeded 1 million tons only once in 1991–92 (see Dowlah 2000).

16. The food rationing system underwent sweeping changes in the early 1990s, when a multidonor task force found that for some food rationing programs it took Tk6.6 for transferring Tk1 to the beneficiaries, and system loss had been between 70 and 80 percent. Moreover, a government-donor joint task force in 1989 linked food aid to various income- and employment-generating development schemes. For details see Dowlah (2000).

17. As Goletti (1994) points out, government-support prices through domestic procurement during the harvest months and putting downward pressure on prices during the lean season had a negligible effect on prices and that even massive increases of domestic procurement would result in very small price increases.

18. In 1998–99, however, food aid flows increased significantly, following the worst floods in the nation's history that wrecked the economy for a prolonged three months, July to October 1998. Otherwise, in recent years, food aid ranged between 0.5 to 0.9 million tons. One reason for the global decline in food aid in recent years may well be that agricultural subsidies are being cut drastically in donor countries under the URAoA.

19. Food subsidy dropped from its peak of Tk3.90 billion in 1990–91 to Tk1.6 billion in 1993–94, then again increased to Tk3.8 billion in 1997–98 (Dowlah 2000).

20. Even without such emergencies, Bangladesh normally experiences seasonal variations in food security during September–November, before the transplanted aman harvest and during March–April, before the boro harvest. These are the most difficult periods for availability as well as accessibility of food, affecting the landless, marginal, and small families the most, as prices soar while agricultural wages drop to the minimum.

21. Table 2.4c also shows that coefficient of variation—a standard measure of dispersion of the tariff structure—remained largely unchanged during the entire period, indicating a rather protective tariff structure.

22. The voluntary preshipment scheme was earlier introduced in 1993–94, but then abandoned, as it was found to be fraught with under-invoicing practices. Government then resorted to what is called the Tariff Value Set, a system of minimum import prices for selected products, which provided an additional degree of protection if the tariff value exceeded the cost including freight price. Reintroduced, the voluntary preshipment scheme has been sending mixed signals again.

23. According to the World Bank (1999c), end-user concessions are a major source of complexity of the tariff structure and a recognized basis of rent seeking by customs personnel. The leakage of customs revenue that could be attributed to such end-use concessions is estimated at around Tk10 billion annually (US$200 million).

24. Illegal cross-border trade, most of which are imports, was equivalent to 13 percent of total official trade of Bangladesh in 1994. Food, agricultural products, and livestock accounted for more than 70 percent of the illegal imports (World Bank 1996). Bangladesh spends about 25 percent of export income for illegal imports from India. Official trade from India consists mainly of intermediate goods, such as cotton yarn and cement, and accounted for 10 percent in 1997 and 8 percent in 1998. Besides having a porous border, the illegal trade with India is facilitated by a more competitive exchange rate policy of India and a relatively less open Indian economy for import of consumer goods vis-à-vis Bangladesh (World Bank 1999c).

25. In response to continued foreign exchange reserve draw downs and appreciation of real exchange rates, a series of mini devaluations have been carried out since the mid-1990s. Between 1992 and 1999, the taka was devalued on at least 30 occasions.

26. The exchange rate distortions are measured through an elasticity or a tax approach. The elasticity approach calculates the equilibrium exchange rate as based on the estimates of implicit import tariff and export tax rates along with estimates of the price elasticities of import demand and export supply. The tax approach uses trade weights to estimate the standard conversion factor, which is expressed as a

ratio in which the numerator represents the value of traded goods at border prices while the denominator indicates the value of the same goods at domestic prices, excluding transport, handling, and trade margins (Shahabuddin 1999).

27. Conventional agriculture in Bangladesh includes crops, fisheries, livestock, and forestry. But agriculture, as defined in the Annex 1 of URAoA, excludes fish and fish products and jute crops, but includes certain tree products, such as essential oils and such other products (GATT 1994). Jute and fish products constitute a large part of Bangladesh's agricultural exportables. In 1997–98, for example, raw jute alone constituted 2.09 percent of the country's total exports compared to a share of 2.63 percent in the previous year.

28. A comparison of effective protection coefficients at official and equilibrium exchange rates for 1991 and 1997 shows that overvalued exchange rates created negative incentives for rice, wheat, and jute growers at both import and export parity prices, both at official and the equilibrium exchange rates.

29. Until 1993, bonded houses were limited to 100 percent exporters in the garment industries that used back-to-back credit lines and to suppliers that sold 100 percent of their output (such as zippers and buttons) to garment exporters. Currently bonded warehouses are also available to all 100 percent exporters and "deemed exporters." A few leather and toy exporters and some jewelry exporters are also using these facilities besides the ready made garments industry.

30. The first export processing zone in the country was established in 1984 in Chittagong, and then a second one was established in Dhaka in 1993. Currently, three other export processing zones in other parts of the country are at various stages of development.

31. Bank credit guarantees are offered to exporters against possible losses on loans received against overseas commercial and political risks. Of the three types of guarantees—preshipment, postshipment, and comprehensive—the first two are extended to the banks that provide export credit and the third is available directly to the exporters.

32. Interest rate subsidies are offered to selected exporters who receive bank credit for export purposes at less than the interest rate applicable for other purposes. In the late 1980s, for example, nontraditional export products were entitled to an interest rate of 9 percent, while the normal rate was 14 percent. In the 1990s, as table 2.16 shows, exporting firms received bank credit at 9–9.6 percent while the market rate for general credit ranged between 13.1 and 17.2 percent.

33. XPB refers to a special foreign exchange rate benefit in excess of the official exchange rate, which was offered to nontraditional export products in the 1980s. Three XPB entitlement rates were maintained at 100 percent, 70 percent, and 40 percent, and all agricultural export products except jute were entitled to the benefits. The nominal value of the XPB benefit, discontinued since 1992, depended on (a) the XPB entitlement rate offered for a particular export product and (b) the difference between the official exchange rate and the exchange rate used for the wage earner scheme.

34. The absolute decline of the sector's export, however, does not seem to be well understood. Some studies suggest that Bangladesh is an efficient producer of rice for import substitution, but not for exports. The production of other crops, such as cotton, onion, and potato are found to be highly competitive with imports,

while tobacco, pulses, vegetables, and tea are found to be moderate to strong contenders for export. Crops like oilseeds, chilies, and sugarcane indicate little or low comparative advantage. See Shahabuddin (1999) and Mitchell (1998).

35. Major reasons for the setback in agro-processing industries lay with the lack of marketing networks as an effective means for reducing variability in prices, poor rural financial services and infrastructures, electrification and communication facilities, and poor functioning of public institutions in rural areas. See World Bank (1999a).

36. Hutcheson (1985) found that exporting activities received an average effective protection rate of a mere 2 percent, compared with 104 percent for import substitution industries. Also see World Bank (1999c).

37. Bangladesh has significantly liberalized its tariff structure, both tariff and nontariff trade barriers, over the years. Even in 1995, when the country declared bound tariff at the 200 percent level, the highest operative tariff (unweighted) was 66 percent and the import weighted average tariff rates (customs duties) on all products, agricultural as well as nonagricultural, were 25.9 percent and 20.8 percent, respectively. It, therefore, seems that Bangladesh may have demonstrated "fear psychology" by declaring the 200 percent bound rate of tariff for selected agricultural goods. Given the current rate of highest tariff at 37.5 percent, the declaration of the bound rate at 200 percent sends misleading signals about the state of trade liberalization in the country.

38. Besides, some subsidy elements can be traced to freight concessions on shipments of exported products by the national airline and shipping line as well as some concessions on fire and shipping insurance charges. These subsidies are, however, exempted from reduction requirements for the developing countries.

39. Also, viewed from the perspectives of a shadow exchange rate, the XPB benefits might have disadvantaged the export products relatively more than some of the export incentives in place.

40. Normally the condition is whether the product showed exports exceeding more than anticipated levels of increase in targets set for the sector.

41. Article 6 of URAoA specifically exempts investment subsidies that are generally available to agriculture and agricultural input subsidies that are generally available to low-income or resource-poor producers. Thus, Bangladesh can legitimately ignore these subsidies or supports in calculating its AMS to agriculture.

42. Government support to agricultural output revolved around 1–3 percent since the late 1980s, with around 2 percent during the base years, and subsequently increasing to a maximum of 3.4 percent.

43. Of the three main types of fertilizers used in Bangladesh—urea, TSP, and MP—none receives any budgetary support, and if the AMS is calculated according to Paragraph 13 in Annex 3 of the Legal Text of the URAoA, Bangladesh has no AMS in fertilizer to report. That, however, does not nullify the fact that the government provides a hidden subsidy to urea production by supplying gas at subsidized prices.

44. In cases of products for which market access opportunity falls short of the target level, minimum access opportunities need to be implemented on the basis of tariff quotas at low rates as provided on most favored nation basis until their share exceeds the current threshold of the specific year of implementation.

45. A significant volume of sugar is imported within the country through illegal trading or by smuggling. In fact, illegal import of sugar constituted about 32 percent of sugar available for domestic consumption in 1994. This means that legal import of sugar will increase if the restrictions on sugar imports are eased.

46. Bangladesh's unilateral trade liberalization, especially in the early 1990s, still remains a highly controversial and politically sensitive issue. Although most of these reforms were carried out under the Enhanced Structural Adjustment Program and the Structural Adjustment Program, sponsored by multilateral donors, the then-finance minister, Saifur Rahman, has been credited, or discredited, for steering those singlehandedly.

47. However, if all agricultural imports handled by government and semi-government bodies are taken into consideration, then the share would range between 5 percent and 24 percent even in the 1990s.

48. A number of top policymakers of Bangladesh were consulted in the preparation of this chapter, including government secretaries of finance, agriculture, and commerce and trade; several key opinion makers, newspaper editors, and professors; and more than 100 attendees at an international seminar on the WTO in Dhaka in August 1999 were interviewed or conferred with. Also, officials of donor agencies, such as the World Bank, the Food and Agriculture Organization, and the U.S. Agency for International Development were consulted.

49. Bangladesh appears to be concerned with Article 27.3 (b) of Trade-Related Aspects of Intellectual Property Rights that relate to patent rights on plants and animals. The viewpoints expressed by policymakers, in both formal and informal meetings, comes closer to what Bhagirath Lal Das (1998), a former Indian ambassador to GATT, proposed.

50. The trade-related labor issues currently relate to the country's main export-earner, the ready-made garments industry. In brief, Bangladesh has made considerable progress in recent years in eliminating child labor in the ready-made garments industry. Still the country is concerned that by pressing hard on trade-related environmental and labor issues, WTO might give a further push to eco-labeling initiatives in the industrialized world for which Bangladesh is not well prepared at this moment (Dowlah 1999).

51. It should, however, be noted that these figures represent up to 1990–97. During the subsequent years of the 1990s, growth rates in exports and manufacturing had been less spectacular.

52. The agricultural sector in Bangladesh consists of four subsectors: crops, livestock, fisheries, and forestry. The URAoA-defined agriculture excludes fish and fish products as well as jute, a major crop of the country, while it includes certain tree products, which are normally not included in agriculture in Bangladesh.

53. Except tea, all other agricultural export commodities—such as jute and jute products, fish and fish products—are excluded from the domain of URAoA agriculture.

54. As shown previously, withdrawal of QRs on potatoes is not likely to increase imports of potatoes and withdrawal of QRs on sugar is likely to reduce illegal trade and increase legal trade in sugar.

55. According to UNCTAD, the 29 member countries of the Organisation for Economic Co-operation and Development (OECD) spent an average $350,000 mil-

lion a year in agricultural support between 1996 and 1998 when agricultural exports from developing countries totaled $170,000 million only. About 39 percent of farm income in the European Union countries came from government production supports, while the percentage was 17 percent for U.S. farm income. The European Union provides nearly 10 times more production support to its farmers than the United States does, about $324 per acre compared with $34 in the United States. The industrialized world does not fall much behind when it comes to tariffs as well. For example, Japan still maintains a 550 percent tariff on imported rice, the countries in the European Union maintain a 215 percent tariff on imported beef, and Canada maintains a 300 percent tariff on butter.

Bibliography

Ahmed, R., S. Haggblade, and T. Chowdhury. 2000. *Out of the Famine: Evolving Food Markets and Food in Bangladesh*. Baltimore: Johns Hopkins University Press.

Anderson, James E. 1997. "The Uruguay Round and Welfare in Some Distorted Agricultural Economies." Working Paper, National Bureau of Economic Research, Cambridge, Mass.

Anderson, James. E., and R. Tyres. 1995. "How Developing Countries Could Gain from Agricultural Trade Liberalization in the Uruguay Round." In I. Goldin and O. Knudsen, eds., *Agricultural Trade Liberalization: Implications for Developing Countries*. Paris: OECD.

Asaduzzaman, A. 1999. "The Uruguay Round, WTO Rules and the Bangladesh Agriculture." Paper presented at the Round Table on the Consequences of the Uruguay Round Agreements for Bangladesh Agriculture, Dhaka, July 1999.

Bakth, Zaid. 1999. "Bangladesh Agriculture: Border Protection and Export Subsidy." Paper presented at the Round Table on the Consequences of the Uruguay Round Agreements for Bangladesh Agriculture, Dhaka, July 1999.

Bangladesh Agriculture Research Council. 1997. "Food Security for the Resource-Poor in Bangladesh." LCG Note, Dhaka.

Bangladesh Ministry of Agriculture. 1997. "Technical Assistance Needs for the Ministry of Agriculture Regarding Compliance of the WTO Agreements." Dhaka.

———. 1998. "The Agreement on Agriculture under the WTO and the Bangladesh Agriculture." Dhaka.

———. 1999a. "Bangladesh Country Paper on the URA, WTO Rules and Implications for Bangladesh Agriculture." Paper presented at the Expert Meeting on Trade in Agricultural Sector, UNCTAD, Geneva, April.

———. 1999b. "Special Presentation of Bangladesh on Agreement on Agriculture." Paper presented at the First Consultative Meeting of the SAARC Commerce Ministers on the WTO Issues. New Delhi, May 10–12.

Bangladesh Ministry of Finance. 1997. *Bangladesh Economic Survey, 1997*. Dhaka.

———. 2000. *Bangladesh Economic Survey, 2000*. Dhaka.

Bergsten, Fred C. 1996. "Competitive Liberalization and Global Free Trade: A Vision for the Early 21st Century." APEC Working Paper 96-15. Institute for International Economics, Washington, D.C.

———. 1998. "Fifty Years of the GATT/WTO: Lessons from the Past for Strategies for the Future." Paper presented at the Symposium on the World Trading System, WTO and the Graduate Institute of International Studies, Geneva, April 1998.
Bhagwati, Jagdish. 1991. *The World Trading System at Risk*. Princeton, N.J.: Princeton University Press.
Bumb, Balu, et al. 1999. "Implications of the Uruguay Round Agreement for Agriculture and Agribusiness Development in Bangladesh." Paper presented at the Round Table on the Consequences of the Uruguay Round Agreements for Bangladesh Agriculture, Dhaka, July 1999.
Das, Bhagirath Lal. 1998. "Proposals for Improvement in the Agreement on TRIPS." *SEATINI Bulletin (Southern and Eastern African Trade, Information and Negotiations Initiative)* 1(8).
Dowlah, C.A.F. 1998. "The Agreement on Textiles and Clothing under the Uruguay Round: A Mixed Bag for the Developing Countries?" *The Journal of Bangladesh International Institute of Strategic Studies*.
———. 1999. "The Future of the Readymade Clothing Industry of Bangladesh in the Post-Uruguay Round World." *The World Economy* 22(7).
———. 2000. "Bangladesh Country Paper on Enabling Development: The Role of Food Assistance in South Asia." Background Paper.
FAO (Food and Agricultural Organization). 1998. *Impact of the Uruguay Round on Agriculture*. Rome.
Faruqee, Rashid, ed. 1998. *Bangladesh Agriculture in the 21st Century*. Dhaka: University Press.
———. 1995. "Structural and Policy Reforms for Agricultural Growth." Working Paper. World Bank, Washington, D.C.
GATT (General Agreement on Tariffs and Trade). 1994. *The Results of the Uruguay Round of Multilateral Trade Negotiations*. Geneva.
Goldin, I., and D. van der Mensbrugghe. 1995. "The Uruguay Round: An Assessment of Economy-Wide and Agricultural Reforms." Working Paper, World Bank.
Goletti, Francesco. 1994. "The Changing Public Role in Rice Economy Approaching Self-Sufficiency: The Case of Bangladesh." *International Food Policy Research Institute Abstract*. September.
Harrison, Glenn, Thomas Rutherford, and David Taylor. 1995. "Quantifying the Outcome of the Uruguay Round." *Finance and Development*.
Hathaway, Dale E., and Merlinda D. Ingco. 1997. "Agricultural Liberalization and the Uruguay Round." In Will Martin and L. Alan Winters, eds., *The Uruguay Round and the Developing Countries*. New York: Cambridge University Press.
Healy, Stephen, Richard Pearce, and Michael Stockbridge. 1998. *The Implications of the Uruguay Round Agreement on Agriculture for Developing Countries*. Rome: FAO.
Hoekman, Bernard, and Kym Anderson. 1999. "Developing Country Agriculture and the New Trade Agenda." Washington, D.C.: World Bank.
Howard, Lyall. 1998. "Unfinished Business: Global Trade Reform in Agriculture." *Agribusiness Review*.
Hutcheson, T. L. 1985. "Effective Protection: An Input-Output Approach." Background Paper. Trade and Industrial Policy Reform Program, Planning Commission, Dhaka.

Ibrahim, Ali. 1998. "The Implications of the Uruguay Round Agreement for Bangladesh." Background Paper. IMF, Washington, D.C.

Islam, Nurul. 1996. "Implementing the Uruguay Round: Increased Food Price Stability by 2020?" In *A 2020 Vision for Food, Agriculture, and the Environment*. Washington, D.C.: International Food Policy Research Institute.

Konandreas, Panos, and Jim Greenfield. 1996. "Uruguay Round Commitments on Domestic Support: Their Implications for Developing Countries." *Food Policy* 21:433–46.

Krueger, A. O. 1999. *Developing Countries and the Next Round of Multilateral Trade Negotiations*. Washington, D.C.: World Bank.

Lindland, Jostein. 1997. *The Impact of the Uruguay Round on Tariff Escalation in Agricultural Products*. Rome: FAO.

Mahmud, W., S. H. Rahman, and S. Zohir. 1994. "Agricultural Growth Through Crop Diversification in Bangladesh." Working Paper. International Food Policy Research Institute, Washington, D.C.

Majd, Nader. 1995. "The Uruguay Round and South Asia." Public Research Working Paper. World Bank, Washington, D.C.

Martin, Will, and L. Alan Winters, eds., 1997. *The Uruguay Round and the Developing Countries*. New York: Cambridge University Press.

Mitchell, Donald. 1998. "Promoting Growth in Bangladesh Agriculture." Working Paper, Washington, D.C.: World Bank.

Mitchell, Donald, and T. Islam. 1998. "Growth Potential in Bangladesh Agriculture." Working Paper. World Bank, Washington, D.C.

Ninno, Carlo D., and Paul Dorosh. 1998. "Government Policy, Markets and Food Security in Bangladesh." Dhaka: International Food Policy Research Institute.

OECD (Organisation for Economic Co-operation and Development). 1997. *The Uruguay Round Agreement on Agriculture and Processed Agricultural Products*. Paris.

Pagiola, Stefano. 1995. "Environmental and Natural Resources Degradation in Intensive Agriculture in Bangladesh." Working Paper. World Bank, Washington, D.C.

Shahabuddin, Quazi. 1999. "Comparative Advantage in Bangladesh Agriculture." Paper presented at the Round Table on the Consequences of the Uruguay Round Agreements for Bangladesh Agriculture, Dhaka, July 1999.

Sharma, Ramesh, and Panos Konandreas. 1999. "Trade and Food Security: Options for Developing Countries." Paper presented at the Round Table on the Consequences of the Uruguay Round Agreements for Bangladesh Agriculture, Dhaka, July 1999.

Shilpi, Forahd. 1998. "Policy Incentives and Comparative Advantage of Bangladesh Agriculture." Working Paper. World Bank, Washington, D.C.

Srinivasan, T. N. 1998. *Developing Countries and the Multilateral Trading System*. Boulder, Colo.: Westview.

Subramanium, Arvind. 1994. "The Case for Low Uniform Tariffs." *Finance and Development*.

Tansey, Geoff. 1999. "Trade, Intellectual Property, Food and Biodiversity: Key Issues and Options for the 1999 Review of the TRIPS Agreement." London: Quaker Peace and Service.

USAID (U.S. Agency for International Development). 1999. "Trade Liberalization, Economic Growth and Food Security: An Example from Bangladesh." Draft paper, Washington, D.C.

Valdés, Alberto. 1999. "Overview of the Global Impact of the Uruguay Round and Lessons from Early Reformers." In Beniot Blarel, Garry Pursell, and Alberto Valdes, eds., *Implications of the Uruguay Round Agreement for South Asia: The Case of Agriculture.* Washington, D.C.: World Bank.

Valdés, Alberto, and A. F. McCalla. 1996. "The Uruguay Round and Agricultural Policies in Developing Countries and Economies in Transition." *Food Policy* 21.

World Bank. 1996. *Trade Policy Reform for Improving the Incentive Regime.* Washington, D.C.: World Bank.

———. 1997. "Policy Notes on Bangladesh Agricultural Policy Issues." Working Paper. Washington, D.C.

———. 1998. "Knowledge for Development." *World Development Report 1998/99.* New York: Oxford University Press.

———. 1999a. "Bangladesh: A Proposed Rural Development Strategy." Working Paper. Washington, D.C.

———. 1999b. " A Proposal for Rationalizing the Tariff Structure in the Forthcoming Budget FY 2000: A Policy Note." Working Paper. Washington, D.C.

———. 1999c. "Bangladesh Trade Liberalization: Its Pace and Impacts." Working Paper. Washington, D.C.

World Food Program (WFP). 1999. *The Bangladesh Foodgrain Digest.* Several issues.

Yusuf, Shahid, and Praveen Kumar. 1995. "Non-Farm Development: Comparative Experience and Bangladesh's Prospects." Working Paper. World Bank, Washington D.C.

3
Sri Lanka

Saman Kelegama

The population of Sri Lanka was 18.8 million in mid 1998. The population growth rate is currently almost 1.2 percent, and the population increases annually by approximately 250,000. This is considered to be a low rate of growth in comparison with other developing countries in the region. Sri Lanka still has an agricultural economy, with one third of the total labor force involved in agriculture activities, but this figure has been shrinking by 4 percent since 1990 (figure 3.1). Though the main occupation of the rural population is agriculture, development in other sectors and high off-farm wages have led to the movement of labor out of the agricultural sector since the latter half of the 1980s, as highlighted in table A3.1. Agriculture's share of the gross domestic product (GDP) declined 5.38 percent between 1990 and 1997 (from 23.22 percent to 17.84 percent; see table A3.2).

Statistics indicate that land used for major agricultural crops has been steadily declining, and only a few crops have shown marginal increases in the extent of cultivation. The extent of land used for paddy (rice in husk) cultivation decreased to 730,000 hectares in 1997, a 15 percent reduction since 1990. However, 848,000 hectares of paddy were cultivated in 1998.

The plantation crops have also demonstrated declining trends during the past decade. Land used for tea cultivation has declined by 10 percent, and land used for rubber cultivation has declined by 20 percent since 1990, along with similar decreases in land used for coconut cultivation. This has been mainly due to the utilization of these lands for residential and industrial purposes. There has also been a remarkable decline in the cultivated land area of other field crops. Potato cultivation fell to 2,328 hectares in 1998, almost a 70 percent reduction in cultivated land area since 1990. During the same period, big onion cultivation declined by 20 percent, and chili cultivation declined by 40 percent. In contrast, the available statistics indicate that the area under cultivation for minor export crops has been increasing during the past decade. In addition, the total forest cover in the country is currently only 20 percent of the total land area (refer to tables A3.3 and A3.4).

Figure 3.1 Agriculture Labor Population, 1990–98

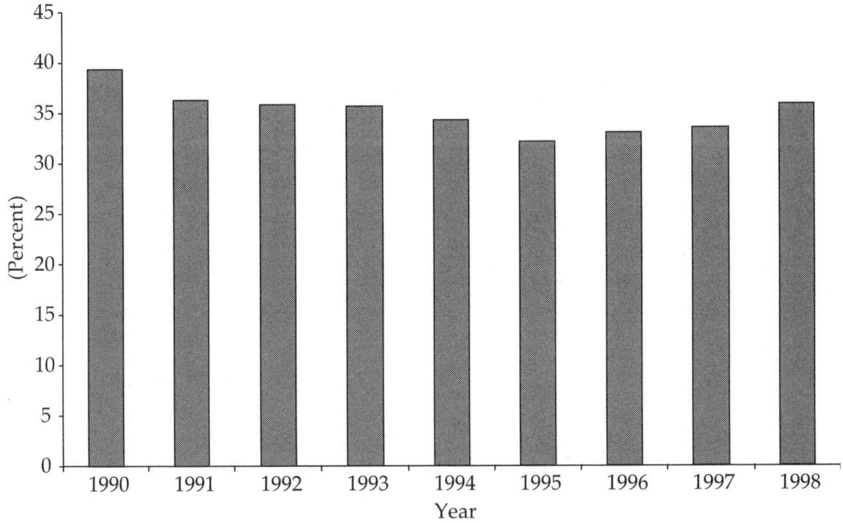

[Bar chart showing agriculture labor population percentages from 1990 to 1998, with values ranging approximately from 32% to 40%]

Source: Plotted using data from the Central Bank of Sri Lanka, Annual Report (various years).

Major Agricultural Commodities

PADDY. Paddy production remained relatively unchanged during the 1990–98 period. Output reached 2.7 million tons in 1998, while the average yield was recorded at 3,636 kilograms per hectare. Production constituted more than 80 percent of the local rice requirement and the remaining 168,000 million tons were imported during 1998. It is estimated that the annual per capita consumption of rice is approximately 106 kilograms, and Sri Lanka is currently 83 percent self-sufficient in rice. Based on the current consumption patterns, projected annual rice requirements will continue to increase (figure 3.2). The government is now debating whether the area under paddy production should be increased by investing heavily in irrigated agriculture, or whether annual paddy yields can be increased from 3.6 to 4.8 tons per hectare with the introduction of high yielding varieties.

TEA. Sri Lanka has more than 130 years of experience in the cultivation of tea and is currently the largest tea exporter in the world, exporting 271

Figure 3.2 Paddy Production, Requirement Projections, 1999–2004

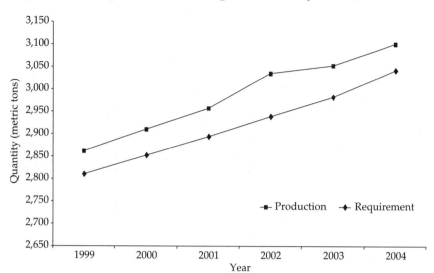

Source: Plotted using data from the Central Bank of Sri Lanka, Annual Report (various years).

million kilograms of tea in 1998. Tea production increased by 20 percent during 1990–98 (figure 3.3), and in 1998 total tea production was recorded at 280 million kilograms. Unfortunately, the increasing cost of production, estimated at Rs106.72 per kilogram in 1998, is a significant issue for this sector. Labor costs account for more than 60 percent of the total cost of production.

Colombo (the capital city of Sri Lanka) houses the largest tea auction in the world, and more than 256 million kilograms of tea were sold in 1998. The gross average price was around Rs134.35 per kilogram during this period. Approximately 96 percent of local tea produced is exported, earning Rs50,000 million in 1998. Tea is exported mainly in bulk and value-added form. Sri Lanka's share of value-added tea exports has been consistently increasing and in 1998 accounted for more than 40 percent of total tea exports.

During the latter half of 1998, and owing to the Russian currency crisis, Sri Lankan exporters were confronted with a liquidity crisis when shipments to the value of US$35 million were unpaid by Russian importers. However, during this period, export volumes increased to the United Arab Emirates and Commonwealth of Independent States (CIS) countries and mitigated the immediate impact of the Russian crisis.

Figure 3.3 Tea and Rubber Production in Sri Lanka, 1990–98

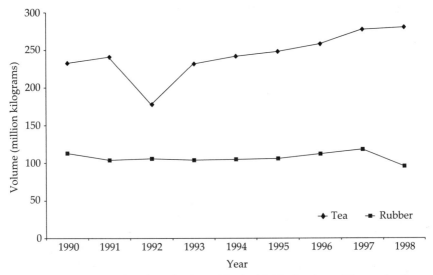

Source: Plotted using data from the Central Bank of Sri Lanka, Annual Report (various years).

The Sri Lankan government levies various types of cesses (surcharges) on tea exports such as the Tea Board cess (Rs2.50 per kilogram), and Tea Medical cess (Rs0.0035 per kilogram). This cess collection is channeled back into the tea sector via the Tea Board, the Tea Small Holdings Development Authority, and the Tea Research Institute for not only the expansion of their activities but also to upgrade tea production, processing, and export through the provision of various subsidies. There are minor quantities of tea imports, mainly for the purpose of re-export. These imports are subject to a 35 percent tariff.

RUBBER. Rubber production declined to 95 million kilograms in 1998, a 20 percent decline in production since 1990. Sri Lanka now contributes less than 2 percent to the global rubber market. The rapid demise of the rubber sector can be attributed to several factors. Primarily, poor yields have led to lower output and unattractive prices, which have in turn resulted in a significant number of producers moving out of rubber production. In addition, the average cost of production of rubber has been continually increasing. It is currently estimated at Rs44.00 per kilogram. This has significantly eroded potential profit margins and has been a significant disincentive for producers.

Rubber exports declined dramatically by 40 percent to 41 million kilograms in 1998. Furthermore, bulk excess rubber stocks dumped on the international market by the United States and Thailand resulted in substantial international price decreases. Currency devaluations in other major rubber exporting countries also adversely affected the competitiveness of Sri Lankan rubber exports.

The impact of these changes in the rubber market affected Sri Lankan smallholders considerably, and these smallholders account for more than 60 percent of the total rubber producers in the country. Thus in May 1998 the Sri Lankan government abolished the rubber export cess to improve producer prices. However, the use of rubber in local industries had been increasing during the past few years, and in 1998 more than 50 percent or around 54 million kilograms of rubber were used locally.

COCONUT. Growth in coconut production has been stagnant since 1990. Fresh nut production was recorded at 2,500 million nuts in 1998. High domestic consumption has constrained the development of the coconut export market, accounting for 70 percent of total production in 1998. Coconut prices have also been fairly high, above Rs8.00 per fresh nut during 1998.

Sri Lanka exports various coconut products including desiccated coconut, coconut oil, copra, and kernel products. The international market prices of these commodities have been subject to a certain amount of fluctuation during the last few years, especially palm oil prices, which have declined. The total export earnings from coconut products were estimated at Rs6,110 million in 1998, a 12 percent reduction from the previous year. The cess for coconut product exports remained unchanged, but increased for desiccated coconut exports in mid-1998. The general tariff rate for the import of coconut products is 35 percent. In particular, Sri Lanka imported 395,600 kilograms in 1997.

Other Field Crops

The production of particularly high value cash crops, such as chilies, potato, and big onion, has been decreasing over the past decade (figure 3.4). In addition, the cost of production of these crops is relatively high when compared to the other countries in the region. Furthermore, local producers have had difficulty competing with imports (figure 3.5). This can be mainly attributed to the relaxation of import restrictions by the government in 1996. Farmers are now confronted with severe difficulties in marketing their products because of the availability of cheaper imports. Bulk purchases of local production have been made by the largest state trading enterprise. Such action has resulted in the transmission of incorrect market signals to producers.

Figure 3.4 Field Crop Production in Sri Lanka, 1994–98

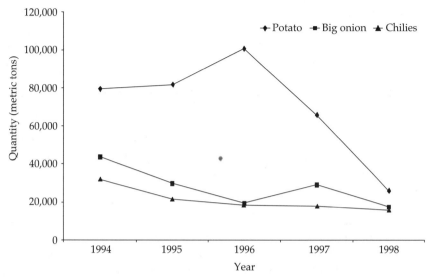

Source: Plotted using data from the Central Bank of Sri Lanka, Annual Report (various years).

Figure 3.5 Field Crop Imports in Sri Lanka, 1994–98

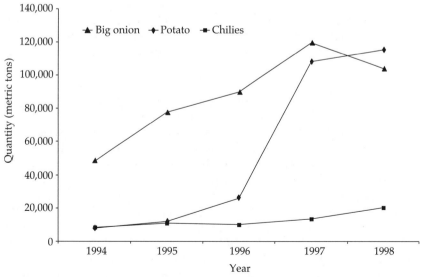

Source: Plotted using data from the Central Bank of Sri Lanka, Annual Report (various years).

In light of the issues facing other field crops producers, the government has maintained a certain degree of protection by retaining a tariff rate of 35 percent, and by also introducing a producer price scheme for these commodities. The recommended prices were Rs50.00–70.00 per kilogram of chilies, Rs12.00–14.00 per kilogram of onion, and Rs20.00–25.00 per kilogram of potato. This guaranteed price scheme was implemented through the Cooperative Wholesale Establishment (CWE) in 1997. However, the CWE's role has been significantly reduced owing to competition from the private sector.

POTATO. Potato production decreased from 84,000 million tons in 1990 to 26,000 million tons in 1998. Potato imports in 1998 were estimated at 115,000 million tons, which accounts for 60 percent of the local requirement. More than 86 percent of total imports are from India and Pakistan. Until 1996 potato remained a highly protected crop. However, in recent years the cost of production, estimated at Rs26.00 per kilogram, has remained extremely high, and poor yield has eroded the profitability of this crop.

CHILIES. Chili production also decreased from 30,000 million tons in 1993 to 15,000 million tons in 1998, while imports increased from 8,000 million tons in 1994 to 20,000 million tons in 1998. The average producer price was Rs100.00 per kilogram during 1998. Import prices of chilies have declined significantly during the last few years owing to increased chili production in India.

BIG ONION. The volume of local production of big onion has demonstrated a declining trend since 1994, when production was recorded at 43,000 million tons. Production accounted for only 15 percent of the domestic requirement in 1998.

SUGAR. Sugar production has remained relatively unchanged during the last decade, though production has decreased more recently from 71,000 million tons in 1994 to 61,000 million tons in 1998. There are four major factories that produce sugar in Sri Lanka: Hingurana, Kantalai, Pelwatte, and Sevanagala. However, the Kantalai factory has not been in operation since 1994, and the Hingurana factory is also currently nonoperational owing to a plethora of problems centered around ad hoc privatization and the ongoing war in the northeast of Sri Lanka. Local production from the factories that are in operation account for only 12–13 percent of the annual domestic sugar requirement. In addition, per capita sugar consumption increased from 20 kilograms in 1988 to 33 kilograms in 1997.

The import of sugar is now subject to a specific tariff rate, and the average annual import volume of sugar has been estimated at around 400,000 million tons during the last five years. During this period sugar prices have shown a declining trend, and in 1998 the price of sugar was recorded at US$291 per metric ton. This sharp decline in international sugar prices has adversely affected the local sugar industry. In response the government has attempted to protect local sugar producers by stabilizing sugar prices at US$500 per metric ton by imposing an ad valorem duty on imports, a heavy burden to the consumer.

Wheat Grain and Wheat Flour

Sri Lanka's wheat grain requirements are solely met by imports from countries such as the United States, Canada, and Australia, and have been increasing over time (figure 3.6). A substantial proportion of this requirement is received as food aid under the U.S. government's special PL 480 aid program. The wheat grain is shipped directly to Prima Ceylon Ltd., with whom the Sri Lankan government has a special contractual agreement.[1] The processing of wheat flour is the only monopolistic business handled by the government through a state trading enterprise, CWE, and the Food Commissioners Department. The CWE plays a significant role in this transaction with regard to the importation of wheat grain while the Food Commissioners Department is directly involved in the storage, transportation, and bulk sale. The department also determines and revises the existing stocks of flour, market situations, and especially the price levels during weekly food security meetings.

Figure 3.6 Wheat Imports, 1990–98

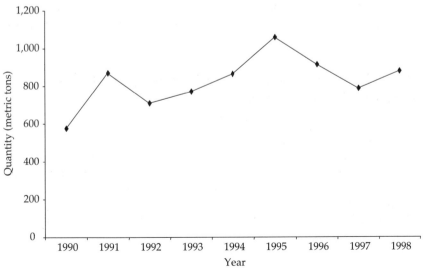

Sources: Cooperative Wholesale Establishment; People's Bank (1999).

The heavy cost borne by the government for the purpose of fulfilling the Prima agreement is influenced by the politically sensitive wheat flour market, which has been controversial in the recent past. The retail price has been fixed by the government from time to time. In particular, the retail price of flour was increased to Rs19.45 per kilogram in 1999 from Rs11.95 per kilogram in 1995. The ultimate cost of production of wheat flour is as high as Rs20 per kilogram. Consumption of wheat flour is only second to the consumption of rice in Sri Lanka, and is estimated at 43 kilograms per annum. Wheat consumption has increased mainly because of urbanization, particularly among low-income groups in society.

Dairy Industry

The dairy cow population in Sri Lanka is currently 697,000, and the total cattle population was 1.5 million in 1997. The buffalo population was estimated at 234,000 cows and 720,000 total head. Local milk production was recorded at 341 million liters in 1998, 256 million liters of which was from cattle and 85 million liters from buffaloes. The collection of milk is dominated by the Kiriya Milk Industry and Nestlé Lanka Ltd, which collected 53 million liters and 29 million liters, respectively, in 1998. Table 3.1 outlines the trends in milk collection between 1990 and 1996.

There are two major issues that have held back dairy production in Sri Lanka. The first is the need to provide a conducive policy environment for the development of the dairy industry. The second is the issue of whether Sri Lanka has a comparative advantage in fluid milk production or powdered milk production. Despite these policy drawbacks, in September 1997 the government initiated the process of reforming the dairy industry by transferring the ownership of the Milk Industry of Lanka Co.

Table 3.1 Milk Collection and Utilization by Local Milk Industries, 1990–96 (million liters)

Industry	1990	1991	1992	1993	1994	1995	1996
Milk Industry of Lanka Co. Ltd. (Kiriya from 1997)	59.3	62.5	43.8	42.5	41.9	46.8	40.9
Nestlé Lanka Ltd.	19.4	20.4	28.1	31.0	27.0	32.4	36.8
International Dairy Products Ltd.	6.0	8.0	9.7	11.1	11.0	9.1	13.3
Ceylon Cold Stores Ltd.	0.8	0.8	0.9	1.0	1.0	1.2	1.1

Ltd. to the Kiriya Milk Industry. It was a major attempt made by the government with the assistance of the National Dairy Development Board of India to develop the dairy industry in Sri Lanka. The broad objectives of this program are to improve industry technology and to increase fluid milk production by setting up a milk processing plant with a production capacity of 300,000 liters of milk per day. Apart from that, a new project has been launched to produce high quality breeding stock to overcome the acute problem of low quality breeding that currently exists in the country's dairy industry.

Prior to 1996 the government set milk prices at Rs10.54 per liter, and during 1996 there were two subsequent price revisions by Rs2.00 per liter and 9 cents per liter. Although the government and milk processing companies negotiated not to pass the full cost of production on to consumers, this milk pricing system was discontinued in 1997, and all milk processors were free to compete directly for milk collection and to set their own prices.

Currently, locally produced milk accounts for only 20 percent of the total requirement, with the balance being imported primarily from Australia and New Zealand (tables 3.2 and A3.5). However, a large proportion of infant milk products is supplied by Indonesia (30 percent) and the United States (55 percent). Notably, 90 percent of total imports was full cream milk powder.

Because costs of production in the dairy industry are high the government imposes a tariff on the import of milk and milk products. Consequently, the import of milk and milk products has been declining in the recent past from 65,000 million tons in 1990 to 42,000 million tons in 1997 as indicated in figure 3.7.

Table 3.2 Dairy Product Imports by Major Source Countries and Market Share, 1995–97

Source of supply	1995		1996		1997	
	Quantity (million tons)	Market share (percent)	Quantity (million tons)	Market share (percent)	Quantity (million tons)	Market share (percent)
New Zealand	25,070	53	26,017	59	27,133	63
Australia	4,786	10	8,306	19	10,162	23
European Union	13,869	29	8,424	19	5,477	13
Other	3,734	8	1,556	3	268	1

Source: Sri Lanka Department of Customs.

Figure 3.7 Volume of Milk Imports, 1990–97

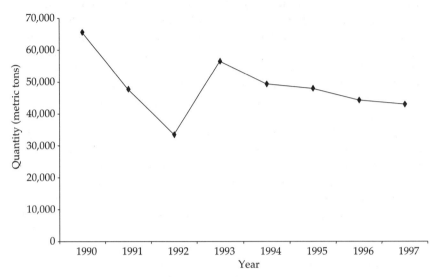

Sources: People's Bank (1999); the Central Bank of Sri Lanka (1999b).

Poultry and Other Meats

The poultry population increased to 9.25 million in 1997 along with an increase in chicken meat production to 47,000 million tons from 9,000 million tons in 1987. Poultry meat consumption also increased, and per capita consumption is currently recorded at 2.12 kilograms per annum. While only 2 percent of the total consumption requirement of poultry meat is being imported, it accounts for approximately 44 percent of total meat imports and was valued at Rs50 million in 1997. There has also been an increase in the export quantities of poultry meat, and 533.1 million tons of poultry meat was exported in 1997 compared with 90 million tons in 1992.

Since 1960, egg production has also increased. Egg exports earned Rs34 million in 1997. Egg consumption has stagnated at around 50 eggs per annum. Moreover, layer production has shown a declining trend up to now.

Since 1992, the export volume of meat has also increased, and the industry earned Rs130 million in 1997. Red meat production has also increased during the last few years, and beef, mutton, and pork production was recorded at 12,000 tons, 980 tons, and 1,129 tons, respectively, in 1996.

Fisheries Industry

Because Sri Lanka has extensive marine resources, 93 percent of the total fish requirement was met by local production in 1998. Total fish produc-

Figure 3.8 Fish Production in Sri Lanka, 1994–98

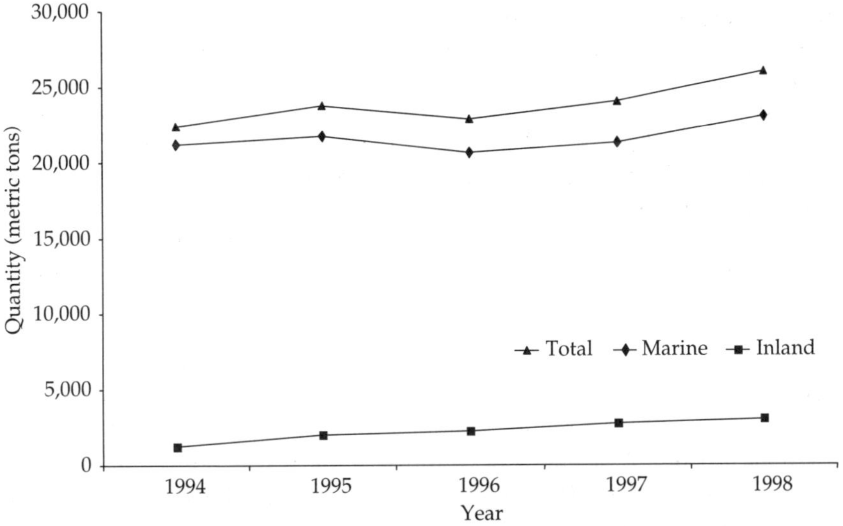

```
        30,000
        25,000
        20,000
Quantity
(metric  15,000
tons)
        10,000
                                    —▲— Total   —♦— Marine   —■— Inland
         5,000
             0
              1994      1995      1996      1997      1998
                                   Year
```

Source: Central Bank of Sri Lanka, Annual Report (various years).

tion has shown increasing trends during the last decade, and fish production was estimated at 260,000 million tons in 1998, which was composed of both marine fish production (230,000 million tons) and inland fish production (30,000 million tons). To meet local consumption requirements, fish has also been imported, and in 1997, 73,950 million tons of fish were imported (see figure 3.8 and table A3.6).[2]

Though the fisheries sector was relatively disorganized during the first half of the 1990s it has recently received considerable support in the form of subsidies. The main objective of the Ceylon Fisheries Cooperation is to promote the fisheries industry in Sri Lanka, and it has refrigerated facilities to store and distribute fish products all around the island. In addition, during 1996 the Ceylon Fisheries Cooperation imported 175 million tons of fish for local consumption.

While fish is considered a cheap source of protein for the local diet it has also generated considerable export revenue. Almost all shrimp production was exported in 1998, and amounted to 6,038 million tons. Although there is significant potential for the export of prawns to Japan, the United States, and the European Union markets, strict quality standards in those countries act as a nontariff barrier for Sri Lankan exports.

Food Security and the Role of Food Aid

FOOD SECURITY. Food security can be primarily considered as the ability of every individual to access sufficient quantities of food at all times. The average person requires 2,200 calories from their food everyday. According to the U.N. World Food Program classifications, Sri Lanka is ranked as a low income, food-deficit country. This indicates that people have low average levels of income and that the country imports food to supplement its domestic production.

Food availability in the country is not sufficient to meet future requirements owing to factors such as low agricultural production, food import and export imbalances, environmental hazards, and civil disturbances. Therefore, Sri Lanka needs to increase its domestic food production by improving yields and efficiency within the farming system and by ensuring sustainable resource use. A sound policy environment is also essential.

FOOD AID. Sri Lanka receives food aid under three types of food assistance programs: Program Food Aid, Project Food Aid, and Emergency Food Assistance. Program Food Aid is mainly delivered in the form of grants or loans from the United States through its PL 480 aid program for wheat grain (as discussed earlier) and from Australia and the European Union.

The U.N. World Food Program governs Program Food Aid. This program provides assistance in the form of food to internally displaced persons and for special development work also. The U.N. World Food Program operational expenditure for Sri Lanka declined from US$5.6 million in 1994 to US$3.9 million in 1997. In comparison to other food aid–receiving countries in the South Asian region, the allocation of food aid seems

Table 3.3 U.N. World Food Program Operational Expenditures, 1993–97 (US$ millions)

Year	Bangladesh	Bhutan	India	Nepal	Pakistan	Sri Lanka	SAARC
1993	25,004	2,425	26,281	9,970	13,034	3,300	80,014
	(31)	(3)	(33)	(12)	(16)	(4)	(100)
1994	66,998	1,020	28,285	7,728	35,229	5,614	144,874
	(46)	(1)	(20)	(5)	(24)	(4)	(100)
1995	40,738	1,479	23,155	8,265	3,249	4,788	81,674
	(50)	(2)	(28)	(10)	(4)	(6)	(100)
1996	28,128	2,107	29,177	12,476	5,691	2,547	80,126
	(35)	(3)	(36)	(16)	(7)	(3)	(100)
1997	60,448	1,923	23,818	10,292	16,378	3,887	116,746
	(52)	(2)	(20)	(9)	(14)	(3)	(100)

Note: Parentheses indicate percentages. SAARC = South Asian Association for Regional Cooperation.
Source: U.N. World Food Program (1998).

to have declined in 1997, receiving only 3 percent of total food aid allocations in 1997 (see table 3.3).

Since 1992, the U.N. World Food Program has assisted with Emergency Food Assistance to some 50,000 internally displaced persons in the country and has contributed US$18 million worth of food aid for relief operations to date. In July 1998, the U.N. World Food Program supplied approximately Rs17 million worth of food aid, consisting of rice, wheat flour, pulses, and canned fish to Jaffna to assist in the reconstruction and rehabilitation of the war-torn northern part of the country. In addition, the U.N. World Food Program has a food-for-work program that provides assistance to the drought-affected farmers in minor irrigation schemes in 13 districts islandwide. This program has contributed US$8.5 million over the last five years.

The Role of Agricultural Trade in the National Economy

While Sri Lanka has traditionally been an agricultural economy, the contribution of the agriculture sector to total GDP declined remarkably during the 1990s. In 1997, the agriculture sector share in GDP was only 17.8 percent compared with 22.6 percent in 1991 (see figure 3.9 and table A3.2). With the liberalization of the economy in 1977, the traditional agriculture sector has been subject to major reforms. In addition, this open economy environment laid a solid foundation for the development of other sectors, particularly the manufacturing and services sectors. The services sector share of GDP grew 50 percent from 1992–97.

Figure 3.9 Sectoral Composition of GDP, 1997

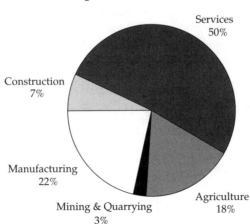

Source: Central Bank of Sri Lanka, Annual Report (various years).

State Trading Enterprises

The Role of State Trading Enterprises in the Economy

COOPERATIVE WHOLESALE ESTABLISHMENT. The CWE is the principal state trading enterprise operating in the agricultural sector. The main objective of the CWE is to stabilize prices and to ensure food security for the Sri Lankan population. The CWE has more than 40 wholesale depots and 120 retail outlets through which they distribute and market imported and local produce.

The CWE purchases bulk quantities of agricultural commodities from local producers, and also imports, based on the recommendations of the Ministries of Agriculture and Trade. The main items imported by the CWE include wheat and wheat flour, rice, lentils, onion, chilies, potato, sugar, and dried fish (the market share for some items is given in table 3.4). For all of these imported commodities, barring the wheat products, the CWE's market share has been declining considerably owing to private trader competition. By 1998, CWE's market share was less than 10 percent of the total market in most agricultural commodities, as highlighted in table 3.4. Since the removal of licensing requirements on essential food items in 1996, the CWE's share of the imported goods market declined even further during 1997 and 1998. The private sector has the largest market share in almost all commodities in which the CWE trades, and there are even a few large firms that currently operate as a trading cartel.

Although the pricing mechanism of most of these commodities is governed by market forces, from time to time the government does intervene, through the CWE, in the determination of commodity prices for both local producers and at the retail level. Regardless of import prices, the government, through the CWE, under a guaranteed price scheme has given priority to local commodity purchases. There is no set policy for determining the quantity that is purchased, so instances of surplus stocks have arisen

Table 3.4 Cooperative Wholesale Establishment's Percentage Share of Food Commodity Imports, 1995–98

Commodity	1995	1996	1997	1998
Potato	11	6	3	2
Chilies	18	5	—	1
Onion	8	—	5	5
Rice	—	10	7	8
Sugar	—	—	7	6

Sources: Cooperative Wholesale Establishment and Sri Lanka Department of Customs.

Sri Lanka

in the past. In 1997, for example, the price of imported potatoes in the market was Rs20.00 while the CWE purchased them from domestic producers at a price of Rs35.00. The resulting loss from this type of protectionist intervention was borne by the government.

The Paddy Marketing Board (PMB) has not been functioning since 1996, so the CWE has taken over the purchasing of paddy under the guaranteed price scheme, which still operates in principle. This arrangement covered 40 purchasing centers and purchased 18,000 million tons up to April 1998. During this period the CWE paid Rs9.40 per kilogram for paddy purchased from a farmer organization while paddy purchases by others were priced at Rs9.00 per kilogram. Despite this, the private sector dominated paddy purchases in 1998, and the CWE's local rice purchases were approximately 3,000 million tons each year.

The CWE does not enter into any long-term contracts on behalf of the government for any of the above mentioned commodities. However, the CWE does have exclusive trading rights over wheat grain because of a contractual obligation between the Sri Lankan government and a Singaporean-owned milling company, Prima Ceylon Ltd., as discussed earlier. The government, through the CWE, also has exclusive trading rights on wheat flour and controls the domestic price. In 1994, the prices of wheat flour and bread were reduced to levels below cost owing to political and economic considerations. The resulting wheat flour subsidy was estimated to cost the government between Rs5–6 billion a year during 1995 and 1996. The CWE currently sells wheat flour at prices above cost, and has been assisted by declines in the international commodity prices of wheat.

While the formal, market-interventionist role of the CWE has been clearly diminishing over time, it still has the potential to ensure adequate stocks of essential commodities in the event of civil unrest, floods, shortages in festive seasons, or black marketeering.

Paddy Marketing Board

The PMB was organized in 1971 to ensure reasonable prices for farmers and to provide milled rice to the consumer at a lower price and owned 359 stores. However, during the 1980s and the 1990s its capacity and role in the purchase of paddy gradually declined (see table 3.5), and in 1996 the operations of the PMB were terminated.

During its life the PMB operated a guaranteed price scheme to ensure a minimum price for paddy farmers. However, as the average farm gate price of paddy was above the guaranteed price during 1989–93, the PMB's paddy purchases were reduced to almost a negligible level. During this period purchases of paddy were about 2 percent of the total paddy mar-

Table 3.5 Paddy Marketing Board Capacity Utilization, 1990–96

Year	Total paddy production (million tons)	Total PMB purchase (million tons)	Capacity utilization (percent)
1990	2,538	31	1.2
1991	2,389	44	1.8
1992	2,340	7	0.3
1993	2,570	46	1.8
1994	2,684	120	4.5
1995	2,810	282	10.0
1996	2,061	1	0.0

Note: PMB = Paddy Marketing Board.
Sources: Central Bank of Sri Lanka, Annual Report (various years), PMB statistics.

ket. In 1995, although PMB purchases increased owing to lower farm gate prices, the PMB sold rice at prices lower than cost, and incurred losses of between Rs150 million and 200 million. While the PMB tried in particular to assist small farmers by guaranteeing prices, the purchase of paddy and the distribution of rice were not sufficient to compete with private sector traders. The maintenance of PMB stores, processing, and distribution systems were also not efficient enough to maintain the quality of rice. As a result, the PMB was rejected by consumers and forced to conclude its activities.

Sri Lanka State Trading Corporation

The Sri Lanka State Trading Corporation (STC) now plays an insignificant interventionist role in the agricultural sector and imports 90 percent of its commodities and trades in items such as crocodile mammoties, generators, sprayers, sprinklers, tree holding machines, irrigation equipment, and chemical mixtures. Though the Sri Lanka STC previously had monopoly rights for more than 90 agriculture-related (and other) commodities, they now only have exclusive rights over three chemical compounds, which are justified by security considerations. They currently operate in direct competition with the private sector. The Sri Lanka STC previously had a 70 percent share in the crocodile mammoty market until 1997, owing to maintaining low pricing by keeping a low profit margin. Subsequently the crocodile mammoty agency was conferred to a large private sector company, and the Sri Lanka STC no longer trades in this brand and has not entered into any long-term contracts on behalf of the government.

Multi-Purposes Cooperative Societies

The Multi-Purposes Cooperative Societies are also state trading enterprises and engage in the marketing of agricultural produce. Though they received government patronage in the early 1990s, operational activities are now completely independent and they purchase local produce during the harvest season in an open, competitive market, import food commodities when necessary, and are subject to the same import tariffs as other organizations and private traders. Multi-Purposes Cooperative Societies also played a significant role in the purchase of paddy and currently operate 119 cooperatives and 1,270 centers and were purchasing approximately 27,000 million tons of paddy until April 1998. They paid farmers between Rs9.00 and Rs12.00 per kilogram for paddy and also undertook the processing in their own mills and distributed the final rice product to the market.

Experience from the Implementation of the Uruguay Round

Reductions in Internal Support

Production subsidies and credit concessions are the most common forms of internal support extended to the agricultural sector. The provision of internal support to the sector continued at varying levels during 1995–98.

TEA SECTOR. Replanting and new planting subsidies are the most significant forms of support extended to the tea sector. As outlined in table 3.6, when examining the levels of replanting and new planting subsidies, it appears that there was no consistent reduction in the total amount of assistance granted to the sector between 1995 and 1998. Although the levels of subsidies declined from Rs76 million in 1995 to Rs38 million in 1997, the subsidies administered increased again in 1998 to Rs77 million.

The Tea Small Holdings Development Authority operates an input subsidy scheme, a fertilizer credit scheme, and provides advisory and extension services for producers. During 1995–98, the Tea Factory Development Scheme and the incentive scheme for machinery were also extended

Table 3.6 Replanting and New Planting Subsidies Granted to the Tea Sector, 1995–98 (Rs millions)

Subsidy type	1995	1996	1997	1998
Replanting subsidy	—[a]	32	30	58.0
New planting subsidy	—[a]	16	8	19.2
Total	76	48	38	77.2

a. Breakdown of subsidies not available for 1995.
Source: Central Bank of Sri Lanka, Annual Report (various years).

Table 3.7 Subsidies Granted to the Coconut Sector, 1997–98
(Rs millions)

Subsidy type	1997	1998
Replanting subsidy	13.0	10.0
New planting subsidy	12.2	13.5
Home Garden Scheme	22.6	15.0
Total	2044.8	2036.5

Source: Central Bank of Sri Lanka, Annual Report (various years).

to the sector, while interest subsidies on tea bagging machinery increased from 50–75 percent (raised from cesses). In 1997 the Tea Small Holdings Development Authority carried out the Small Holder Tea Development Project under which Rs300 million was given as loans for replanting, new planting, and nursery development and initiated an insurance scheme for small holders, and Rs44 million was disbursed among 93 factories under the Factory Development Assistance Scheme.

COCONUT SECTOR. The Coconut Development Board has also utilized funds raised from the export cess to provide support for the sector in the form of subsidies. Coconut subsidy rates remained at Rs25,000 per hectare for replanting and new planting and Rs12,000 for staggered planting, Rs7,500 for moisture conservation, and Rs10,000 for inter-cropping in 1995. However, in 1996 the Coconut Development Board restructured these support schemes in order to better utilize the cess funds, and the subsidies increased to Rs38,750 per hectare for replanting and Rs40,000 per hectare for new planting, while home gardens received a maximum of 10 coconuts free of charge. The subsidies have continued at these rates until the present. In 1997 and 1998 other subsidies were allocated to the coconut sector (see table 3.7). In addition an allocation of Rs8 million was made for a credit scheme extended to producers.

A financial assistance scheme for the installation of continuous drying schemes for desiccated coconut was introduced by the Coconut Development Authority in 1993, and allocations were made in 1995 (Rs7 million to 15 mills), 1996 (Rs15 million to 17 mills), and 1997 (Rs17 million to 20 mills) for machinery costs.

In 1997 a Fiber Mill Modernization Scheme was initiated to provide producers with financial support for items such as de-fibering machines and husk crushing machines (maximum allocation of Rs300,000). In addition, grants were provided to cover 50 percent of the cost of obtaining the main supply of electricity. During 1997, the Fiber Mill Modernizing Scheme disbursed Rs2.6 million to 21 fiber mills.

OTHER EXPORT CROPS. Production subsidies for other export crops such as cloves, cardamom, cinnamon, pepper, nutmeg, cocoa, coffee, and citronella oils consistently increased during 1994–98, from 15 million in 1994 to 32 million in 1998. Throughout this period subsidies have primarily been in the form of new planting and replanting subsidies, over 50 percent of which is received by pepper and cinnamon producers. In 1998, Rs32 million was allocated to this sector, and an additional budgetary allocation of Rs150 million was made for the development of this sector to improve crop production in four districts.

RUBBER SECTOR. Rubber producers have also received replanting and new planting subsidies over time, and in 1996 the rubber replanting subsidies amounted to Rs400 million and were raised from the collection of the export cess on rubber. However, in May 1998 the rubber cess was abolished to minimize a rapidly declining price trend in the sector that resulted from the East Asian currency crisis.

FISHERIES SECTOR. The fisheries sector has continued to receive support under producer subsidy schemes in the form of items such as multi-day boats, traditional crafts, fishing gear units, and radios supplied to producers. However, there has been no consistent trend in the allocations of these subsidies as in 1994 when Rs75 million were allocated; this rose to Rs83 million in 1996 but fell to Rs65 million in 1997.

FERTILIZER SUBSIDY. The most important subsidy accruing to the agriculture sector is the fertilizer subsidy, which is now considered an essential component of the new planting/replanting subsidy package. While the fertilizer subsidy has been in place since the 1970s it was removed in 1989 and reintroduced in 1994. The fertilizer subsidy applied to four major fertilizer ingredients: urea, sulphate of ammonia, muriate of potash, and triple super phosphate. The subsidy reduced the retail price of the major fertilizers by 30 percent. Again, in 1995, the fertilizer subsidy was removed owing to price increases in urea and triple super phosphate, and a new scheme was introduced, which fixed ceiling rates of subsidies payable to importers and readjusted subsidy ceilings depending on the fluctuations of the world market price of these items. In September 1997, the fertilizer subsidy scheme was further revised, and was applicable only to urea fertilizer to target the subsidy toward more needy farmers (75 percent of urea users are paddy cultivators). In 1998, the fertilizer subsidy amounted to Rs2.2 billion, an increase over the Rs1.3 million allocated in 1995.

IRRIGATION SUBSIDY. The irrigation subsidy is another important indirect subsidy that is granted primarily to the paddy sector in the form of free irrigation water from irrigation schemes constructed and maintained by the government. In 1995, an annual equivalent of irrigation subsidies (based on operation and maintenance costs) was estimated at Rs1,350 per hectare (World Bank 1996).

ISSUE OF SEEDS. The Seed and Planting Material Center of the Department of Agriculture continues to issue a variety of seed material. In 1995, 4,100 million tons of seed material was issued for a range of other food crops, such as maize, soya bean, green gram, and paddy. In 1996 there was a 7 percent decline in issue of seeds, followed by a further 2 percent decline in issue of seeds during 1997. The government's current policy is to gradually hand over seed production to the private sector.

CREDIT. Interest subsidies are provided by credit facilities granted by commercial banks under the New Comprehensive Rural Credit Scheme. The amount of credit provided to producers has shown a declining trend, having peaked in 1995 at Rs1,200 million and declined to Rs442 million in 1998. Approximately two thirds of all allocated credit is granted to paddy producers while the balance accrues to producers in the other food crops sector. An interest subsidy of 7.5 percent was conferred in 1995 and continued until 1998 when this subsidy component was increased to 10 percent to increase the movement of credit into the agriculture sector.

Reductions in Tariffs

Sri Lanka's agricultural trade is now governed predominantly by a progressive tariff regime. While tariffs on agricultural commodities are currently bound at 50 percent, in 1995 the tariff structure was reformed to a 3-band system from a 13-band system in 1990 and 4-band system in 1991. Import duty rates in 1995 were levied at 10, 20, and 35 percent and were subsequently revised in November 1998 to 5, 10, and 30 percent across the board. Import duties on agricultural products, however, remain outside the bounds of this tariff structure, and agricultural commodities are subject to a standard duty rate of 35 percent. This departure from the three-band tariff system is justified by the need for the agricultural sector's requiring more time to adjust in the medium term to lower tariff rates after the recent liberalization of all nontariff barriers in the sector in 1996.

Commodities such as sugar, tobacco, cigarettes, and liquor are governed by specific duty rates (ad valorem) outside the bounds of the three-band system. Import duties levied on wheat, lentils, and dried fish are currently at a zero level. There is a zero duty rate on agricultural inputs such as seeds and planting material.

Preferential tariffs have been granted for certain countries under preferential trading arrangements such as the Bangkok Agreement, the Agreement on the Global System of Trade Preferences (GSTP), and the South Asian Preferential Trading Arrangement (SAPTA). Under SAPTA Sri Lanka has offered tariff concessions to member countries on more than 120 items, of which the largest category of concessions was for imports of live animals and animal products. Sri Lanka also entered into a bilateral trade agreement with India—the Indo-Sri Lanka Free Trade Agreement—in December 1998. Under this agreement Sri Lanka is due to offer complete duty exemptions on approximately 300 items, and a 50 percent preferential margin on a further 600 items once the negative lists of the two countries have been agreed upon. Furthermore, customs surcharges have been levied from time to time on agricultural commodities as a measure of emergency protection based on harvest seasons and production levels. However, the bound rate of 50 percent applies to both tariffs and these surcharges. The GSTP and defense levies are also charged on duty-inclusive import prices.

Ad hoc duty waivers and exemptions still exist for some agricultural commodities and have had distortionary effects on agricultural commodity markets and domestic production. The granting of waivers and exemptions has typically disrupted predetermined trade policies and distorted market signals in the past. Some of the changes to the tariff structure from 1995–98 are outlined in table 3.8.

Complete duty exemptions exist for the import of seed cleaning machines, sorting and grading machines, seed testing equipment, seed packing machines, tea bag packaging machinery, and color separators and fertilizer. Duty free concessions apply to the import of agricultural tractors, lorries, prime movers, refrigerated trucks, and buses. These duty exemptions are as follows (Sri Lanka Department of Customs 1999):

- Ayurveda and prepared drugs, medicinal plants.
- Ornamental fish imported for re-export or under such conditions.
- Fish caught by fishing vessels operating from a Sri Lankan port that have been duly registered in Sri Lanka or issued with landing permits by the Sri Lanka Ministry of Fisheries.
- Ingredients for the manufacture of animal and poultry food.
- Technical grade chemicals used in formulation of pesticide and plant growth regulators for the agriculture industry.
- Parts, components, and accessories for the manufacture and assembly of machines for cleaning, sorting, or grading seed, grain or dried leguminous vegetables; machinery used in the milling industry or for processing of cereals or dried grain or leguminous vegetables.

Table 3.8 Major Changes to Import Tariffs in the Agriculture Sector, 1995–98

Commodity	1995	1996	1997	1998
Milk powder (full cream, >26% fat)	10% duty waiver granted	10% duty waiver granted	10% duty waiver granted	Reclassified at 10% duty
Inputs and engines for fishing boats	Exempt from duty			
Fishing nets	Duty free from 35% to 20%			
Agricultural implements	Duty free from 35% to 10%			
Rice	35% duty applicable	Full duty waiver granted (April–December)	Duty waiver removed	35% duty applicable
Sugar	25% duty applicable	• Exempt from turnover tax • Duty reduced to 18%	Duty reduced further to 10%	Specific duty rate of Rs3.50/km levied
Desiccated coconut		Exempt from turnover tax		
Tea packing materials		Exempt from turnover tax		
Edible oils	35% duty applicable	30% duty waiver granted	Duty waiver reduced to 20%	30% duty waiver applied
Copra	35% duty applicable	30% duty waiver granted	Duty waiver reduced to 20%	20% duty waiver applied
Shrimp and poultry feed	30% duty applicable	Duty waiver granted	Full duty waiver	Full duty waiver granted
Chilies	35% duty applicable	Duty reduced to 20%		
Onion	35% duty applicable	Duty reduced to 20%		Duty rate of 20% continued
Potato	35% duty applicable	Duty reduced to 20%		Duty rate of 20% continued
NPK fertilizer and agro-chemicals			Exempt from duty	

Seed cleaning, sorting and grading machines, seed testing equipment, and seed packing machines		Duty free
Tea packing machinery and color separators		Duty free
Agricultural tractors, lorries, and refrigerated trucks		Duty free
Navigation equipment, spare parts for fishing boats, fish finding devices, and raw materials for fishing nets	10% duty applicable	Duty free
Red split lentils	35% duty applicable	Exempt from duty
Dried sprats and dried prawns	10% duty applicable	Exempt from duty
Canned fish	10% duty applicable	Partial duty waiver applied
		Duty free
Wheat	35% duty applicable	20% duty applicable
		Full duty waiver
Wheat flour	35% duty applicable	Full duty waiver
		Full duty waiver
Live animals for breeding	10% duty applicable	Duty free

Source: Central Bank of Sri Lanka, Annual Report (various years).

- Raw material components, parts, and accessories for the manufacture of fishing boats.
- Green houses, poly tunnels, sprinklers, drip irrigation systems, and netting for agriculture and related activities.
- Multilayered packing material/packs consisting of laminated papers, polythene film, and aluminum foil used for packaging of milk, vegetables, and fruit juice.

Decreases in both the rates of duty and dutiable imports have become evident in the past two years. The ratio of import duty collection to total adjusted imports declined by 0.3 percent between 1997 and 1998, reflecting decreases in dutiable rates. Similarly, dutiable imports as a proportion of total imports declined by 1.6 percent between the same period, reflecting decreases in dutiable imports.

REDUCTIONS IN APPLIED IMPORT PROTECTION. Until recently the imports of many agricultural products were subject to import control systems such as licensing that had been implemented stringently in the past. Some agricultural items such as red onions and potatoes were at one time subject to a complete import ban.

However, from 1994 to 1998 many of these licensing requirements were relaxed for most agricultural commodities. In 1994 paddy was liberalized, and in 1996 license controls for major commodities such as potato, big onion, red onion, and chilies were also eliminated.

Licensing requirements now only exist for a select list of commodities on the grounds of national security, public health, environmental protection, and domestic producer protection. However, these license controls are usually implemented in an ad hoc manner. Prior to 1995 a special cess was levied on imports that were at or above a 45 percent duty rate. As recently as 1996 the import of paddy was brought under license control to protect local producers and to prevent pests and diseases. Maize is still bound by licensing requirements for reasons of domestic producer protection. Imports of wheat and meslin as well as wheat and meslin flour currently remain under license control owing to contractual obligations between the government and Prima Ceylon Ltd. Some of the major agricultural (and related) commodities currently subject to licensing requirements are as follows (Sri Lanka Department of Customs 1999):

- Other live animals for human consumption
- Meat of bovine
- Meat of sheep or goat
- Guts/bladders/stomachs
- Paddy or rough rice
- Wheat or meslin flour
- Soups/composite food
- Chemicals for fertilizer manufacture

- Acid treated bores/ivory/tortoise
- Sausages and similar products
- Preserved meat
- Wheat, meslin
- Maize seed
- Cane molasses
- Other maize
- Animal fertilizer
- Vegetable fertilizer
- Tractors
- Blast freezers for preserving poultry meat
- Milk chilling tanks

REDUCTIONS IN EXPORT SUBSIDIES. There are a limited number of export subsidies provided for commodities in the agricultural sector. Some of these subsidies granted since 1995 are outlined in table 3.9. Subsidies on nonplantation export crops have been estimated at less than 1 percent of export earnings from the specified commodities (Athukorala and Kelegama 1996).

DUTY CONCESSIONS FOR EXPORTERS. Imports of capital goods are fully exempt from duty if more than 90 percent of the resulting output is exported or sold to Board of Investment–approved firms and paid in foreign currency. A duty exemption of 50 percent is granted to firms exporting between 50 and 90 percent of their output. Tax and duty exemptions or rebates may also be granted for inputs used for export processing.

EXPORT INCENTIVES AND INSTITUTIONAL SUPPORT. There is a fiscal incentive scheme currently in place that permits duty free imports for investments of more than Rs4 million for new investors and more than Rs1 million for existing investors. In the 1999 budget the minimum investment requirement was revoked to grant smaller industries the same benefits. Items used for the advancement of the agriculture sector, such as greenhouses, planting material, packaging material, and refrigerated trucks, are exempt from import duty and GSTP.

There are two main government institutions that provide institutional support for exporters: the Sri Lanka Export Development Board (SLEDB) and the Sri Lanka Export Credit Insurance Corporation (SLECIC). The SLEDB provides technical and skills development support to exporters as well as financial assistance under the agricultural products and rubber products rebate scheme. The SLECIC provides export insurance and guarantee services for the development of exports. The development authorities for tea, rubber, and coconut also provide institutional support to the respective industries utilizing funds raised by export cesses on each of the products.

EXPORT CHARGES AND QUANTITATIVE RESTRICTIONS. Since the elimination of export duties on all plantation crops in 1992 there are currently a limited

Table 3.9 Export Subsidies Granted to the Agriculture Sector, 1995–97

1995	1996	1997
Duty rebate scheme	Duty rebate scheme continued	Duty rebate scheme, bonded-warehouse scheme, inward processing scheme abandoned
Manufacture-in-bond scheme	Manufacture-in-bond scheme continued	
Duty free clearance of machinery scheme	Duty free clearance of machinery scheme	
Joint venture with Russia (bondsmen concept)		
Joint venture with Pakistan to re-establish lost tea market		
Bank guarantees and insurance schemes provided by Sri Lanka Export Credit Insurance Corporation		
Financial assistance for small and large scale exporters		
• 10-year tax holiday and duty free imports of machinery and equipment for existing and new companies engaged in the export of fresh and processed fruits and vegetables that undertake a cultivation of a minimum area of 5 hectares		
• 100 percent rebates on quoted freight rates on Air Lanka for exporters of cut flowers, foliage, fruits, and vegetables		
• Grants for nontraditional agricultural exports in first year of operation		
• 50 percent interest rate subsidy on loans for the purchase of tea bagging machinery		
• Import duty and other tax exemptions on capital goods used for the processing of tea for export		
• Cash grants for exporters who increase the volume and export price of processed tea over the previous year		
• Subsidies on imported packing materials for exports of fresh fruit and vegetables.		

Source: Central Bank of Sri Lanka, Annual Report (various years).

Table 3.10 Export Cesses and Surcharges, 1999

Commodity	Amount levied	Beneficiary
Crustaceans (shrimp or prawns)	Rs10.00/km	SLEDB
Coconut	• Rs2.00/km	CDA
Desiccated shell/seed	• Rs0.75/km	
Pure Ceylon tea	• Rs2.50/km	SLTB
	• Rs0.0035/km (Tea medical levy)	
Coconut milk powder	Rs0.45/km	CDA
Copra	Rs0.90/km	CDA
Coconut	Rs0.10/km	CDA
Coconut shell pieces	Rs0.20/km	CDA
Coconut (oil, palm kernel)	Rs0.40/km	CDA
Fruit juices and vegetable juices of coconut (cream)	Rs0.45/km	CDA
Extracts, essences, and concentrates of coffee and tea	Rs2.50km	SLTB
Instant tea	Rs0.0035/km (Tea medical levy)	
Animal leather	Rs40.00/ft^2	SLRDB
Coconut abaca	Rs0.25/km	CDA

Note: CDA = Coconut Development Authority; Rs = rupees; SLEDB = Sri Lanka Export Development Board; SLTB = Sri Lanka Tea Board.
Source: Sri Lanka Department of Customs (1999).

number of agricultural export commodities subject to export cesses and surcharges, as outlined in table 3.10. The revenue raised from these charges is channeled back into each sector through the relevant development authority in the form of incentives and institutional support. Until May 1998 there was an export cess of Rs0.0165/kilogram levied on natural rubber, which was then removed to prevent declines in rubber prices. There are currently no quantitative restrictions on exports, though a select list of commodities are subject to licensing requirements and other export restrictions for reasons of cultural value and health and environmental safeguards.

Impact of the Implementation of the Uruguay Round Agreement on Agriculture by Major Trading Partners

Impact on Exports

Export quantities have not been significantly influenced by the implementation of the Uruguay Round (UR) Agreement on Agriculture (AoA) in trading partner countries. Export quantities of commodities such as coconut and rubber have been declining during the post-URAoA period, as highlighted in table A3.9. This trend can be primarily attributed to decreases in world demand for these commodities, in addition to increasing costs of production in each of the above-mentioned sectors. Export quantities of tea, on the other hand, have increased, especially in the post-URAoA years (1995–98) and can be attributed to such internal factors as the improved efficiency of the sector after privatization of tea plantations, the increase in value-added tea exports, and the targeting of exports to new markets such as the Commonwealth of Independent States (countries of central Asia and eastern Europe) and Turkey.

Export prices have not been affected directly by URAoA measures in trading partner countries. While prices of rubber declined considerably between 1994 and 1998, coconut prices remained relatively unchanged. However, prices of tea and other agricultural exports have demonstrated significant increasing trends in the post-URAoA period owing to an increase in international demand, especially from the CIS and Middle Eastern countries, most of which are currently not members of the WTO.

Impact on Imports

Imports of most agricultural commodities have demonstrated marginal increases during the post-URAoA period. This can be attributed in part to the liberal changes in Sri Lanka's tariff structure and the relaxation of license controls on many agricultural commodities. However, certain internal factors have had a significant influence on the levels of agricultural commodity imports. Sugar imports increased during this time owing to reduced local production, while wheat imports increased owing to higher local consumption. However, rice imports fluctuated significantly during 1994–98 and were directly due to seasonal and environmental changes such as drought. Fertilizer imports have remained relatively unchanged during the post-URAoA period despite the increasing fertilizer subsidy and low duty on fertilizer imports (see table A3.10).

The nominal prices of major agricultural imports show a declining trend during the post-URAoA period and this can be attributed to international liberalization in those markets. However, import prices have remained relatively constant when taking the continual devaluation of the Sri Lankan rupee into account.

Impact on the Availability of Food Aid

Sri Lanka currently receives food aid under three distinct assistance programs, predominantly from the United States, the European Union, Australia, and the U.N. World Food Program. In comparison to other food aid–receiving countries in the South Asian region, the allocation of food aid seems to have declined in 1997. Sri Lanka received only 3 percent of total food aid allocations in 1997.

When analyzing cereal aid shipments to Sri Lanka, it appears that donor contributions have also been decreasing in the post-URAoA period. It is, however, difficult to ascertain whether this is the direct result of the URAoA.

Difficulties and Benefits Owing to URAoA

The implementation of the URAoA has not resulted in the expected increase in market access for the exports of the developing and least industrialized countries of the South Asian Association for Regional Cooperation (SAARC) as a whole mainly because of "dirty tariffication"[3] practices, tariff escalation, and the use of a range of nontariff barriers by industrialized countries. Tariff escalation has been found to be high, for example, in the case of rubber products to the European Union, Japan, and the United States, and has discouraged the exports of processed goods from the region.

However, there has been no significant change in trading patterns for Sri Lanka's largest exports as a result of implementing the URAoA. In the tea sector, exports had been subject to a liberal trade environment prior to the URAoA, and some of the industrialized country importers such as the United Kingdom, the European Union, and the United States did not impose import duties or other restrictions on bulk or packeted tea. While many of the developing country importers of tea did impose tariff and nontariff measures, some of those importers were not signatories to the URAoA during this period.

Many of the main industrialized country markets had already imposed low or zero tariffs before the URAoA on the imports of Sri Lanka's other major agricultural exports such as rubber and coconut products. Thus, the overall impact on Sri Lanka's trade and traders during the implementation of the URAoA has been minimal. Likewise, importers of agricultural commodities have not been affected significantly by the implementation of the URAoA, other than the benefits resulting from reductions in import duties and the increase in competitiveness and demand for their products.

One special case, however, has been the exporting of desiccated coconut and coconut milk powder to Brazil. In February 1996 Sri Lanka lodged a formal complaint against Brazil with the WTO, claiming that Brazil's imposition of countervailing duties on Sri Lanka's exports of desiccated coconut and coconut milk powder contravenes GATT Articles I, II, VI, and 13(a) of the URAoA.

Impact on Sanitary and Phytosanitary Standards

Though Sri Lanka is still in the process of fully complying with the Sanitary and Phytosanitary (SPS) Agreement there are a number of emerging issues that have impeded the country's ability to thoroughly assess the legitimacy of national as well as international SPS standards. One such impediment is the lack of information regarding prevailing SPS measures and their degree of consistency with the SPS Agreement. As a result, estimates of the impact of SPS regulations have been found to be unreliable. There are a limited number of accredited laboratory facilities and a significant lack of financial resources to acquire such expertise in the assessment of SPS standards. This has caused critical problems not only for exporters but also for importers, especially of foliage material. The Special and Differential (S&D) clauses governing developing countries such as Sri Lanka have not been visible in their application to local exporters, and have only exacerbated the prevailing issues. In general, there is also a lack of awareness of the contents of these S&D clauses, and inadequate use has been made of the benefits granted within them as a result.

However, despite these constraints, there are some mechanisms in operation that are attempting to adapt to the changing international environment. The Sri Lanka Standards Institution (SLSI) is the national body responsible for setting and monitoring food standards, and it is also a national inquiry point for the implementation of the SPS Agreement. In this capacity SLSI is responsible for the dissemination of information to exporters regarding changes to trade partners' product standards in various industries.

SLSI adheres to international health and safety standards and guidelines for food items, such as Codex standards, as strictly as possible. Sri Lanka is a member of the Codex Alimentarius Commission, which has set 237 food commodity standards, 41 hygienic practice codes, and more than 3,200 maximum residue limits for pesticides. By adhering to harmonized food standards and testing and inspection procedures, potential nontariff barriers can be eliminated.

SLSI has recently proposed the initiation of an independent National Accreditation Body that will assist in facilitating the smooth flow of exports by being the umbrella organization that will govern a national standards group and a national measurement laboratory.

The SPS Agreement states that: "Members shall ensure that any sanitary and phytosanitary measure is applied only to the extent necessary to protect human, animal or plant life or health, is based on scientific principles and is not maintained without sufficient scientific evidence...." However, the current national plant quarantine regulations in particular are deemed restrictive, especially by the private sector. The restrictions of plant material and seed imports are decided on international listings of plant diseases and pests in the country of origin as opposed to conducting case-by-case analyses at the point of entry. This has created significant problems for importers of seed and planting materials and the agriculture sector in general.

The restrictive elements of the measures have resulted in a limited transfer of essential technology to the agricultural sector, thus agricultural industries have had significant difficulty in accessing high yielding plant material and improved livestock breeds necessary for improved production levels. In addition, the restrictive quarantine practices have encouraged the smuggling of seeds and other materials into the country, thereby increasing the risk of the spread of pests and diseases.

There have been some discrepancies in the enforcement of these regulations, and special import permits have been issued in an ad hoc manner for prohibited materials from time to time. Unofficial bans have also been placed on certain seed imports for purposes other than plant quarantine (Youngberg 1998b).

However, a Plant Protection Act[4] has recently been revised in line with some of the SPS requirements. The biggest constraint facing the government in amending plant quarantine regulations is the government's inability to provide the necessary and complementary testing facilities because of lack of money. There is also currently no legal structure governing intellectual property rights of plant materials entering Sri Lanka. As a result, new high yielding varieties and special hybrid plant breeds are not commonly brought into the country.[5]

Impact on Agricultural Incomes

Agricultural income declined by 14 percent in real terms between 1986–87 of Rs809 per month to Rs693 per month in 1996–97 and currently constitutes the lowest income occupation. This can be explained mainly by increases in costs of production in the sector and the resulting decline in profit margins received by agricultural producers. Since the liberalization of the agricultural sector, increased competition from lower-priced imports of agricultural commodities has also resulted in lower producer prices, and this in turn has led to lower agricultural incomes. Accordingly, in 1986–87, 41 percent of income receivers were employed in the agriculture sector while in 1996–97 this proportion was reduced to 28 percent.

Impact on Food Availability

While the availability of food has depended on the level of agricultural production in the country, the liberalization of agricultural commodity markets in the post-URAoA period has also played a significant role in food availability. Agricultural production demonstrated declining trends during the 1990s in almost all sectors except tea, paddy, fisheries, and milk production. The increasing population, decreasing land availability, rising costs of production, declining profit margins, and the inability to access high yielding varieties are all factors that have contributed toward agricultural productivity declines. These trends are visible in table 3.11. In contrast, the paddy sector has achieved 83 percent self-sufficiency in rice. The liberalization of agricultural markets has resulted in increased imports of major commodities in recent years. This has resulted in greater availability of low-priced food items in the market. Any production shortfalls are now met by imports and there is less risk of supply shortages (in the absence of external supply shocks).

Impact on Agricultural Prices

Both agricultural producer and retail prices (in real terms) have demonstrated declining trends during the post-URAoA period. Sri Lanka is a net importer of most agricultural commodities, and these declining prices can be specifically attributed to the recent changes in the licensing structures under the auspices of URAoA implementation. The resulting inflows of low-priced agricultural imports have exerted downward pressure on both producer and retail prices during this period.

Current Nominal and Effective Rates of Protection

Table 3.12 denotes the results of the most recent study, conducted in 1995 (updated nominal and effective rates of protection are presently unavailable in Sri Lanka).

Summary and Conclusions

While Sri Lanka has traditionally been an agricultural economy, the contribution of the agriculture sector to total GDP declined during the 1990s. In 1997 the agriculture sector share in GDP was only 17.8 percent, compared with 23.2 percent in 1990. The traditional agriculture sector has been subject to major reform with the liberalization of the economy in 1977. This open economic environment has laid a solid foundation for the development of other sectors.

Sri Lanka now has a relatively liberal trade policy that focuses on the simplification of the tariff structure and reduction of tariff rates, quantitative restrictions, and other market distorting factors. While this process of reform was initiated prior to the URAoA, during 1994–99 the tariff

Table 3.11 Total Availability of Selected Agricultural Commodities, 1994–98

Year	Paddy/rice (million tons)			Onion (million tons)			Potato (million tons)			Chilies (million tons)			Sugar (million tons)		
	Local production	Imports	Total availability	Local production	Imports	Total availability	Local production	Imports	Total availability	Local production	Imports	Total availability	Local production	Imports	Total availability
1994	2,684	58	2,742	44	48	92	79	8	87	32	8	40	72	491	563
1995	2,810	9	2,819	30	78	108	82	12	94	21	11	32	71	418	489
1996	2,061	341	2,402	20	90	110	100	26	126	18	10	28	70	381	451
1997	2,339	306	2,645	29	120	149	66	108	174	18	13	31	64	545	609
1998	2,692	168	2,860	17	104	121	26	115	141	16	20	36	61	444	505

Sources: Central Bank of Sri Lanka (1999a); Sri Lanka Department of Customs.

Table 3.12 Incentive Structure for Agriculture, 1993

Category	Import duty (percent)	NPC	EPC	ESC
Import-competing agriculture	n.a.	1.33	1.53	1.68
Rice	35	1.30	1.36	1.56
Others (average)	n.a.	n.a.	1.70	1.79
Chilies	10	1.50	n.a.	n.a.
Big onion	10	2.40	n.a.	n.a.
Potato	5	1.60	n.a.	n.a.
Lentils 1990–93	10	1.20	n.a.	n.a.
Export-oriented agriculture	n.a.	n.a.	1.02	1.06
Nonplantation crops	n.a.	n.a.	1.35	1.45
Plantation crops	n.a.	n.a.	1.00	1.03
Tea	15	n.a.	n.a.	1.04
Rubber	36	n.a.	n.a.	1.04
Coconut	10	n.a.	n.a.	1.02
Agriculture, average	n.a.	n.a.	1.24	1.32
Manufacturing	n.a.	n.a.	1.30	n.a.
Import-competing manufacturing	n.a.	n.a.	1.70	n.a.
Export-oriented manufacturing	n.a.	n.a.	1.00	n.a.

n.a. Not applicable.

Note: EPC = effective protection coefficient; ESC = effective subsidy coefficient of agricultural consumers; NPC = nominal protection coefficient.

Sources: Edwards (1993); World Bank (1996).

became the main instrument of regulation in the agricultural sector. Sri Lanka's tariffs are well below the bound rate of 50 percent for all agricultural commodities. Sri Lanka now adheres to a three-band tariff structure of 5, 10, and 30 percent duty rates, with a 35 percent rate applicable to agricultural commodities. This tariff system is due to be reformed further to a two-band structure.

While most quantitative restrictions have been reduced, select restrictions still do apply to certain commodities mainly because of national security, health, and environmental considerations. Some export subsidies and producer subsidies are also still applicable to certain commodities in the sector. State trading enterprises still operate in agricultural markets and are primarily engaged in commercial activities. While this formal, market-interventionist role has been clearly diminishing over time, the state trading enterprises still have the potential to ensure adequate stocks of essential commodities in the event of civil unrest, floods, shortages in festive seasons, or black marketeering.

Both Sri Lankan export quantities and prices have not been significantly influenced by the implementation of the URAoA in trading partner countries. However, there has been an increase in import quantities and prices and this can be attributed to a liberalization in these particular agricultural commodity markets.

Though Sri Lanka is still in the process of fully complying with the SPS Agreement, there are a number of emerging issues that have impeded the country's ability to thoroughly assess the legitimacy of national, as well as international, SPS standards. The S&D clauses governing developing countries such as Sri Lanka have not been visible in their application to local exporters, and have only exacerbated the prevailing issues. There is also a lack of awareness of the contents of these S&D clauses, and inadequate use has been made of the benefits granted within them as a result.

The implementation of the URAoA has not resulted in the expected increase in market access for the exports of countries such as Sri Lanka, and this may be because of so-called dirty tariffication practices, the occurrence of tariff escalation, and the use of a range of nontariff barriers by industrialized countries. Sri Lanka's agricultural trade is now governed predominantly by a progressive tariff regime, but there are still a range of market distorting elements visible within the sector.

Taking all of these factors into consideration, it is apparent that the overall impact on Sri Lanka's trade and traders during the implementation of the URAoA has been minimal.

Table A3.1 Total Population and Labor Force and Agriculture Sector Labor, 1990–98

Year	Total population (millions)	Total labor force (millions)	Total agricultural labor force (millions)	Percent
1990	16.9	6.00	2.36	39.33
1991	17.2	5.87	2.13	36.29
1992	17.4	5.80	2.08	35.86
1993	17.6	6.03	2.15	35.66
1994	17.8	6.07	2.08	34.27
1995	18.1	6.10	1.96	32.13
1996	18.3	6.24	2.06	33.01
1997	18.5	6.21	2.08	33.49
1998	18.7	6.69	2.40	35.87

Note: Data exclude northern and eastern provinces.
Source: Sri Lanka Labor Force Survey and the Consumer Finance Survey.

Table A3.2 Agriculture Sector Share of GDP, 1990–97

Year	GDP (Rs millions)	Share of agriculture (Rs millions)	Percentage share
1990	129,244	30,011	23.22
1991	135,204	30,556	22.60
1992	140,990	30,079	21.33
1993	150,783	31,554	20.93
1994	159,269	32,593	20.46
1995	167,953	33,659	20.00
1996	174,261	32,109	18.43
1997	185,500	33,095	17.84

Source: Central Bank of Sri Lanka (1999a).

Table A3.3 Crop Cultivation Land Extent, 1990–98 (hectares)

Crop	1990	1991	1992	1993	1994	1995	1996	1997	1998
Paddy	857,000	817,000	803,000	835,000	930,000	915,000	749,000	730,000	848,000
Tea	221,758	221,691	221,836	192,730	187,426	188,970	189,354	193,676	194,736
Rubber	199,048	198,451	194,550	161,477	160,909	161,600	162,000	158,200	158,140
Coconut	383,500	379,500	375,000	416,000	416,000	416,000	417,000	417,000	439,000
Potato	7,699	3,499	5,310	7,733	7,210	7,428	7,925	6,469	2,328
Big onion	1,776	2,400	2,460	3,514	3,761	3,687	2,662	2,956	1,413
Chilies	38,095	34,176	31,399	42,753	36,516	30,597	26,098	24,146	21,632
Cinnamon	20,190	20,310	20,210	24,257	24,218	24,248	24,304	24,358	—
Pepper	15,600	17,000	17,190	25,840	25,590	26,990	26,983	27,028	—

— Not available.
Sources: Central Bank of Sri Lanka, Annual Report (various years); Central Bank of Sri Lanka, Agricultural Abstracts (various years).

Table A3.4 Agricultural Commodity Production in Sri Lanka, 1990–98

Commodity	1990	1991	1992	1993	1994	1995	1996	1997	1998[a]
Tea (million km)	233.1	241	178	232	242	248	258	277	280
Rubber (million km)	113.1	104	106	104	105	106	112	118	95.7
Coconut (million tons)	2,532	2,184	2,296	2,164	2,622	2,755	2,546	2,631	2,547
Paddy (million tons)	2,528	2,389	2,340	2,570	2,684	2,810	2,061	2,339	2,692
Potato (million tons)	84,347	42,200	45,054	77,163	79,385	81,657	100,755	65,800	25,900
Big onion (million tons)	18,777	21,400	27,639	38,023	43,726	29,719	19,367	29,100	17,400
Chilies (million tons)	39,100	33,200	33,500	40,400	31,900	21,300	18,400	17,900	15,600
Vegetable (million tons)	558,840	567,190	572,390	879,430	587,520	—	427,380	419,000	352,000
Manioc (million tons)	253,985	358,808	301,878	299,572	298,402	288,928	270,596	249,779	—
Sugar (million tons)	57,165	66,440	59,710	68,603	72,275	710,00	70,000	63,897	61,000
Milk (million liters)	249	280	318	326	332	333	331	331	341
Fish (million tons)	177,063	198,063	206,168	220,900	224,000	238,000	228,000	240,000	260,000

— Not available.

a. Provisional data series are taken from the Central Bank of Sri Lanka, Annual Report (various years).

Source: Central Bank of Sri Lanka, Economic and Social Statistics of Sri Lanka (various years).

Table A3.5 Major Dairy Product Imports, 1995–97

Source of supply	1995 Quantity (million tons)	1995 Market share (percent)	1996 Quantity (million tons)	1996 Market share (percent)	1997 Quantity (million tons)	1997 Market share (percent)
Full cream milk powder over 26 percent milk fat						
New Zealand	24,568	58.7	25,300	66.2	25,502	67.9
Australia	3,456	8.3	5,141	13.5	7,261	19.3
European Union	12,147	29.0	7,403	19.4	4,729	12.6
Other	1,659	4.0	376	0.9	49	0.2
Skim milk powder						
New Zealand	501	12.0	717	16.9	1,632	39.1
Australia	924	22.1	2,467	58.1	2.273	54.5
European Union	906	21.7	409	9.6	192	4.6
Other	1,850	44.2	656	15.4	72	1.9
Infant milk products						
European Union	356	81.3	344	73.6	2	10.3
Other	81	18.7	123	26.4	14	89.7
Whey products and other						
Australia	405	36.2	698	53.6	628	47.7
European Union	459	33.1	267	20.5	554	42.1
Other	142	29.8	339	26.0	133	10.2

Source: Sri Lanka Department of Customs.

Table A3.6 Fish Production and Imports in Sri Lanka, 1994–98
(million tons)

Item	1994	1995	1996	1997	1998
Marine fish production	212,000	217,550	206,300	213,000	230,200
Inland fish production	12,000	20,000	22,250	27,000	30,000
Total production	224,000	237,550	228,550	240,000	260,200
Total imports	61,675	71,432	65,892	76,000	—

— Not available.
Source: Fisheries Day Book statistics.

Table A3.7 Quantity and Value of Food Imported by the Cooperative Wholesale Establishment, 1994–98 (million tons)

Year	Chilies	Onion	Potato	Red lentils	White sugar	Rice
1994	—	12,099	—	14,537	—	—
		(8,924)		(331)		
1995	2,000	6,312	1,350	28,281	20,673	—
	(189)	(140)	(30)	(847)	(598)	
1996	450	649	1,535	4,940	15,125	29,990
	(39)	(133)	(32)	(153)	(403)	(483)
1997	—	5,863	3,189	17,166	39,250	20,886
		(102)	(57)	(666)	(1,044)	(388)
1998	198.4	5,148	2,837	10,704	26,250	14,953
	(24)	(154)	(62)	(395)	(698)	(315)

— Not available.
Note: Parentheses indicate values in Rs million.
Source: Cooperative Wholesale Establishment statistics.

Table A3.8 Local Purchases of Agricultural Commodities by the Cooperative Wholesale Establishment, by Volume, 1994–98 (million tons)

Commodity	1994	1995	1996	1997	1998
Black gram	—	29	61	7	100
White	1	23	49	5	100
Green gram	194	553	—	323	211
Lanka kadala	—	—	—	—	—
Rice	—	—	—	—	—
Potato	76	—	—	91	360
Tamarind	15	—	—	21	60
Dry chilies	1,120	—	—	1,798	90
Prima flour	34,700	—	—	10,453	20,704
Vegetable	—	—	—	—	—
Turmeric	56	—	—	—	45
Black pepper	29	—	—	—	100
Big onion	3,700	3,772	—	1,571	29
Cinnamon	6	5	—	—	48
Goraka	6	—	—	—	190
White sugar	16,000	—	—	—	—
Brown sugar	200	—	—	—	—

— Not available.
Source: Cooperative Wholesale Establishment statistics.

Table A3.9 Total Agriculture Exports, by Volume, 1994–98
(million kilograms)

Commodity	1994	1995	1996	1997	1998
Tea	229,561	240,802	244,109	268,537	271,868
Rubber	69,100	68,300	72,100	61,500	41,300
Coconut	436,500	578,600	474,500	505,200	435,000
Minor agricultural products	52,458	53,545	16,030	13,820	16,838
Vegetable	16,299	8,371	6,734	6,869	7,705
Fruit	5,774	5,868	5,810	9,886	3,590
Coffee	4,371	1,281	692	1,150	1,588
Pepper	3,490	2,768	2,997	3,484	5,494
Cinnamon	11,040	9,852	10	10,661	9,401
Cardamom	26	19	6	8	16
Cloves	850	1,116	1,429	2,461	1,909
Betel leaves	1,846	1,811	2,580	1,729	1,321
Cocoa products	15	190	43	153	88
Cashew nuts	390	349	334	599	421
Oilseed	176	144	128	257	168
Nutmeg and mace	666	755	1,084	760	898
Areca nuts	311	2,763	3,109	3,338	5,026
Unmanufactured tobacco	3,540	3,021	3,229	1,832	2,611
Meat exports	168	79	727	1,202	—

— Not available.
Source: Sri Lanka Department of Customs; Central Bank of Sri Lanka (1999a).

Table A3.10 Total Agriculture Commodity Imports, by Volume, 1994–98 (million tons)

Commodity	1994	1995	1996	1997	1998
Rice	58,000	9,000	341,000	306,000	168,000
Wheat	865,000	1,057,000	913,000	789,000	880,000
Potato	7,849	11,981	25,738	108,332	115,507
Big onion	48,001	77,741	90,005	119,625	104,070
Sugar	491,000	418,000	381,000	545,000	444,000
Milk and products	1,427,000	1,072,000	579,000	—	—
Chilies	8,346	10,804	9,945	13,415	20,203
Meat and products	2,286	1,517	1,188	1,935	1,799
Fertilizer	427,000	452,000	361,000	391,000	440,000

— Not available.
Source: Central Bank of Sri Lanka, Annual Report (various years) and socioeconomic data.

Endnotes

1. This contract was signed by the government and Prima in 1978 and extends to 2004. The company guarantees the milling of approximately 435,000 million tons of wheat grain and provides the government with 74 percent of the wheat flour milled for every 100 units of wheat grain supplied. The balance of wheat flour is retained by Prima as payment for its milling cost. By using this excess wheat flour, Prima supplies the local market with animal feed, over which it now essentially has a monopoly. In addition, the government bears the transportation cost from the mills in the northeast of the country to Colombo, an amount of Rs210 million annually. This contract has served to prolong the liberalization of the wheat flour market as well as the animal feed market.
2. Importation would have been much less if the northeast coastal belt were available for fishing. However, the ongoing war has restricted this belt from fishing.
3. Refers to a situation that occurs in the process of converting nontariff barriers to tariffs, where the countries concerned can manipulate base rate data, so that the resulting tariff equivalents are high.
4. Taken from the Plant Protection Ordinance (Chapter 447) of the *Gazette of the Democratic Socialist Republic of Sri Lanka*, issued on May 14, 1999.
5. Information taken from field interviews.

Bibliography

Athukorala, P., and S. Kelegama. 1996. *The Uruguay Round Agreement on Agriculture: Implications for Sri Lanka*. Colombo: Institute of Policy Studies.

Bhalla, S. 1991. "The Political Economy of Agricultural Pricing Policy, Sri Lanka." In A. Krueger, ed., *The Political Economy of Agriculture Pricing Policy*. Vol. II. Baltimore: Johns Hopkins University Press.

Blarele, B., Gary Pursell, and Alberto Valdés, eds. 1996. *Implications of the Uruguay Round Agreement for South Asia: The Case for Agriculture*. Washington, D.C.: World Bank.

Central Bank of Sri Lanka. Various years. *Agricultural Abstracts*. Colombo.

———. Various years. *Annual Report*. Colombo.

———. Various years. *Economic and Social Statistics of Sri Lanka*. Colombo.

———. 1998. *Economic Progress of Independent Sri Lanka*. Colombo.

———. 1999a. *Bulletin, January 1999*. Colombo.

———. 1999b. "Report on Consumer Finances and Socio Economic Survey, Sri Lanka 1996/97, Part I." Colombo.

———. 1999c. *Budget at a Glance 1999*. Colombo.

Dhanasekera, D. M. U. B. 1998. "Cut Flower Production in Sri Lanka." In *Cut Flower Production in Asia*. Bangkok: FAO Regional Office for Asia and the Pacific.

Ediriweera, N. D. 1998. "Food Security Situation in Sri Lanka." In *People's Bank (1998) Economic Review, April–May 1998*. Colombo: People's Bank.

Edwards, C. 1993. *A Report on Protectionism and Trade Policy in Manufacturing and Agriculture, Sri Lanka*. Colombo: Institute of Policy Studies.

Eriksen, J. H. 1998. *An Assessment of Dairy Industry Policy in Sri Lanka.* Colombo: Agro-Enterprise Development Project.
FAO (Food and Agriculture Organization). 1995a. *Impacts of the Uruguay Round Agreement on the World Tea Economy.* Rome.
———. 1995b. *This is Codex Alimentarius.* Rome.
———. 1998. *Selected Indicators of Food and Agriculture Development in the Asia Pacific Region.* Bangkok: Regional Office for Asia and the Pacific.
Healy, S., Rachel Pearce, and Michael Stockbridge. 1998. *The Implications of the Uruguay Round Agreement on Agriculture for Developing Countries: A Training Manual.* Rome: FAO.
Hector Kobbekauwa Agrarian Research and Training Institute (HARTI). 1997. *Food Commodity Prices, 1985–1996.* Colombo.
Indraratna, A. D. V. de S. ed. 1998. *Fifty Years of Sri Lanka's Independence, A Socio Economic Review.* Colombo: Sri Lanka Institute of Social and Economic Studies.
Institute of Policy Studies. 1996. "Strategy for National Agricultural Development Horizon 2010: Sri Lanka." World Food Summit, Colombo.
———. 1999. *Investment Incentives for Manufacturing Industries in Sri Lanka: Rural Urban Differences, Preliminary Report.* Colombo.
Kelegama, S., and Y. Casie Chetty. 1993. *Consumer Protection and Fair Trading in Sri Lanka.* Colombo: The Law and Society Trust.
Lakshman W. D., ed. 1997. *Dilemmas of Development, Fifty Years of Economic Change in Sri Lanka.* Colombo: Sri Lanka Association of Economists.
Linland, J. 1997. *The Impact of the Uruguay Round on Tariff Escalation in Agricultural Products.* Rome: Trade Policy Group, Commodities and Trade Division, FAO.
Mendis, H. 1996. *Seminar on Hatchery Management and Practices/Economic Factors of Livestock Production, An Assessment of the Poultry Industry in Sri Lanka.* Colombo: Agro-Enterprise Development Project.
National Development Council. 1996. "Agricultural Policy Recommendations." Report of the National Development Council Working Group on Agricultural Policy. Colombo.
Peiris, G. L. 1998. "Budget Speech 1998." Government Press, Colombo.
People's Bank. 1999. *Economic Review, Paddy Sector Development, January–March 1999.* Colombo.
Presidential Tariff Commission. 1991. "Report of the Presidential Tariff Commission, November 1991." Colombo.
Shilpi, F. 1995. "Policy Incentive, Diversification, and Comparative Advantage of Non-Plantation Crops in Sri Lanka." Working Paper 2. World Bank, Washington, D.C.
Sri Lanka Department of Commerce. 1997. *Trade Statistics, December 1997.* Colombo.
Sri Lanka Department of Customs. 1998. *External Trade Statistics, Sri Lanka 1998.* Colombo.
———. 1999. *Sri Lanka Customs Tariff Guide 1999.* Colombo.
Sri Lanka Ministry of Agriculture, Lands, and Forestry. 1996. World Food Summit Position Paper. Colombo.
Sri Lanka Ministry of Finance and Planning. 1998. *Trends in Public Finance 1998.* Colombo
———. 1997. *Statistical Abstract 1997.* Colombo.

Sri Lanka Ministry of Policy Planning and Implementation. Various years. *Public Investment*. Colombo.

———. 1992. *Food and Nutrition Statistics, 1950–1990*. Colombo.

Sri Lanka Ministry of Public Administration, Home Affairs, and Plantation Industries. 1998. *Plantation Sector Statistical Pocket Book, 1998*. Colombo.

UNCTAD (United Nations Conference on Trade and Development) Secretariat. 1999. "WTO Agreement on Sanitary and Phytosanitary Measures: Issues for Developing Countries." In "Trade Related Agenda, Development and Equity (TRADE)." Working Paper 3. Geneva.

U.N. World Food Program. 1998. *Thirty Years of Cooperation 1968–1998*. Colombo.

Valdés, A. 1996. "Surveillance of Agricultural Price and Trade Policy in Latin America during Major Policy Reforms." World Bank Discussion Paper 249. Washington D.C.

World Bank. 1996. *Sri Lanka, Nonplantation Crop Sector Policy Alternatives*. Washington, D.C.

WTO (World Trade Organization). 1996a. *Trading into the Future: World Trade Organization*. Geneva.

———. 1996b. "Agreement on the Application of Sanitary and Phytosanitary Measures." Geneva.

———. 1997. "Draft Anti-Dumping Legislation." Geneva.

Youngberg, H. W. 1998a. *A Proposed Seed Act for Sri Lanka*. Colombo: Agro-Enterprise Development Project.

———. 1998b. *A Review of Issues Relating to Seed Policy in Sri Lanka*. Colombo: Agro-Enterprise Development Project.

4
Pakistan

Safraz Khan

One of the major initiatives toward the establishment of a liberal world trading system was the signing of the Uruguay Round (UR) of the General Agreement on Tariffs and Trade (GATT) and the establishment of its successor, the World Trade Organization (WTO). The UR global trade accord is seen by most observers as the most comprehensive and ambitious of all rounds of talks among member countries because it includes new areas such as agriculture, services, textiles and clothing, intellectual property rights, and investment measures. The UR Agreement on Agriculture (AoA), however, is seen as being among the most contentious subjects of the UR accord by the farming community in both industrialized and developing countries because both fear that dislocation will occur from cheaper agricultural exports.

Decisions on agricultural trade have far-reaching implications considering the importance of agriculture to most economies. For most developing countries like Pakistan where agriculture is the dominant sector and contributes a large proportion of export earnings, the implementation of the agreement will have profound implications for a majority of the population. Because the agreement requires that the economic policies in member countries will need to be modified to conform to the provisions of the Final Act, political economy considerations need to be understood.

With the implementation of the UR agreement there will clearly be winners and losers. In the short run some will be affected as a result of adjustments from policies that will need to be aligned with the accord. Countries dependent on agricultural imports, for instance, will suffer from increased prices of commodities owing to the phasing out of export subsidies in the exporting countries. However, in the long run, the increased competitiveness among WTO-member countries is expected to result in greater efficiency in production, generate more employment, and increase farm incomes. Agricultural exporting developing countries like Pakistan are expected to gain from the increased access to foreign markets under the WTO.

The UR accord will definitely impinge on the performance of the agriculture sector of Pakistan. A study of the implications of the accord, therefore, is required to identify the opportunities, problems, and programs/ actions to maximize the gains and minimize the costs from the implementation of the agreement.

Agriculture and the Economy

Agriculture is a major economic activity in Pakistan. It employs half the country's labor force and generates nearly a fourth of the gross national product (tables 4.1 and 4.2). So far the agricultural strategy of Pakistan has successfully met the food requirements of a rapidly growing population and has played a pivotal role in earning foreign exchange through the export of rice and cotton. Crops are the most important agricultural subsector, constituting around 60 percent of agricultural gross domestic product (GDP), with production concentrated in three broad agro-ecological zones: irrigated lowlands, rain-fed lowlands, and mountain areas. Crop production is well diversified, with more than half the area devoted to cereals, one fifth to cash crops, and the rest to fodder, pulses, vegetables, and fruits. Of 22 million hectares of cultivable land, 18 million are irrigated and 4 million are rain fed. Almost 60 percent of this land is found in the Punjab and about 30 percent in the Sindh. The irrigated plains are used mainly for the production of cotton, rice, and sugarcane, while wheat is the main crop in the rain-fed areas. Another 9 million hectares are classified as being cultivable but undeveloped either because of environmental damage (wind and water erosion, salinity, and water logging) or because of a lack of irrigation. Mixed crop-livestock farming dominates agriculture in most mountain regions. Livestock are of considerable economic importance, accounting for almost 30 percent of agricultural GDP and more than 10 percent of the country's foreign exchange earnings.

Agriculture and Economic Growth

Agriculture has provided a significant boost to Pakistan's overall economic growth in recent years. In 1986–91 agricultural growth averaged 4.3 percent a year, or 1.3 percent a year in per capita terms (the population grew by 3 percent a year). Assuming that a 1 percent increase in per capita agricultural income generates a 1.5 percent increase in per capita nonagricultural income, the 1.3 percent agricultural growth likely gave rise to about 2 percent per capita nonagricultural growth and almost 5 percent in overall nonagricultural growth (the actual growth rate was 5.3 percent). Within the nonagricultural sector, manufacturing appears to benefit the most from agricultural expansion, especially those industries with strong linkages to agriculture, such as food and beverage processing, tobacco, and textiles and clothing.

Table 4.1 Performance of Overall Economy, 1990–99 (at constant market prices: 1980–81 = 100)

Fiscal year	Agriculture	Mining and quarrying	Manu-facturing	Construction	Electricity and gas	Transport storage and commerce	Wholesale and retail trade	Finance and insurance	Ownership dwelling	Public administration and defense	Services	Taxes minus subsidies
1990–91	22.91	0.50	15.80	3.69	3.09	8.54	14.68	1.98	4.86	6.34	6.82	10.79
1991–92	23.26	0.48	15.83	3.44	3.12	8.75	14.61	1.92	4.75	6.03	6.74	11.08
1992–93	21.62	0.48	16.36	3.77	3.26	9.16	14.75	2.01	4.90	6.06	7.04	10.58
1993–94	21.90	0.48	16.59	3.69	3.23	9.14	14.60	2.21	4.97	5.91	7.22	10.05
1994–95	22.20	0.44	16.37	3.54	3.59	9.06	14.54	2.24	4.98	5.80	7.30	9.94
1995–96	23.62	0.45	16.34	3.48	3.77	8.62	14.69	2.43	4.99	5.70	7.43	8.50
1996–97	23.36	0.45	16.35	3.48	3.62	8.91	14.61	2.80	5.19	5.76	7.82	7.66
1997–98	23.48	0.41	17.07	3.41	3.81	9.33	14.56	2.01	5.30	5.68	8.06	6.87
1998–99	22.68	0.42	17.20	3.31	3.77	9.45	14.18	2.11	5.36	5.65	8.56	7.33

Source: Pakistan Ministry of Finance (1999).

Table 4.2 Basic Data on Agriculture, 1990–99

Fiscal year	Cropped area (million hectares)	Cultivated area (million hectares)	Irrigated area (million hectares)	Population (millions)	Employed labor force (millions)	Agricultural labor force (millions)	Agricultural as a percent of employed labor force (millions)	GDP (Rs millions)	Agricultural value-added as a percent of GDP	Average annual growth of agricultural value-added (percent)
1990–91	21.82	20.96	16.75	110.79	29.01	13.77	47.47	499,960	22.91	—
1991–92	21.72	21.06	16.85	113.61	30.07	14.51	48.25	539,131	23.26	9.50
1992–93	22.44	21.40	17.33	116.47	30.92	14.70	47.54	549,455	21.62	–5.29
1993–94	21.87	21.51	17.13	119.39	31.68	15.85	50.03	570,859	21.90	5.23
1994–95	22.14	21.55	17.20	122.36	31.80	14.98	47.11	600,086	22.20	6.57
1995–96	22.59	21.68	17.58	125.38	32.58	15.24	46.78	630,151	23.62	11.72
1996–97	22.93	22.05	17.83	128.42	34.59	15.25	44.09	637,876	23.36	0.12
1997–98	23.04	22.04	18.00	131.51	35.42	15.62	44.10	658,928	23.48	3.82
1998–99	23.04	21.92		134.51	36.23	15.98	44.11	684,683	22.68	0.35

Source: Pakistan Ministry of Finance (1999).

HISTORICAL TRENDS IN AGRICULTURAL PRODUCTION. Since the early 1970s agricultural GDP has more than doubled, increasing from Rs51 billion in 1970 to Rs115 billion in 1991. It increased to Rs155 billion in 1999 showing a steady growth of about 3 percent a year. Agriculture's share of total GDP fluctuated around 22–23 percent during the period 1990–99. Crop production accounted for the largest share of agricultural GDP (59 percent in 1998–99), with livestock contributing 37 percent and fisheries and forestry making up the remaining 4 percent. The share of livestock in total agricultural GDP rose by 5 percent, while crop production fell by 5 percent. Fishery and forestry have not shown any change.

The shares for the 1990s are significantly different from those for the 1970s, indicating that important structural changes have taken place in the sector. In particular, livestock has emerged as an important subsector, contributing more than one-third of agricultural GDP, compared with less than 15 percent 20 years ago. Similarly, fisheries and forestry, while still minor contributors to agricultural GDP, have grown rapidly. Structural changes have also taken place within the crop sector itself. For example, cotton is now as important as wheat in terms of value-added, with a one-third share of total crop earnings. As the share of cotton in value-added expanded, there was a decline in the relative importance of rice and sugar; that is, the shares of both crops fell from 20 percent in the early 1970s to close to 12 percent in 1991–92. (Please see tables 4.3, 4.4, and 4.5 for more detail.)

The strong annual growth of the 1960s was driven by a number of factors, including greater certainty in the use of irrigation water (owing to an agreement with India), the introduction of productivity-enhancing fertilizer-seed packages, the emergence of tubewells and electrification of rural

Table 4.3 Agriculture Sector Performance, 1990–99
(percent share in agriculture)

Fiscal year	Major crops	Minor crops	Livestock	Fishing	Forestry
1990–91	47.79	17.30	29.78	3.87	1.26
1991–92	50.40	16.18	28.81	3.71	0.91
1992–93	44.91	17.75	32.25	4.13	0.95
1993–94	43.21	19.00	32.48	4.35	0.95
1994–95	44.07	19.06	32.16	3.79	0.91
1995–96	41.80	17.90	36.40	3.29	0.61
1996–97	39.94	18.04	37.89	3.45	0.67
1997–98	41.65	17.95	36.23	3.58	0.59
1998–99	41.26	17.95	36.64	3.70	0.44

Source: Pakistan Ministry of Finance (1999).

Table 4.4 Agricultural and GDP Growth, 1960–98

Years	Value-added in agriculture	GDP
1960–70	6.7	4.9
1970–80	4.9	2.3
1980–92	6.1	4.5
1992–98	3.5	3.1

Source: Pakistan Ministry of Finance (1999).

areas, and policy changes that improved the profitability of farming. (See table 4.4.)

Growth in the 1970s declined following the uncertainty created by land reforms (and their selective implementation) in 1972 and 1977, severe climatic shocks, a cotton virus that reduced production for most of the 1970s, and political instability. The recovery in the 1980s and early 1990s can be attributed to the introduction of new cotton varieties and improved management techniques, as well as to a gradual improvement in economic incentives. Correspondingly, growth performance weakens when the cotton crop is poor.

The dependence on cotton for strong growth and export performance means that economic stability is threatened when the cotton crop suffers any setbacks. Recent developments indicate that the cotton-driven boom has now run its course and that new sources of growth will have to be found. There are clear signs that productivity growth in other major crops also is leveling off. Except for cotton there have been few upward trends in productivity.

Table 4.5 Growth of Agriculture Sector, 1970s to 1990s (percent)

Commodity	1970s	1980s	1990s
Sector crops	3.3	4.1	–0.9
Wheat	2.6	3.0	12.4
Rice	1.7	1.4	0.7
Cotton	6.6	9.3	–1.4
Sugar	1.9	1.7	0.8
Noncrops	4.2	2.7	5.9
Livestock	2.8	5.4	6.6
Fisheries	29.7	2.0	3.3
Forestry	23.1	6.5	–9.1
Total	4.0	4.1	1.8

Source: Pakistan Ministry of Finance (1999).

Pakistan

Rice. Rice is both exported and consumed domestically, although production has barely increased since the early 1980s. While the area under rice fluctuated moderately around 2 million hectares during the 1980s, the yield increased from almost 1,543 kilograms per hectare in 1990–91 to just under 1,928 kilograms per hectare in 1998–99. During the 1990s the area under rice increased from 2.1 million hectares in 1990–91 to 2.4 million hectares in 1998–99.

Food Crops. Wheat is by far the most important foodgrain and is estimated to contribute more than half of per capita caloric intake and 85 percent of total protein intake. Some wheat is also fed to livestock. Total consumption in 1992–93 was about 17.5 million metric tons. The area under wheat increased from 7.4 million hectares in 1982–83 to about 7.9 million hectares in 1991–92 and to 8.3 million hectares in 1998–99. Yields also rose, from just under 1,700 kilograms per hectare in 1982–83 to nearly 1,900 kilograms per hectare in 1991–92 and to 2,167 per hectare in 1998–99. The area under maize grew only slightly, from about 0.79 million hectares to 0.86 million hectares during the 1982–83/1992–93 periods while in 1998–99 it rose to 0.88 million hectares. Maize yields increased modestly from 1,250 kilograms per hectare to 1,400 kilograms per hectare during the same period.

Like many other countries, Pakistan has pushed for self-sufficiency in sugar, and production has increased slowly since the mid-1980s. Sugar area averaged about 0.85 million hectares during the 1980s, while yields increased moderately: from 35,700 kilograms per hectare in 1982–83 to 43,300 kilograms per hectare in 1991–92.

Livestock and Related Products. The livestock sector grew rapidly and contributed about 37 percent of agricultural GDP during the 1980s. About 5.5 million households own livestock, generally in small mixed farming systems, with 70–80 percent of households owning fewer than four head of cattle or buffalo and 60 percent owning fewer than five goats.

Since 1981–82 the volume of red meat and milk production has grown by 5–6 percent a year. The poultry sector has been even more dynamic, growing by 12–13 percent a year in recent years. Poultry in 1992–93 accounted for almost 14 percent of total meat production, compared with 9 percent in 1984–85 and 6 percent in 1980–81. Milk is the most important animal product, with 70 percent coming from buffalo.

The livestock sector is secondary to the crop sector and is not very commercialized. There are many questions about the performance and potential of the livestock subsector (such as a possible trade off between the growth of crops and livestock), and further analysis is needed before sound policy recommendations can be made with regard to its commercialization.

HORTICULTURAL PRODUCTS. A favorable climate gives Pakistan a strong comparative advantage in horticulture, as indicated by its rapid growth in the absence of policy interventions. The country's climatic zones provide valuable niche crops in several areas of the horticulture market, notably off-season (relative to the European market) midwinter harvests, year-round tropical fruits, low-chilling temperate fruits (such as berries and some types of stone fruit), and high-chilling temperate fruits (stone fruit). For example, peaches in Pakistan have lower production costs than in Greece, India, or California. But the perishability of horticultural products requires efficient processing and marketing infrastructure that is largely deficient in Pakistan. Nonetheless, the Pakistan Horticulture Export Development Project has estimated that with appropriate planning, the country can have annual horticulture exports in excess of $100 million within 10 years.

Agricultural Policy

Policy related to the agrarian sector has been one of the major concerns of planners and policymakers in Pakistan. Agricultural policy can be essentially divided into two major types: structural and nonstructural. Structural policies attempt to change the basic structure of the agrarian sector through reforms aimed at altering the size and distribution of land holdings and tenancy relationships, formalizing such relationships, and imposing direct taxes on agriculture. Such policies are general in nature and cover the whole sector. Nonstructural policies are more specific and relate mainly to price manipulations, whether of inputs or factors of production or output, and indirect taxes on agricultural activities. While both policies affect agricultural production and economic welfare of the agrarian sector, the following discussion relates to the nonstructural policy framework and discusses some of the broad policy issues and changes that are directly related to agricultural pricing and production.

PRICING POLICIES, AGRICULTURAL PRODUCTION, AND INCOME DISTRIBUTION. The argument for higher agricultural prices is based on the microeconomic effects of price changes on individual farmers. Higher prices can stimulate agricultural production by encouraging better and greater use of resources, particularly labor and other variable inputs, by encouraging further investment in the adoption of new technologies resulting in lower average costs. The price elasticity of agricultural supply, though not always substantial, does in general indicate a positive and significant response. To assume that subsistence farmers do not respond favorably to price changes is misleading. They can also be encouraged to use more and better resources, to apply more labor, and to adopt more efficient agricultural practices through appropriate price changes. A link also exists between price incentives and private investment in land leveling and improvement, irrigation, and other farm development. It is also accepted that a large part of farm incomes, particularly for small to medium farmers, is reinvested. Thus, if farm incomes are raised through higher prices then there is likely to be greater investment in agriculture.

The argument used for keeping food prices low is based on the view that it benefits the urban poor and that the losers are mainly nonsubsistence farmers. This has been the reason why major food commodities in Pakistan have been subject to both quantity rationing and price controls ever since the early 1950s. In the absence of an egalitarian agrarian structure and a highly skewed distribution of land, power, and benefits, there is some doubt about the beneficiaries of any policy changes. Even subsistence farmers have to sell their produce to buy other essentials. The effect on urban consumers through black marketing and other means may also be negated. In Pakistan, the effect of subsidized food prices on income distribution has never been determined, and there are various proponents, both for and against, keeping food prices low. The overall effect on agricultural production is likely to have been negative. Moreover, in the absence of such price controls, production of food crops may have been higher.

This line of reasoning is further strengthened when the price subsidies on inputs given to farmers are examined. Modern inputs, particularly high yielding varieties (HYVs) of seeds and chemical fertilizers, have been subsidized ever since they were first introduced in Pakistan in the late 1950s and early 1960s. Such farm subsidies mostly benefit middle and upper income farmers. Poorer farmers lack the money and the ability to obtain credit at subsidized rates to buy adequate amounts of pesticides, fertilizers, or HYVs. The agrarian structure reinforces this inequality, further increases the dependence of tenants on their landlords (who provide these inputs on credit to tenants), and pushes small farmers closer to subsistence farming. Large farmers manage to benefit from these subsidies, which generally result in a worsening of real income distribution. What is generally ignored when such subsidies are advocated is that because of the existing distribution of assets and power all farmers do not have equal access to inputs. Since this structure is unaltered the benefits of any subsidy are also skewed. Subsidies on water is such an example. Water rates in Pakistan are highly subsidized, supposedly to benefit small farmers, but most of this subsidy goes to large farmers because of unequal access to water.

Over time there have been substantial increases in prices paid to farmers for food crops. Price controls on cash crops have also been relaxed. Subsidies on inputs have been greatly reduced since the late 1970s. Such moves can be considered rational in light of the evidence regarding transfer of resources between producers, consumers, and the government as a result of price policies. Gotsch and Brown (1980) have estimated these transfers for wheat in Pakistan. They show a large income transfer from wheat producers to consumers through lower than world market prices for domestic wheat, including that procured by the government. For 1976, Gotsch and Brown estimated that these transfers amounted to 52 percent of the income received by all farmers from marketed wheat. On the other hand, in the same year, farmers received government subsidies on inputs used in wheat production amounting to only 10 percent of the value of domestic marketed wheat. The net result has been a large income transfer from producers to consumers, estimated at more than the total payment to domestic farmers for their entire crop of marketed wheat.

An analysis of the domestic subsidy policy must be based on the costs and benefits of these subsidies. All consumers are beneficiaries. The costs may be borne disproportionately by small and subsistence level farmers who market as much as 30 percent of all marketed wheat in Pakistan, receiving only a minor fraction of input subsidies. Higher farm prices will affect the incomes of small farmers and agricultural workers. Perhaps, a direct food subsidy program for the urban poor will not only be cheaper but also reach the desired target more effectively. In any event, the general structure and the effects of a particular pricing policy needs to be studied in detail to come to any conclusion regarding the kinds of policies that have been pursued. The little evidence that exists suggests that the pricing policy may not have had the desired effects either on production or income distribution in the agricultural sector.

CREDIT POLICY. Major suppliers of farm credit have been noninstitutional sources. These include landlords, commission agents, shopkeepers, agricultural input suppliers, friends, and relatives. Although the relative share of noninstitutional sources in total credit has declined, they still remain dominant. The institutional sources of credit have grown as a result of much publicized policies. These sources include the Agricultural Development Bank of Pakistan, commercial banks, cooperative societies, and taccavi loans. The share of institutional credit has also increased owing to the need for greater resources since the introduction of new innovations and technologies in Pakistan. Taccavi loans are the oldest form of institutional credit and are given directly to farmers in times of distress or famine. Such loans are also given on a long-term basis for land improvement and protection, flood control, and for canal and irrigation purposes.

The Agricultural Development Bank of Pakistan was formed in 1961 through a merger of the former Agricultural Development Bank and the Agricultural Development Finance Corporation. This bank extends long, medium-, and short-term loans for all agricultural activities including forestry, fisheries, and animal husbandry. It is supposed to give preference to the needs of small farmers but for various reasons most of the beneficiaries are large farmers. Before 1972, commercial banks played little part in providing loans for agricultural purposes. With increasing commercialization of agriculture, this role has increased but is mainly confined to large landlords for obvious reasons. Cooperative credit societies have also recently gained some success in providing credit for farmers, and, if properly supported, can become a useful source of credit for small farmers.

Most of the credit from the banks (both the Agricultural Development Bank of Pakistan and others) has gone to larger farmers whereas small farmers continue to rely on informal sources. Banks prefer giving loans for technological improvements that include modern input packages; new machines including tractors, threshers, and tubewells; post-harvesting storage facilities; and processing and refining of crops. It is clear that these are not always the priorities of small farmers who may require short-term loans for emergency or consumption reasons. When institutional loans are unavailable, they have to resort to noninstitutional sources or use their production resources.

The Agricultural Development Bank of Pakistan and, more recently, the commercial banks have played a major role in financing mechanization, confined to tractors and tubewells. Most of these have, until recently, been purchased by farmers in the Punjab. The government has actively promoted mechanization. All the five-year plans have advocated mechanization, and credit policy has been geared to encourage the provision of subsidized loans to purchase tractors and tubewells. These loans have been made to large landholders since they are likely to benefit from mechanization and desire it. With the bias toward larger tractors and, until recently, the ban on the import of small tractors, small farmers are hardly likely to invest in a tractor for use on a small holding. Tubewells too have been only of medium to large sizes. Both tractorization and tubewell installation received major support in the mid-1960s through the early 1970s.

Recently, the Agricultural Development Bank of Pakistan has attempted to increase its lending to small farmers as have the commercial banks, but despite much publicity the results have not been very effective. The basic nature of the credit policy remains biased toward large farmers. There appears to be little chance of resolving the problem of providing small farmer credit while still maintaining a low risk of default policy or reducing collateral requirements.

Experience with Adapting Agricultural and Trade Policies to World Trade Organization Commitments

Under the URAoA the ceilings of tariff bindings had to be submitted for all agricultural products. For developing countries there was no limit on the level of these bindings and no obligations to reduce them during the 10 year phase-in period, provided the tariffs had been previously bound under the GATT. Quantitative restrictions, such as quotas, had to be converted into tariffs.

In the UR Pakistan committed to bind more than 90 percent of its agricultural import tariffs (Harmonized System (HS) chapters 1–24). About 6 percent agricultural tariff lines will remain unbound, mainly in alcoholic beverages, swine, and pig meat and products (Ingco and Winters 1996), with bound tariff ceilings in the range of 100–150 percent for about 78 percent of the agricultural products included in the Pakistan customs tariff schedule (that is, 633 out of 813 tariff lines under HS chapters 1–24 [minus 3] and 72 out of 91 tariff lines under other chapters). Pakistan has not bound commodities like tobacco and cotton; interestingly these exceptional cases are the export commodities of the country. Pakistan like many other developing countries bound its tariff on the higher side. This decision was to safeguard the perceived dislocation in the short run from anticipated increased imports owing to the dismantling of nontariff restrictions resulting from the URAoA. Details in table 4.6 indicate that Pakistan has not made a commitment to reduce protection in agriculture.

Besides tariffs, Pakistan used to apply a number of nontrade barriers (NTBs) to limit or control imports. Sometimes these NTBs were used in conjunction with tariffs. In addition, the Trading Corporation of Pakistan (a public sector agency) imports specific commodities.

The aggregate of quantitative restrictions or NTBs on various commodity groupings can be seen in table 4.7. The number of commodities included in each restriction—negative list, procedural requirement, and health and safety—has remained the same from 1996 to 2000, except for a few variations. In the grouping of tobacco substitutes, the four commodities in the negative list in 1996 were reduced to two in 1997. The one commodity of "wood and articles of wood" included in the health and safety restriction in 1996 was removed. The number of items (three) of "works of art, collectors' pieces, and antiques" included in the negative list restriction were reduced to two after 1998.

The trend of declining tariff rates over time can be seen clearly in table 4.8. As shown in the table, the maximum tariff rate has gone down in most cases from around about 65 percent in 1996–97 to 35 percent in 1999–2000 although the maximum tariff range for beverages, spirits, and vinegar was from 45 to 250 percent (table. 4.6). At present the tariff rate varies from 0 percent to 35 percent, which is much below the bound tariff ceilings. Table 4.9 provides the distribution of commodities by different tariff slabs of tariff bands, showing the tariff rate for most agricultural commodities below 40 percent.

Table 4.6 Tariff Range for Agricultural Commodities, 1996–2000
(percent)

		Tariff range			
Code	Commodity	1996–97	1997–98	1998–99	1999–2000
01	Live animals	65–20	45–18	35–10	35–10
02	Meat and edible meat offal	65–15	45–15	35–10	35–10
03	Fish and crustaceans, mollusks, etc.	65–41	45–33	35–23	35–23
04	Dairy produce, birds' eggs, etc., n.e.s.	65–28	45–30	35–27	35–27
05	Products of animal origin, n.e.s.	65–35	45–35	35–25	35–25
06	Live trees and other plants, bulbs, roots, etc.	35–15	35–15	25–10	25–10
07	Edible vegetables and certain roots and tubers	35–10	35–0	28–0	28–0
08	Edible fruit and nuts, peel of citrus fruit, etc.	65–53	45–45	35–30	35–29
09	Coffee, tea, mate, and spices	65–21	45–21	35–14	35–14
10	Cereals	65–0	25–0	15–0	15–0
11	Products of the milling industry, malt, etc.	25–10	25–10	25–10	25–10
12	Oilseed and oleaginous fruits, etc.	55–14	45–10	30–0	30–0
13	Lac, gums, resins, and other vegetable sap, etc.	48–47	45–43	35–33	35–35
14	Vegetable planting materials, etc., n.e.s.	65–62	45–45	35–25	35–25
15	Animal or vegetable fats and oils, etc.	65–25	45–25	35–13	35–13
16	Preparations of meat, fish, etc.	65–35	45–45	35–35	35–35
17	Sugars and sugar confectionery	65–15	45–15	35–15	35–15
18	Cocoa and cocoa preparations	55–25	44–25	30–15	30–15
19	Preparations of cereals, flour, starch, etc.	65–42	45–36	35–25	35–25
20	Preparations of vegetables, fruit, nuts, etc.	65–45	45–45	35–25	35–25
21	Miscellaneous edible preparations	65–45	45–42	35–27	35–27
22	Beverages, spirits, and vinegar	250–45	250–45	250–37	50–35
23	Residues and waste from the food industries	45–15	45–10	35–10	35–10
24	Tobacco and manufactured tobacco substitutes	65–10	45–10	35–10	35–10
25	Salt; sulphur, earths, and stone; lime and cement	45–10	40–10	35–10	35–10
26	Ores, slag, and ash	10–10	10–10	10–10	10–10
27	Mineral fuels, mineral oils, mineral waxes	45–14	27–14	19–11	19–10

(Table continues on the following page.)

Table 4.6 Tariff Range for Agricultural Commodities, 1996–2000
(percent) *(continued)*

Code	Commodity	Tariff range 1996–97	1997–98	1998–99	1999–2000
28	Inorganic chemicals, etc.	42–15	27–10	23–10	23–10
29	Organic chemicals	40–10	16–10	13–10	13–10
30	Pharmaceutical products	55–0	42–0	32–0	32–0
31	Fertilizers	28–0	25–0	28–0	28–0
32	Tanning or dyeing extracts	45–25	45–25	35–25	35–24
33	Essential oils and resinoids, perfumery, etc.	62–42	45–38	35–25	35–25
34	Soap, organic surface-active agents, etc.	65–30	45–31	35–25	35–25
35	Albuminoidal substances, glues, enzymes	65–35	45–35	35–25	35–25
36	Explosives, pyrotechnic products	65–32	45–32	35–22	35–22
37	Photographic or cinematographic goods	52–15	45–15	25–15	25–9
38	Miscellaneous chemical products	45–25	45–24	35–21	35–18
39	Plastics and articles thereof	48–45	35–30	28–20	28–20
40	Rubber and articles thereof	50–10	45–10	35–10	35–10
41	Raw hides and skins (not furskins) and leather	25–10	23–10	9–0	16–0
42	Articles of leather, etc.	56–15	45–15	35–15	35–15
43	Furskins and artificial fur, manufactures thereof	55–10	45–10	35–10	35–10
44	Wood and articles of wood, wood charcoal	55–10	45–10	35–10	35–10
45	Cork and articles of cork	65–10	45–10	35–10	35–10
46	Manufactures of straw, basketware	65–51	45–43	35–33	35–33
47	Pulp of wood or other fibrous cellulosic material	25–10	10–10	10–10	10–10
48	Paper and paperboard, articles of paper	50–45	35–10	35–10	35–10
49	Printed books, newspapers, pictures, etc.	55–0	45–0	35–0	35–0
50	Silk	61–15	45–10	35–10	35–10
51	Wool, fine or coarse animal hair	55–10	45–10	35–0	35–0
52	Cotton	65–10	45–10	35–0	35–0

n.e.s. Not elsewhere specified.

Sources: Pakistan Ministry of Finance (various years); *Pakistan Gazettes* (various years); Pakistan Ministry of Commerce (various years); *Trade Policy.*

Table 4.7 Quantitative Restrictions on Various Commodities, 1996–99

Section	Classification	1996			1997			1998			1999		
		NL	PR	HS	NL	PR	HS	NL	PR	HS	NL	PR	HS
I	Live animals, animal products	13	10	1	13	10	1	13	10	1	13	10	1
II	Vegetable products	3	0	1	3	0	1	3	0	1	3	0	1
III	Animal or vegetable fats and oils and products; prepared edible fats; animal or vegetable waxes	2	0	1	2	0	1	2	0	1	2	0	1
IV	Prepared foodstuffs; beverages, spirits, and vinegar; tobacco and manufactured tobacco substitutes	4	0	1	2	0	1	2	0	1	2	0	1
V	Mineral products	0	2	1	0	2	1	0	2	1	0	2	1
VI	Products of chemical or allied industries	4	3	23	4	3	23	4	3	22	4	3	22
VII	Plastics and articles thereof; rubber and articles thereof	1	1	1	1	1	1	1	1	1	1	1	1
VIII	Raw hides and skins, furskins and articles thereof; saddlery and harness; travel goods, handbags, and similar containers; articles of animal guts (other than worm gut)	3	0	0	3	0	0	3	0	0	3	0	0
IX	Wood and articles of wood; wood charcoal; cork and articles of cork; manufactures of straw, esparto, or plastic materials; basketware and wickerwork	0	0	1	0	0	0	0	0	0	0	0	0
X	Pulp of wood or of other fibrous cellulosic material; waste and scrap of paper or paperboard; paper and paperboard and articles thereof	0	2	1	0	2	1	0	2	1	0	2	1
XI	Textile and textile articles	68	0	0	68	0	0	68	0	0	68	0	1

(Table continues on the following page.)

Table 4.7 Quantitative Restrictions on Various Commodities, 1996–99 (continued)

Section	Classification	1996			1997			1998			1999		
		NL	PR	HS	NL	PR	HS	NL	PR	HS	NL	PR	HS
XIII	Articles of stone, plaster, cement, asbestos, mica, or similar materials; ceramic products; glass and glassware	1	0	0	1	0	0	1	0	0	1	0	0
XIV	Natural or cultured pearls, precious or semi-precious stones, precious metals, metals clad with precious metal and articles thereof, imitation jewelry; coin	0	2	0	0	2	0	0	2	0	0	2	0
XV	Base metals and articles of base metal	0	0	1	0	0	1	0	0	1	0	0	1
XVI	Machinery and mechanical appliances; electrical equipment; parts thereof; sound recorders, television image and sound recorders, parts and accessories of such articles	2	0	2	2	0	2	2	0	3	2	0	3
XVII	Vehicles, aircraft, vessels, and associated transport equipment	2	10	1	2	10	1	2	10	1	2	10	1
XVIII	Optical, photographic, cinematographic, measuring, checking, precision, medical, or surgical instruments; clocks and watches; musical instruments; parts and accessories thereof	1	0	0	1	0	0	1	0	0	1	0	0
XIX	Arms and ammunition; parts and accessories thereof	6	0	4	6	0	4	6	0	4	6	0	4
XX	Miscellaneous manufactured articles	3	0	0	3	0	0	3	0	0	3	0	0
XXI	Works of art, collectors' pieces, and antiques	3	0	0	3	0	0	3	0	0	2	0	0

Note: HS = health and safety; NL = negative list; PR = procedural requirement.

Table 4.8 Average Tariff Rates for Various Commodities, 1996–2000 (percent)

		Average			
Code	Commodity	1996–97	1997–98	1998–99	1999–2000
01	Live animals	34.56	25.48	16.87	16.39
02	Meat and edible meat offal	50.00	36.00	27.50	27.50
03	Fish and crustaceans, mollusks, etc.	56.93	38.68	28.81	28.81
04	Dairy produce, birds' eggs, etc., n.e.s.	44.29	38.79	31.79	31.67
05	Products of animal origin, n.e.s.	61.54	43.94	33.74	33.74
06	Live trees and other plants, bulbs, roots, etc.	27.68	27.68	19.38	19.64
07	Edible vegetables and certain roots and tubers	26.25	21.61	13.99	13.99
08	Edible fruit and nuts, peel of citrus fruit, etc.	56.31	45.00	34.64	34.59
09	Coffee, tea, mate, and spices	41.50	37.75	24.39	24.49
10	Cereals	26.56	20.94	12.50	12.50
11	Products of the milling industry, malt, etc.	21.67	21.67	21.67	21.67
12	Oilseed and oleaginous fruits, etc.	27.34	22.68	13.25	13.25
13	Lac, gums, resins, and other vegetable sap, etc.	47.58	44.17	34.17	35.00
14	Vegetable planting materials, etc., n.e.s.	63.89	45.00	31.67	31.67
15	Animal or vegetable fats and oils, etc.	53.80	41.40	30.79	30.85
16	Preparations of meat, fish, etc.	53.00	45.00	35.00	35.00
17	Sugars and sugar confectionery	37.50	32.50	25.00	30.00
18	Cocoa and cocoa preparations	38.33	33.10	19.92	19.92
19	Preparations of cereals, flour, starch, etc.	59.43	43.29	31.86	31.86

(Table continues on the following page.)

Table 4.8 Average Tariff Rates for Various Commodities, 1996–2000 (percent) (continued)

Code	Commodity	Average			
		1996–97	1997–98	1998–99	1999–2000
20	Preparations of vegetables, fruit, nuts, etc.	61.72	45.00	28.33	26.70
21	Miscellaneous edible preparations	59.85	44.55	32.65	32.65
22	Beverages, spirits, and vinegar	98.06	92.50	90.28	88.89
23	Residues and waste from the food industries	25.00	22.86	23.57	23.57
24	Tobacco and manufactured tobacco substitutes	40.00	30.71	25.00	25.00
25	Salt; sulfur, earths, and stone; lime and cement	21.43	17.86	14.29	14.29
26	Ores, slag, and ash	10.00	10.00	10.00	10.00
27	Mineral fuels, mineral oils, mineral waxes	30.36	22.07	14.50	13.96
28	Inorganic chemicals, etc.	24.88	15.24	12.62	12.62
29	Organic chemicals	29.54	13.90	10.74	10.38
30	Pharmaceutical products	17.76	15.24	13.48	13.48
31	Fertilizers	7.62	7.14	7.62	7.62
32	Tanning or dyeing extracts	32.62	30.88	28.19	28.00
33	Essential oils and resinoids, perfumery, etc.	52.23	43.35	28.89	28.89
34	Soap, organic surface-active agents, etc.	51.27	40.95	30.22	30.36
35	Albuminoidal substances, glues, enzymes	49.29	40.71	30.00	30.00

36	Explosives, pyrotechnic products	60.24	43.10	33.10	33.10
37	Photographic or cinematographic goods	31.95	30.42	21.93	14.35
38	Miscellaneous chemical products	40.71	37.95	30.60	30.19
39	Plastics and articles thereof	45.36	32.94	23.85	23.85
40	Rubber and articles thereof	31.93	18.86	17.86	17.86
41	Raw hides and skins (not furskins) and leather	13.82	13.46	1.25	7.32
42	Articles of leather, etc.	40.83	36.90	29.29	27.86
43	Furskins and artificial fur, manufactures thereof	23.10	20.83	17.98	17.98
44	Wood and articles of wood, wood charcoal	26.96	23.93	19.46	19.46
45	Cork and articles of cork	38.00	31.14	24.00	24.00
46	Manufactures of straw, basketware	58.00	44.00	34.00	34.00
47	Pulp of wood or other fibrous cellulosic material	12.14	10.00	10.00	10.00
48	Paper and paperboard, articles of paper	46.43	25.18	25.18	25.55
49	Printed books, newspapers, pictures, etc.	25.79	22.07	18.14	18.14
50	Silk	44.39	36.94	28.57	28.57
51	Wool, fine or coarse animal hair	33.15	30.00	23.38	23.38
52	Cotton	51.80	40.63	25.83	25.83

n.e.s. Not elsewhere specified.
Sources: Pakistan Ministry of Finance (various years); *Pakistan Gazettes* (various years); Pakistan Ministry of Commerce (various years); *Trade Policy*.

Table 4.9 Number of Agricultural Commodities in Various Tariff Slabs, 1996–99 (percent)

Tariff rate	1996	1997	1998	1999
71–250	4	4	4	4
61–70	91	0	2	0
51–60	98	2	0	2
41–50	99	217	0	0
31–40	134	90	206	205
21–30	80	102	135	136
11–20	46	106	100	98
0–10	53	84	158	159
Total	605	605	605	604

Sources: Pakistan Ministry of Finance (various years); *Pakistan Gazettes* (various years); Pakistan Ministry of Commerce (various years); *Trade Policy.*

Pakistan has made appreciable progress in reducing NTBs. The quantitative quotas have been almost eliminated. Licensing fees had already been abolished in 1993–94. Negative and restrictive lists of imports have also undergone reductions. Only a few agricultural items are subject to the restrictions, but those have been retained on account of health, environment, and security grounds.

Export restrictions included an outright ban on export quotas, specific conditions (which include taking permission from different ministries or departments), and exports through rice and cotton export corporations. Most of these restrictions have been lifted. Temporary restrictions like banning of exports and levy of export duties are resorted to for the imports of some essential consumer items, but that is mainly to ensure adequate domestic availability and to check abnormal increases in their prices under food security considerations. Nevertheless, exports are not, as a matter of general policy, taxed or restricted by Pakistan. The overall picture of implementing commitments and market access obligations under the URAoA is quite satisfactory. The country has greatly enhanced its market access opportunities to other member countries for their exports.

Nominal Rate of Protection

This rate is measured by the ratio of minimum support price and import/export parity price. This has been calculated for four major crops (counting two rice varieties as one) in table 4.10. The rate varies from crop to crop and fluctuates over the years in the case of an individual crop. With

Table 4.10 Nominal Protection Coefficients by Crops, 1990–99

Number		Unit	1990–91	1991–92	1992–93	1993–94	1994–95	1997–98	1993–94 to 1997–98	1998–99
	Wheat									
1	Support price	Rs/ton	2,800	3,100	3,250	4,000	4,000	6,000	4,865	6,000
2	IPP by APC	Rs/ton	4,818	3,547	5,019	4,385	4,697	9,574	9,625	70,455
3	NPC (1/2)		0.58	0.87	0.65	0.91	0.85	0.63	0.51	0.85
	Rice basmati									
1	Support price	Rs/ton	7,075	7,700	8,500	9,000	9,720	7,750[a]	5,912[a]	8,250[a]
2	EPP by APC	Rs/ton	11,988	8,796	10,833	8,171	9,743	8,968	9,100	10,403[b]
3	NPC (1/2)		0.59	0.88	0.78	1.1	1	0.86	0.65	0.79
	Rice coarse									
1	Support price	Rs/ton	3,750	4,000	4,250	4,528	4,875	3,825[a]	2,932[a]	4,375[a]
2	EPP by APC	Rs/ton	3,983	3,503	4,498	3,709	2,960	3,867	3,725	4,640[b]
3	NPC (1/2)		0.94	1.14	0.94	1.22	1.65	0.99	0.79	0.94
	Seed cotton									
1	Support price	Rs/ton	6,125	7,000	7,500	7,875	10,000	12,500	10,575	14,375
2	EPP by APC	Rs/ton	10,362	10,996	9,935	9,486	12,408	21,471	22,502	20,182[b]
3	NPC (1/2)		0.59	0.64	0.75	0.83	0.81	0.58	0.47	0.71
	Sugarcane								1992–93 to 1996–97	
1	Support price	Rs/ton	385	421	440	462	515	875	508	875
2	IPP by APC	Rs/ton	577	581	481	458	641	713	1,195	706[b]
3	NPC (1/2)		0.67	0.72	0.91	1.01	0.8	1.23	0.43	1.24

a. Paddy price.
b. Computed by author.
Note: APC = Agricultural Prices Commission; EPP = export parity price; IPP = import parity price; NPC = nominal protection coefficient; Rs = rupees.
Sources: Pakistan Ministry of Finance (various years); Blarel and others (1999).

the exception of one or two crops the nominal protection rate has been less than one. This implies that the minimum support policies have been persistently pegged at below the level of export/import parity prices and that the policy has created a distortion in the marketplace; that is, agriculture is negatively protected in Pakistan. On the input side, the farmer pays more than the international prices, as fertilizers and tractor industries are protected under tariffs.

The aggregate measurement of support (AMS) of Pakistan has essentially two components: market price support and input subsidies (the URAoA covers the latter under "other nonexempt measures"). Every year the Pakistan government fixes minimum support prices for important crops—10 crops in 1980–87 increased to 11 in 1990–91. Wheat has a minimum price support because the government directly procures wheat from farmers. The government does not buy other crops.

Subsidies on inputs (that is, agricultural credit, electricity, and fertilizer) have been covered by nonproduct-specific AMS. The agricultural credit subsidy was discontinued in 1995–96, and the fertilizer subsidy was discontinued the following year. Only the electricity subsidy was retained.

Official estimates of the AMS submitted by Pakistan during the negotiations for the base years of 1986–87, 1987–88, and 1988–89 and the updated estimates of AMS for the years 1990–91 to 1993–94 are shown in table 4.11. The average amount of the product-specific AMS for 11 crops was –11,524.2 million rupees during 1986–87 to 1988–89. This turns out to be –7.57 percent of the total value of agricultural production. The nonproduct-specific support for the same period was 3,582 million rupees, which is –2.35 percent of the total value of agricultural production. The AMS, amounting to –7,942.23 million rupees, is –5.22 percent of the total value of agricultural production. For the period 1990–91 to 1993–94, the average amount of product specific support, nonproduct–specific support, and AMS is –19,387, +1,767 and –17,620 million rupees, respectively. As a percentage of the total value of agricultural production, the AMS are –6.90 percent, –0.63 percent, and –6.27 percent, respectively. Because the AMS figures are negative, Pakistan is not required to reduce its support level as required by the URAoA.

Since 1995–96 Pakistan has calculated AMS in U.S. dollars rather than the Pakistan rupee. The rupee version of AMS was reported to be giving a distorted picture of domestic support because of the depreciation of the rupee and continued inflation. The product-specific AMS was calculated at –$202.6 million for 1995–96 and –$72.41 million for 1996–97. The nonproduct–specific AMS has remained positive and in fact has increased over time. The total AMS, however, has been negative during these two years. The position did not change even in 1997–98. Trends in AMS up to 1997–98 can be seen in table 4.11.

Table 4.11 Product-Specific and Nonproduct-Specific Aggregate Measurement of Support, 1986–98
(Rs millions, US$ millions,[a] and as percentage of value-added of agricultural crops livestock products)

Support type	1986–87	1987–88	1988–89	1990–91	1991–92	1992–93	1993–94	Average 1986–87 to 1988–89	Average 1990–91 to 1993–94	1995–96	1996–97	1997–98
Product-specific AMS												
Wheat	−5,699.62	−4,038.6	−3,857.38	−1,801	−3,481	−3,126	803	−4,531.87	−1,901	−172	−72.41	−143.42
Seed cotton	4,020.14	−7,442.38	−6,681.85	−21,150	−23,293	−9,776	−1,297	−3,368.03	−13,879	0	0	0
Rice basmati	−1,518.29	−1,432.39	−3,388.32	−507	−323	−1,346	−787	−2,113	−741	−20.1	0	0
Rice coarse	−489.36	−855.63	−1,280.75	−114	−307	−493	−450	−875.24	−341	−10.4	0	0
Sugarcane	598.48	782.56	−73.21	−1,017	−918	−2,482	—	435.94	−1,104	0	0	0
Onion	0	−0.04	−0.08	−1,525	−469	−483	−2,030	−0.04	−1,125	−0.1	0	0
Potato	−5.66	0	−2.3	−6.91	−131	−216	−446	−2.66	−371	0	0	0
Gram	−4.37	−1,566.9	−1,550.4	0.5	27	−2	—	−1,040.53	6.4	0	0	0
Soybean	−28.64	−11.51	—	2	3	—	—	−20.08	1.25	0	0	0
Sunflower	29.4	38.58	−89.1	57	210	—	—	−7.04	67	0	0	0
Safflower	—	—	—	2	—	—	—	−1.68	0.5	0	0	0
Total: all crops	−12,335.2	−14,580.5	−16,923.4	−26,743.5	−28,682	−17,924	−4,200	−11,524.2	−19,387	−202.6	−72.41	−143.42
Total specific support	(−9.50)	(−9.70)	(−9.57)	(−11.92)	(−10.52)	(−6.28)	(−1.23)	(−7.57)	(−6.90)	(−2.44)	(−0.93)	(−1.72)

(Table continues on the following page.)

Table 4.11 Product-Specific and Nonproduct-Specific Aggregate Measurement of Support, 1986–98 *(continued)*
(Rs millions, US$ millions,[a] and as percentage of value-added of agricultural crops livestock products)

Support type	1986–87	1987–88	1988–89	Average 1986–87 to 1988–89	1990–91	1991–92	1992–93	1993–94	Average 1990–91 to 1993–94	1995–96	1996–97	1997–98
Nonproduct-specific AMS												
Agriculture credit subsidy	735	607	80	697	688	805	863	550	726	0	—	0
Electric subsidy	784	1,143	1,210	1,046	732	829	746	92	600	10.4	15.5	22.5
Fertilizer subsidy	1,284	1,819	2,415	1,839	625	564	351	223	441	0.4	—	0
Total nonproduct-specific support	2,803	3,569	3,705	3,582	2,045	2,198	1,960	865	1,767	10.8	15.5	22.5
	(–2.16)	(–2.37)	(–2.1)	(–2.35)	(–0.91)	(–0.81)	(–0.69)	(–0.25)	(–0.63)	(–0.13)	(–0.2)	(–0.26)
AMS	–9,532.16	–11,012.5	–13,218.4	–7,942.23	–24,698.5	–26,484	–15,964	–3,335	–17,620	–191.8	–56.88	–120.92
	(–7.34)	(–7.33)	(–7.48)	(–5.22)	(–11.02)	(–9.71)	(–5.59)	(–0.98)	(–6.27)	(–2.31)	(–0.73)	(–1.45)

a. Since 1995–96 Pakistan calculated its AMS in U.S. dollars.

Note: AMS = aggregate measurement of support. Figures in parentheses represent AMS as percentage of value-added of the agriculture sector minus fishing and forestry.

Sources: Data for the years 1986–87 to 1988–89 have been obtained from WTO (1995a); data for the remaining years have been obtained from the Pakistan Ministry of Food and Agriculture; Blarel and others (1999).

REDUCTIONS IN EXPORT SUBSIDIES. The Pakistan government had occasionally resorted to freight subsidies on the exports of fruits and vegetables, but those have been discontinued. Previously, when all exporting of cotton and rice was through government-sponsored monopolies there was a subsidy, but since the involvement of the private sector the subsidies have basically stopped. To promote exports there is a rebate on duties on some exports and imports of raw material and farm equipment and machinery, but agriculture has not benefited from these rebates. There is also an export refinance plan under which credit is made available at concessional interest rates to exports, basically high value-added exports and some agricultural products such as fish and packed rice. In 1998–99, eggs for hatching and day old chicks were included in the export refinancing plan. Higher and specific credit limits are allowed for cotton and sugar, which ultimately enter into the export market.

EXPORT PROHIBITIONS AND RESTRICTIONS. Article 12 of the URAoA sets out disciplines on export prohibitions and restrictions. The member countries are required to give due consideration to the effects of such measures on importing countries' food security when they institute any new export prohibition or restriction on foodstuffs. This would be applicable to a country that is a net food exporter of the specific foodstuff concerned.

Pakistan has a long history of using quantitative export restrictions on a number of major agricultural products. Until 1995 the major exports that were prohibited included certain live animals, beef and mutton, grains and pulses, wheat flour, edible oils, hides and skins, nonferrous metals, sugar, and re-exports of imports except in cases where the re-export value exceeded the customs, insurance, and freight (c.i.f.) import value by at least 10 percent. Pakistan has also used procedural requirements for exports of rice and has fixed minimum export prices in the case of some commodities (for example, breeding animals). In an effort to support domestic cotton users, Pakistan has also imposed export taxes and limited exports.

In 1996–97 a 10 percent value-added tax on exports was reduced to 2.5 percent and the additional condition of authorization, issued by the Ministry of Commerce, was rescinded. In 1997–98 the export of packed meat was allowed against the import of live animals with the condition that 60 percent of the gross weight of the live animals be exported as packed meat/beef. Duty free import of raw sugar was also allowed for re-export after refining.

In 1998–99 Pakistan decided to lift the ban on exports of 15 items: live animals, beef and mutton, grains, pulses, blood meals and meat meals, bran and fodder, hides and skins, wet blue leather, ferrous and nonferrous metals, paper waste, and oilseeds. However, exports will be regulated by an imposition of export duties, if required, and will also be subject to registration of export contracts with the Export Promotion Bureau. The quota restrictions on exports of maize, gram and gram split, soda ash, breeding camels, endemic birds, cement, and clinker have also been removed.

To curb smuggling Pakistan decided in 1998–99 to allow exports of kitchen items via land routes to Afghanistan and through Afghanistan to the Central Asian Republics against advance payment of letters of credit in foreign currency without the duty drawback facility. However, exports to the Central Asian Republics via Iran will continue to be allowed with duty drawback. The validity of a special regulatory order concerning export/import of raw cotton had been extended to June 30, 1999, with the amount restricted to 200,000 bales. Restrictions on exports of fruits and vegetables to border countries were removed.

With a view to ensuring adequate availability in the local market and to check an abnormal rise in their prices, regulatory duties were occasionally imposed on some essential kitchen items, such as chilies and onions to protect the interests of the consumers. In 1998–99 a 20 percent export duty was imposed on hides, skins, and wet blue leather to ensure their availability to the local industry for producing more exportable surplus.

A cess (that is, an assessment) mostly at a half percent ad valorem was levied on primary agricultural commodities such as fish, fruits, and hides. This is basically to finance agricultural research. Some of the subsidies and export restricting measures appear export distortionary and conflict with the interests of food importing countries. But in practice these are either of a temporary nature or not important enough to cause any serious harm to other member countries.

SANITARY AND PHYTOSANITARY MEASURES. There is a separate Sanitary and Phytosanitary (SPS) Agreement measure that discusses standards for human, animal, or plant life or health. This agreement is integrated into the URAoA under Article 14 and is to ensure inter alia that the consumers in the importing country are supplied with food safe to eat. However, the importing country is advised against making any restrictions, whether they be health or safety related, that will knowingly favor domestic producers at the expense of the exporting producer.

Member countries are encouraged to use standards based on science, and they are required to observe the standards only to the extent necessary to protect human and plant life or health. It does allow some freedom to member countries to apply higher standards based on an appropriate assessment of risk as long as their approach is consistent and not arbitrary and is not designed to discriminate against imports. This freedom is necessary because of varying geographical and sanitary conditions among the member countries. Nevertheless, the SPS Agreement emphasizes that the member countries should review their domestic regulations and standards and methods of inspecting products and encourages the member countries to use international standards, guidelines, and recommendations where these exist. It also emphasizes harmonization and transparency with regard to SPS regulations.

Pakistan has a number of regulations and standards to prevent food adulteration and to ensure hygienic and quality standards. These are used both at the domestic production level and import level. The WTO Secretariat's report (1995) observed that Pakistan has made some efforts to base its standards on international norms and that national standards on a small number of items are inferior to international norms owing to a lack of required technology. However, Pakistan's standards do not seem to constitute a major impediment to trade. In some cases controls on imports have been made more lenient. For example, in its trade policy for 1995-96 the prescribed shelf life of imported edible oil products was reduced from 75 percent to 50 percent at the time of import. The exporting countries have often taken undue advantage of the poor local and physical infrastructure of Pakistan to enforce SPS standards.

Under the Agricultural Produce (Grading and Marketing) Act of 1937 (Pakistan) different rules have been formulated to check and control the quality of agricultural commodities for export of wool animal hair, lamb skins of grades I-V, casings, eggs, dry fish and shell fish, fish meal, bones (either crushed or in powdered form), citrus fruits (lime and lemon), chilies, turmeric, ginger, garlic and onion, potato, radish, brinjal, peas, asparagus, Brussels sprouts, pumpkin, cauliflower, tomato, cucumber (kheera), cucumber (Kari), carrot, fresh beans, artichokes, celery, turnip, green chilies, lady finger, guava, molasses, dates, banana, mango, oilseed, and oil cake (including solvent extracted meals).

However, quality control restrictions on export of fruit and vegetables are not applicable on exports to border countries. The government announced in 1998-99 a system for inspection of all rice shipments by the Export Promotion Bureau in consultation with the Rice Exporters Association of Pakistan to ensure quality exports. A similar system is in use for the European Union for exports of basmati rice.

Pakistani consumers have directly suffered because of the inferior quality of some imports of foodstuffs. However, Pakistan's inability to enforce strict SPS standards has hurt its exports. Pakistan expected that the UR talks would give its export business a needed push, but it did not owing to the SPS standards many countries have enforced.

PAKISTAN'S EXPERIENCE WITH AGRICULTURAL TRADE. Pakistan has made substantial progress in implementing its commitments to liberalize its agricultural trade, but expected gains have not materialized.

Exports. Cotton and rice are the two major traditional exports of Pakistan, with a worldwide share of 9 percent for cotton and 1 percent for rice. Pakistan is thus labeled a net exporter by the WTO. Total exports of primary agricultural commodities fluctuated markedly from year to year in both the pre-UR and post-UR periods. The annual average of exports of cotton and rice during July 1990 to June 1995 was $902 million and rose to $1,038 million during July 1995 to June 1998. This shows some improvement in agricultural exports in the post-UR period. Insects and bad weather affected the cotton surplus, though. Export prices of cotton have also decreased. Pakistani cotton enjoyed perfect market conditions for its export outlets. No trade barrier affected it.

Pakistan produces two types of rice varieties, and both are exported. Basmati rice has its traditional markets, but it faces some competition with Indian basmati rice. The export of coarse rice faces competition from other low-priced competitive countries, but it is still exported to Asian and African countries. Even the two rice-producing countries of Sri Lanka and Indonesia import it. The special basmati variety is exported to high-income Middle East countries and the United Kingdom (which has a relatively large Pakistani population). During the post-UR period no market diversification has been noticed. While total Pakistani rice exports have increased substantially during this period, exports to industrialized countries have not owing to lack of market access. The average export prices, however, have been fluctuating from year to year, but no significant change in the price trends has been observed in the post-UR period when compared with the pre-UR period.

The export of fruits has shown an improvement in the post-UR period, particularly during the two years of 1996–98. Even though Pakistan exports some fruits to a few countries (such as the United Kingdom), many industrialized countries have SPS standards that Pakistan does not meet. Pakistan considers these standards unfair, but has not brought up the issue with the WTO. Instead, Pakistan is dealing with each country separately. In response, for example, Japan has offered a food-processing plant. Certainly the vast potential for fruit exports remains untapped.

Raw cotton, cotton waste, rice, and fruit account for roughly 94 percent of the total agricultural exports (excluding fish). Their aggregate share has not experienced any significant change for a number of years. Thus like the country concentration of exports, the degree of commodity concentration of exports is fairly high.

Quantities of primary agriculture exports and their total value are given in table 4.12. The trend of concentration of agricultural exports of the four items is given in table 4.13.

Imports. Despite being an agricultural country, Pakistan has had to import a huge amount of foodstuffs every year. Its import bill has increased in the post-UR period, and in 1997–98 it was $2 billion (19.8 percent of total imports and 23.2 percent of total export earnings). Because of its persistent dependence on the import of essential items Pakistan has been classified by the WTO as a net food importing developing country. Quantities of major agricultural imports and their total value for 1990–99 are given in table 4.14.

Wheat and edible oil are the two largest imported products in Pakistan, at times as high as 80 percent of all imports. Edible oil imports have remained constant, but wheat fluctuates because of domestic production, from 2 million tons to 4 million tons. Wheat is mainly imported from North America, palm oil from Malaysia, and soybean oil from North America and Europe.

Tea is the next largest import, and is imported from Asian and African countries. Tea is not domestically produced. Sugar, pulses, and milk are also imported, and, again, their import varies depending on domestic production. All in all, wheat, edible oil, tea, sugar, pulses, and milk account for about 90 percent of total agricultural imports (table 4.14) and the value of these key imports (table 4.15).

The countries exporting to Pakistan have not been using export barriers because they want to promote their exports. Pakistan, though, depending on the commodity, has been using import duties as a means of regulating domestic production. Wheat, sugar, and pulses have basically no import duties. But that has changed from year to year to ensure domestic production, particularly in sugar and pulses, and to prevent dumping. Edible oils, though, have been subject to relatively high duties to increase domestic production by ensuring a parity price with domestic oils.

Terms of Trade and Trade Balance in the Context of Agriculture. Because of the imbalance of agricultural trade, Pakistan was in a deficit in 1990–99, with agricultural imports more than double exports. The indices of terms of trade are given in table 4.16. Unit prices of principal agricultural export and import commodities are given in tables 4.17 and 4.18. The value of agricultural exports and the value of agricultural imports in terms of total exports and imports during 1995–99 are provided in tables 4.19 and 4.20.

Table 4.12 Quantities of Major Primary Agricultural Exports and Their Total Value, 1990–99 (thousand tons)

Export	1990–91	1991–92	1992–93	1993–94	1994–95	1995–96	1996–97	1997–98	1998–99
Raw cotton	282.6	456.3	264.9	76.6	33.6	313.5	25.2	94.9	1.8
Cotton waste	67.7	81.1	77.5	100.2	84.3	72.6	74.4	79.2	
Raw wool	5.6	7.4	11.8	8.4	8.3	9.1	10.8	5.2	1.7
Fish	47.6	61.2	86.5	67.2	61.3	64.5	78.1	75.6	
Rice	1,204.6	1,511.8	1,032.1	984.3	1,852.3	1,600.5	1,767.2	2,091.2	1,730.7
Fruit	111.8	124.6	120.8	127.5	138.5	135.1	218.8	202.2	177.3
Onion	5.5	12.2	1.8	28.8	5.6	11.9	18.7	65.0	
Spices including chilies	10.7	23.7	9.4	8.7	6.2	3.9	5.4	7.2	
Seed poppy	4.4	1.4	3.6	9.0	6.7	3.4	1.9	7.2	
Fish meal	0.7	2.9	3.0	1.7	1.3	1.2	1.4	1.5	
Live animals and products bones	27.6	31.5	29.9	20.8	29.0	30.7	31.6	22.8	
Total value (millions) including the above items and honey, vegetables, potato, castor oilseed, cumin, and coriander seed	Rs22,800.0 US$1,008.8	Rs29,607.6 US$1,189.1	Rs23,263.0 US$894.7	Rs18,501.1 US$612.6	Rs24,855.7 US$804.4	Rs43,776.0 US$1,291.3	Rs31,457.2 US$804.5	Rs43,973.6 US$1,017.9	
Total value minus fish	Rs20224.1 US$894.9	Rs26776.5 US$1,075.4	Rs18531.2 US$712.8	Rs13869.7 US$459.2	Rs20110.1 US$650.8	Rs39096.5 US$1,153.3	Rs25655.4 US$656.1	Rs33631.8 US$848.0	

Sources: Pakistan Ministry of Food and Agriculture (various years); Pakistan Ministry of Finance (1999).

Table 4.13 Value of Major Primary Agricultural Exports, 1990–99

Export	1990–91	1991–92	1992–93	1993–94	1994–95	1995–96	1996–97	1997–98	1998–99
Raw cotton	9,560.4	12,945.8	7,014.8	2,391.6	1,957.6	17,458.8	1,285.9	5,554.5	116.0
Cotton waste	1,108.2	1,328.3	1,150.6	1,680.6	1,728.2	1,696.2	1,491.0	1,673.0	
Rice	7,847.6	10,339.6	8,213.9	7,318.9	14,025.6	17,141.0	18,453.0	24,562.5	26,231.0
Fruit	935.2	965.5	1,178.7	1,324.3	1,256.1	1,486.8	2,775.7	2,784.3	2,735.0
Subtotal (Rs millions)	19,451.4	25,579.2	17,558.0	12,715.4	18,967.5	37,782.8	24,005.6	34,574.3	
Subtotal (US$ millions)	860.7	1,027.3	675.3	421	613.8	1,114.5	613.9	800.3	

Note: Rs = rupees.
Sources: Pakistan Ministry of Food and Agriculture (various years); Pakistan Ministry of Finance (1999).

Table 4.14 Quantities of Major Primary Agricultural Imports and Their Total Value, 1990–99 (thousand tons)

Import	1990–91	1991–92	1992–93	1993–94	1994–95	1995–96	1996–97	1997–98	1998–99
Wheat	972.0	2,018.0	2,868.0	1,902.0	2,617.0	1,968.0	2,500.0	4,088.0	3,237.5
Edible oil	959.6	1,045.9	1,330.9	1,131.4	1,394.5	1,142.8	1,056.8	1,178.6	1,301.0
Milk and milk products	22.6	26.2	31.4	12.6	10.6	14.9	9.2	12.4	19.1
Tea	104.0	106.6	119.4	112.4	113.7	114.8	85.4	98.6	119.8
Fruit	37.6	36.5	42.0	69.3	69.4	104.0	102.4	83.5	
Vegetables	n.a.	0.6	4.3	7.4	1.0	10.9	2.8	5.5	
Wool	8.2	9.3	5.3	3.9	3.9	3.8	2.6	2.6	
Jute	95.1	117.4	92.2	70.2	87.1	59.8	80.0	88.0	
Rubber (N.S.)	5.6	5.5	7.2	4.3	3.9	13.8	13.1	13.1	
Natural rubber	15.9	19.0	19.4	24.4	21.8	15.8	17.6	21.4	
Betel leaves and nuts	22.8	27.6	29.0	27.6	28.8	32.6	35.4	40.7	
Sugar, refined	434.6	116.6	75.0	47.8	4.9	3.3	680.9	110.4	10.2
Pulses	77.9	116.7	238.3	153.7	190.9	261.8	79.9	118.3	191.5

Ginger	n.a.	18.9	18.0	20.4	18.3	42.9	23.8	28.0
Copra	13.0	12.7	12.0	9.4	11.9	8.6	8.3	8.8
Tallow animals	84.2	81.4	51.0	70.4	47.3	54.2	36.0	62.5
Spices (other)	9.1	9.3	9.3	6.6	8.7	5.2	10.7	8.4
Seed cloves	8.6	4.7	5.1	8.9	3.1	6.4	7.1	6.0
Seed vegetable	2.6	2.7	4.2	4.2	2.8	0.7	1.1	0.3
Total value (millions) including above items and honey, tobacco, and seeds (flower, seed grass, and seed for growing)	Rs24,520.7	Rs30,190.4	RS39,974.5	Rs34,971.8	Rs57,580.1	Rs61,042.4	Rs71,642.0	Rs86,259.6
Total value (millions)	US$1,089.8	US$1,212.5	US$1,537.5	US$1,158.0	US$1,863.4	US$1,811.3	US$1,832.3	US$2,001.4

Note: Rs = rupees; n.a. = not available.

Sources: Pakistan Ministry of Food and Agriculture (various years); Pakistan Ministry of Finance (1999).

Table 4.15 Value of Major Primary Agricultural Imports, 1990–99 (Rs millions and US$ millions)

Import	1990–91	1991–92	1992–93	1993–94	1994–95	1995–96	1996–97	1997–98	1998–99
Wheat	3,118.1	8,485.7	12,080.0	7,235.2	12,755.2	15,189.0	18,925.0	30,304.3	19,004.0
Edible oils	9,020.3	10,025.2	15,185.7	14,698.5	30,780.8	28,674.7	23,906.0	33,304.4	40,002.0
Tea	3,728.7	4,158.7	5,183.5	5,475.8	5,692.6	5,706.7	93,56.6	9,818.1	11,169.0
Sugar, refined	3,593.3	913.1	551.9	445.1	65.7	51.2	9,859.6	1,676.6	154.0
Pulses	651.8	1,269.2	1,735.5	1,319.0	1,916.3	2,965.5	1,133.2	1,753.0	3,104.0
Milk	707.5	869.6	807.3	629.1	547.7	1,054.4	674.3	966.5	1,847.0
Subtotal (millions)	Rs20,819.7	Rs25,721.5	Rs35,543.9	Rs29,802.7	Rs51,758.4	Rs53,641.5	Rs63,854.7	Rs77,822.0	
Subtotal (millions)	US$925.3	US$1,033.0	US$1,367.1	US$986.8	US$1,675.0	US$1,591.7	US$1,633.1	US$1,805.6	

Note: Rs = rupees.
Sources: Pakistan Ministry of Food and Agriculture (various years); Pakistan Ministry of Finance (1999).

Table 4.16 Unit Value Indices and Terms of Trade, 1991–99 (1990–91 = 100)

Item	1991–92	1992–93	1993–94	1994–95	1995–96	1996–97	1997–98	1998–98	June–March 1998–99
Food and live animals group									
Unit price index of exports	106.61	118.30	127.47	137.17	159.21	180.63	203.20	203.64	217.36
Unit price index of imports	111.66	115.32	127.25	152.02	181.19	191.78	217.54	211.13	222.26
Terms of trade	95.48	102.58	100.17	90.23	87.87	94.19	93.41	96.45	97.80
Beverages and tobacco group									
Unit price index of exports	122.06	150.13	138.85	155.04	128.51	141.10	143.35	131.48	111.35
Unit price index of imports	119.04	158.71	232.30	280.40	357.50	381.24	399.60	399.74	610.62
Terms of trade	102.54	94.59	59.77	55.29	35.95	37.01	35.87	32.89	18.35

Source: Pakistan Ministry of Finance (1999).

Table 4.17 Unit Value of Major Agricultural Exports, 1990–99

Fiscal year	Rice (US$/ton)	Raw cotton (US$/ton)	Cotton waste (US$/kilogram)	Fruit (US$/kilogram)
1990–91	288.3	1,500.4	0.70	0.37
1991–92	274.7	1,142.0	0.64	0.31
1992–93	306.1	1,024.1	0.56	0.38
1993–94	246.2	1,039.7	0.55	0.34
1994–95	245.0	2,008.3	0.66	0.29
1995–96	315.8	1,652.4	0.71	0.32
1996–97	267.1	1,509.4	0.52	0.32
1997–98	271.9	1,431.6	0.49	0.32
July–March				
1997–98	265.6	1,444.1	0.49	0.32
1998–99	296.4	1,168.2	0.42	0.31

Sources: Pakistan Ministry of Food and Agriculture (various years); Pakistan Ministry of Finance (1999).

Table 4.18 Unit Value of Major Agricultural Imports, 1990–99

Fiscal year	Wheat (US$/ton)	Tea (US$/kilogram)	Edible oil (US$/kilogram)	Milk (US$/kilogram)	Sugar (US$/kilogram)	Pulses (US$/kilogram)
1990–91	142.5	1.6	0.42	1.39	0.36	0.37
1991–92	168.9	1.6	0.39	1.33	0.31	0.44
1992–93	162.0	1.6	0.47	0.99	0.28	0.28
1993–94	126.0	1.6	0.43	1.65	0.31	0.28
1994–95	157.7	1.6	0.71	1.70	0.44	0.32
1995–96	229.0	1.5	0.74	2.10	0.46	0.34
1996–97	193.6	1.6	0.58	1.90	0.37	0.36
1997–98	172.0	2.3	0.66	1.80	0.35	0.34
July–March						
1998–99	115.1	1.8	0.64			

Sources: Pakistan Ministry of Food and Agriculture (various years); Pakistan Ministry of Finance (1999).

STATE TRADING ENTERPRISES. WTO members can retain import or export monopolies in the public or private sector as recognized in Article XVII of the GATT 1994 agreement. Pakistan has two agricultural export corporations, the Rice Export Corporation and the Cotton Export Corporation, and one agricultural import corporation, the Trading Corporation of Pakistan. Pakistan maintains that these corporations are operating on commercial lines. More private companies are involved in both exporting and importing.

Table 4.19 Exports of All Commodities, 1995–99
(Rs millions)

Code	Commodity	1995–96	1997–98	1998–99
00	Live animals other than division 03	64.58	12.29	10.41
01	Meat and meat preparations	9.97	1.32	3.52
02	Dairy products and bird eggs	13.23	8.95	9.92
03	Fish, crustaceans, mollusks, and preparations	4,210.62	1,922.33	1,057.58
04	Cereals and cereal preparations	14,002.22	3,010.34	3,720.30
05	Vegetable and fruit	1,762.98	604.90	964.26
06	Sugar, sugar preparations, honey	2,839.97	576.05	4,163.44
07	Coffee, tea, etc., and manufactures	345.06	108.01	103.93
08	Feeding stuff for animals	13.17	15.35	2.54
09	Miscellaneous edible products and preparations	96.22	74.01	89.13
11	Beverages	0.56	0.31	0.43
12	Tobacco and tobacco manufactures	87.33	29.23	47.18
22	Oilseeds and oleaginous fruits	10.48	83.95	212.78
23	Crude rubber (including synthetic, reclaimed)	7.91	4.19	1.07
24	Cork and wood	6.99	0.04	0.00
25	Pulp and waste paper	0.85	1.44	0.12
26	Textile fibers and their waste	19,598.60	1,676.68	562.59
27	Crude fertilizers and minerals excluding coal, etc.	117.72	51.76	79.33
28	Metalliferous ores and metal scrap	270.92	59.81	129.86
29	Crude animal and vegetable materials, n.e.s.	2,397.51	462.43	600.38
32	Coal, coke, and briquettes	25.66	0.00	0.00
33	Petroleum products and related materials	1,604.26	447.56	436.80
41	Animal oils and fats	0.00	0.00	0.30
42	Fixed vegetable fats and oils	0.00	0.79	0.00
43	Animal, vegetable fat, oil, wax, etc., n.e.s.	1.12	0.00	138.85
51	Organic chemicals	96.54	0.96	9.73
52	Inorganic chemicals	8.79	3.50	2.10
53	Dyeing, tanning, and coloring materials	19.20	13.20	16.13
54	Medicinal, pharmaceutical products	1,296.11	333.82	382.95
55	Essential oils, perfume, etc.	104.47	13.64	46.83

(Table continues on the following page.)

Table 4.19 Exports of All Commodities, 1995–99
(Rs millions) *(continued)*

Code	Commodity	1995–96	1997–98	1998–99
56	Fertilizer except group 272	77.13	2.55	1.14
57	Plastics in primary form	116.31	3.35	6.68
58	Plastics, nonprimary form	9.58	0.16	1.13
59	Chemical materials, n.e.s.	161.30	53.97	72.94
61	Leather, leather goods	7,697.68	2,313.91	2,138.28
62	Rubber manufactures, n.e.s.	17.01	3.45	9.22
63	Cork, wood manufactures	51.31	35.42	29.11
64	Paper, paperboard, etc.	10.86	27.80	8.32
65	Textile yarn, fabric, etc.	133,157.99	44,081.36	46,399.46
66	Nonmetal mineral manufactures	398.31	212.30	134.62
67	Iron and steel	5.97	11.12	26.68
68	Nonferrous metals	2.65	0.41	8.97
69	Metal manufactures, n.e.s.	780.77	295.55	346.11
71	Power generating machines	6.79	3.48	2.87
72	Special industrial machinery	188.06	208.71	210.05
73	Metal working machinery	20.25	3.58	4.93
74	General industrial machinery, n.e.s.	48.64	18.76	27.99
75	Office machines, adp. machines	0.00	2.98	0.47
76	Telecomm., sound equip., etc.	12.49	0.79	0.32
77	Electrical machinery appar., parts, n.e.s.	66.97	65.17	95.69
78	Road vehicles	51.22	18.59	32.25
79	Other transport equipment	27.13	59.47	22.35
81	Prefab buildings, fittings, etc.	2.04	1.27	0.17
82	Furniture, parts thereof	97.55	23.67	37.29
83	Travel goods, handbags, etc.	93.38	35.58	39.56
84	Clothing and accessories	48,422.36	18,447.39	22,016.80
85	Footwear	1,468.79	356.44	315.77
87	Scientific equipment, n.e.s.	3,902.29	1,372.62	1,391.47
88	Photography apparat., n.e.s.; colors	6.30	5.96	15.68
89	Misc. manufactured goods, n.e.s.	8,899.67	4,806.82	4,165.99
93	Special transactions	510.62	54.10	199.62

n.e.s. Not elsewhere specified.
Source: Federal Bureau of Statistics (various years).

Table 4.20 Imports of All Commodities, 1995–99
(Rs millions)

Code	Commodity	1995–96	1997–98	1998–99
00	Live animals other than division 03	58.62	2.40	13.89
01	Meat and meat preparations	30.87	0.82	0.17
02	Dairy products and bird eggs	1,039.01	174.21	391.49
03	Fish, crustaceans, mollusks	2.16	0.09	2.74
04	Cereals and cereal preparations	15,272.75	9,992.03	3,265.00
05	Vegetables and fruits	5,123.57	809.57	1,842.09
06	Sugar, sugar preparations, honey	240.01	1,962.85	164.29
07	Coffee, tea, cocoa, spices	5,718.79	2,218.09	3,329.79
08	Feeding stuff for animals	18.55	92.28	262.90
09	Miscellaneous edible products, etc.	875.17	155.47	280.94
11	Beverages	229.60	34.90	56.77
12	Tobacco and tobacco manufactures	5.35	1.11	4.79
21	Hides, skins, furskins, raw	766.52	232.50	99.01
22	Oilseeds and oleaginous fruit	1,007.64	78.30	131.58
23	Crude rubber	2,007.06	506.55	535.84
24	Cork and wood	416.49	178.97	345.13
25	Pulp and waste paper	1,065.37	289.57	299.97
26	Textile fibers	8,305.36	2,209.74	4,161.06
27	Crude fertilizers and minerals	1,123.51	291.89	439.92
28	Metalliferous ores and scrap	3,941.42	1,018.18	679.52
29	Crude animal and vegetable material	1,211.88	364.52	361.51
32	Coal, coke, briquettes	1,676.23	826.99	743.14
33	Petroleum, petrol product	60,658.91	20,631.31	13,781.27
34	Gas, natural, manufactured	1,674.53	526.02	675.53
41	Animal oils, fats, etc.	1,119.48	254.60	488.81
42	Fixed vegetable fats and oils	26,780.65	6,774.44	9,955.68
43	Processed animal, veg. oil, etc.	915.63	318.21	330.13
51	Organic chemicals	16,504.37	5,152.49	6,563.75
52	Inorganic chemicals	2,074.69	590.75	844.90
53	Dyes, coloring materials	4,428.89	1,240.35	1,630.80
54	Medicinal, pharmaceutical products	9,913.61	2,539.50	2,871.50
55	Essential oils, perfume, etc.	1,253.32	332.02	591.53
56	Fertilizer except group 272	9,929.44	584.56	862.88
57	Plastics in primary form	10,717.43	2,225.83	3,047.16
58	Plastics, nonprimary form	1,688.91	257.52	411.36
59	Chemical materials, n.e.s.	8,548.71	3,413.46	4,418.00
61	Leather, leather goods	252.51	85.04	159.32
62	Rubber manufactures, n.e.s.	2,489.01	784.37	1,012.23

(Table continues on the following page.)

Table 4.20 Imports of All Commodities, 1995–99
(Rs millions) *(continued)*

Code	Commodity	1995–96	1997–98	1998–99
63	Cork, wood manufactures	172.01	87.57	87.93
64	Paper, paperboard, etc.	4,703.13	1,134.55	1,259.34
65	Textile yarn, fabric, etc.	3,973.43	795.45	1,078.53
66	Nonmetal mineral manufactures	1,771.72	411.48	520.25
67	Iron and steel	14,522.84	3,608.58	3,618.90
68	Nonferrous metals	5,499.47	886.43	1,036.43
69	Metal manufactures, n.e.s.	4,383.08	1,185.89	938.16
71	Power generating machines	21,233.74	4,976.00	2,268.74
72	Special industrial machinery	21,448.08	7,392.19	6,955.88
73	Metal working machinery	790.40	115.24	222.22
74	General industrial machinery, n.e.s.	10,925.44	3,071.87	3,773.75
75	Office machines, adp. machines	2,059.06	720.02	1,535.60
76	Telecomm., sound equip., etc.	5,006.79	685.93	1,951.37
77	Electrical machinery appar., parts, n.e.s.	13,449.49	4,320.99	1,526.01
78	Road vehicles	13,452.17	4,003.09	3,398.74
79	Other transport equipment	2,293.70	1,219.77	2,662.54
81	Prefab buildings, fittings, etc.	255.41	45.63	61.83
82	Furniture, parts thereof	42.04	15.85	29.59
83	Travel goods, handbags, etc.	9.61	2.45	4.24
84	Clothing and accessories	73.36	16.49	28.02
85	Footwear	48.68	41.80	27.52
87	Scientific equipment, n.e.s.	3,153.03	715.89	786.49
88	Photography apparat., n.e.s.; colors	1,395.19	366.80	484.78
89	Misc. manufactured goods, n.e.s.	4,107.52	842.33	1,101.53
93	Special transactions	681.14	3,435.44	437.55
97	Gold, nonmonetary, n.e.s.	9,789.14	3,150.69	9.41

n.e.s. Not elsewhere specified.
Source: Federal Bureau of Statistics (various years).

Some Implications for Policy Options

Production Policy Options

AMS-RELATED SUPPORT. At no point does the URAoA ban any specific production policy, for either industrialized or developing countries, even for those policies that have a production or trade distorting effect. What has been agreed to is that in the future the aggregate level of support associated with all such policies (the total current AMS) should not exceed that provided in the past and it has to be reduced by at least 13.3 percent in 10 years in the case of developing countries and 20 percent in six years for industrialized countries.

This reduction on direct price support does not appear to be too onerous for developing countries (that is, it is smaller and more gradual than that for industrialized countries). Nevertheless, on closer examination developing countries may be more constrained as a result of their zero or insignificant levels of AMS included in their schedules. There is a view that most developing countries believe that it was to their advantage to try to exempt most of their policies under the green box provisions instead of including them under the AMS. However, their claims of nonuse of direct price support measures in the past essentially limits their options for the use of such measures in the future.

SPECIAL AND DIFFERENTIAL TREATMENT–RELATED SUPPORT. This is a special category of production support policies specific to developing countries: generally available investment subsidies and agricultural input subsidies to low-income or resource-poor producers, as well as support to producers to encourage diversification from the growing of illicit narcotic crops. These are an important set of exemptions that allow considerable room to support agricultural producers in a way that may entail less distortion of the market and a more efficient allocation of resources.

PRODUCTION-LIMITING SUPPORT. The inclusion of these policies among those exempted from reduction commitments was to accommodate certain ongoing policies pursued by the United States and the European Union. However, limiting production is of little interest to most developing countries because their problem is normally under-production rather than over-production.

GREEN BOX–RELATED SUPPORT. The measures included under the green box are potentially desirable for all countries because they result in minimum market distorting effects. However, such policies, especially those that entail decoupled income support to producers, are unusual in developing countries because this assistance requires an administrative capacity for designing and implementing targeted policies, which often goes beyond that available in many developing countries.

Green box measures as well as the other forms of assistance have real costs associated with them. Moreover, in many cases these policies go beyond other constraints that countries may face. In particular, many developing countries have been undertaking policy reforms under Structural Adjustment Programs (SAPs). These reforms call for less government intervention in both the input and output markets and, more importantly, require reductions of budgetary outlays associated with such interventions. Thus, although the URAoA does not include any restrictions on public expenditures (or foregone revenue), aside from those transferred to producers, it is unlikely that countries undertaking SAPs would be able to pursue certain expensive policies even though permitted under the URAoA.

Consumption Policy Options

Provision of food commodities at prices that the majority of the population can afford has often been a key food security objective in many developing countries. Many have this objective in place through consumption support programs either operating under generalized price subsidies or through specific programs targeted to poor households. Are such policies and programs in accordance with the URAoA?

The main provision of the URAoA that relates to consumer support is included under the green box category of "domestic food aid." The URAoA stipulates that eligibility to receive food assistance shall be subject to clearly defined criteria related to nutritional objectives. However, there is an important exception for developing countries to this general prescription that allows them to provide foodstuffs at subsidized prices with the objective of "meeting food requirements of urban and rural poor in developing countries on a regular basis at reasonable prices." This is an important concession to countries that provide subsidized food through fair price shops on a regular basis.

In practice, both industrialized and developing countries have included their domestic food assistance programs under the "domestic food aid" category and have seldom made a distinction in their schedules as to the characteristics of the beneficiary population. None of these submissions has been challenged so far by other signatories to the URAoA. This is understandable because the URAoA is primarily concerned with production- and trade-distorting measures. Although consumption subsidization is market distorting, as it generally leads to higher overall food consumption than it would be otherwise, it is nevertheless trade enhancing.

Budgetary costs for stockholding activities, or expenditures (or revenue foregone) in relation to consumer support, are not subject to reduction commitments. However, again, the constraint on consumption support for most developing countries will not come from the URAoA rules but largely from budgetary limitations. Already SAPs have required many developing countries to cut consumer subsidies.

While the URAoA does not attempt to address the budgetary constraint problems of many developing countries, it nevertheless contains a commitment that in principle should not aggravate it. Article 16 provides for action within the framework of the Decision on Measures Concerning the Possible Negative Effects of the Reform Programme on Least-Developed and Net Food-Importing Developing Countries. The promise is that if food import prices rise because of the implementation of the UR liberalization process, net food importing developing countries and the least-industrialized countries would be eligible for "action" by industrialized country members. This could result in increased food aid, financing to help them maintain normal imports of food, and technical assistance for, and eventually favorable treatment on, agricultural export credits. Such aid could help those countries dampen consumer price increases while allowing prices to rise for farmers.

Domestic Market Stability Options

Another concern of developing countries is the effect a more open trade regime will have on domestic price stability, especially on sensitive food commodities, and whether world market price variability will decrease or increase in the future. By opening up national agricultural markets it is expected that the absorption of production shocks will increase, having a de-stabilizing effect on the market. Also, the location of production may shift somewhat from countries with relatively high levels of protection to countries where protection is relatively low. If production is more unstable in the latter, then overall variability of production can increase. There is also the issue of the level and ownership of stocks. Reduced government intervention implies that the level of public stocks will be reduced and privately held stocks may not increase sufficiently to fill the gap.

Issues of Concern to Pakistan in the New Round

Pakistan's experience with the implementation of the URAoA highlights many useful insights that can be helpful for future rounds. Pakistan has not gained much in terms of agricultural exports and growth. This cannot be blamed wholly on Pakistan's ability, or inability, to bring its agricultural sector into line with the URAoA. Some blame must also be placed on the countries that have, for instance, created an unequal playing field, where domestic producers are protected to the detriment of those exporting countries trying to compete. However, it is important to remember that SPS measures have a role to play, and if Pakistan cannot meet those requirements, then the importing country does have a right to refuse entry.

Since the launching of the Marrakesh Agreement in January 1994 Pakistan has flagged its concerns at different meetings of the WTO's Committee on Agriculture and ministerial conferences.

Complexity of Implementing Commitments

Administration of the tariff rate quota system and other quota commitments involve a number of issues that have to be further developed and streamlined so that the URAoA can be smoothly implemented to the benefit of all member countries. These issues include the allocation of access under most favored nation tariff quotas to preferential suppliers and nonmembers and the allocation of import access to state trading enterprises and producer organizations, auctioning of tariff quota licenses, limitations on imports of particular products under broadly defined tariff quota commitments, and making imports under tariff quotas conditional on absorption of domestic production of the product concerned. Under the URAoA the actual allocation and administration of the quotas are left to each member. There is a need to have a transparent method of quota administration that does not cause a breach of the market access commitments.

LACK OF DISCIPLINE ON CALCULATION OF TARIFF EQUIVALENT. The calculations of tariff equivalents of NTBs were left to the member countries. There is a need for incorporating a provision in the URAoA for independent monitoring of member countries' adherence to the guidelines in reducing the peak tariffs. Criticism has been made on a number of occasions that the tariff equivalents by some countries are much higher than the effective level of the existing NTBs. The harmonization approach to tariffs implies that the higher the initial tariff rates the larger the reduction, and this should be applied on a product-to-product basis. This approach was used for industrial tariffs in the Tokyo Round.

NEED FOR UNIFORM TARIFF RATES. The reduction commitments for tariffs were made both on average and per product at a minimum rate. When the base tariff levels are different across the countries, the required reduction even after implementation will leave a great dispersion of tariff rates and peak tariffs among the member countries. There is a need to have a uniform tariff level, allowing preferential treatment to the developing countries.

DOMESTIC SUPPORT COMMITMENTS. Domestic support reduction has to be made by a specific reduction in the current total AMS. The apportionment of reduction across different products is left to the discretion of member countries. This provides the country the opportunity to protect a product that could harm the interests of other trade partners. By rebalancing the support among crops/sectors, the protection to sensitive products has been increased.

The blue box measures that allow exemptions tailored to the requirements of the U.S. deficiency payments and the European Union compensation payments emerged out of the concessions made under the Blair House Accord. These are the government's direct payments under a production limiting scheme. In some cases some nonexempt measures and the green box measures are not so clearly distinguishable. There is a need to have another look at more transparency and misuse of green box measures by industrialized countries.

The AMS is calculated with reference to a base period of 1986–88. The cost of production continues to change. Using the reference price of a base period for calculating AMS after some period of time will not provide for a proper assessment of realistic support to agriculture. Therefore, this needs to be addressed.

OBSCURITY OF PRODUCT SPECIFICITY. The reduction commitment is unclear on product specificity, especially in those cases where outlays and quantity commitments were allowed to be established for a group of products. For instance, the category "coarse grains" covers 46 products classified under HS 6-digit. In such cases, it is uncertain how the reduction commitments will affect individual products when they have been grouped together in the reduction commitments.

Circumvention of export subsidy commitments, noted in the meetings of the WTO Committee on Agriculture involves the case where several members were allegedly starting a new export subsidy that they claim was not subject to the reduction commitment. Other loopholes in the reduction commitments have also been identified, such as an "inward processing" program, which involves "exporting" of a subsidized product to an export processing zone where the product is processed into another product and then exported to other countries. For example, the European Union allowed a subsidy for cheese production through this mechanism. In such cases this may be considered as an input subsidy to the final processed product.

STRINGENT SPS STANDARDS. The SPS Agreement also covers fishery and forestry. This SPS Agreement under Article 10 provides for Special and Differential Treatment. In practice the Agreement has been used by industrialized countries as a barrier against imports from developing countries. The European Union banned the import of Pakistan fish in July 1998. The United States tried to ban the import of Pakistan tuna fish, and the WTO Dispute Settlement Committee decided the case in favor of Pakistan. It is widely recognized that the developing countries are far behind the industrialized countries in the SPS standards area. Developing countries do not have adequate financial, technical, and staffing capability to cover this gap anytime soon. Industrialized countries should give support to the developing countries so that they can in due course have compatible standards with their industrialized trade partners.

ASSISTANCE FOR NET FOOD IMPORTING DEVELOPING COUNTRIES. The Marrakesh Ministerial decision on Least Developed and Net Food Importing Developing Countries established a measure to respond to possible negative affects of the reform process. This decision has not been implemented as yet. Some mechanism has to be evolved so that the grievances of the countries concerned can be redressed. This issue was to be discussed in collaboration with the Food and Agriculture Organization, the Food Aid Committee, and the World Bank.

SPECIAL SAFEGUARD PROVISIONS. Since 1995, industrialized countries have mainly used special safeguard provisions, and the developing countries have considered these provisions a form of protection. There is a need either to completely eliminate or to minimize the provisions.

ADDITIONAL ISSUES. Future negotiations on agriculture should stop the industrialized countries from backsliding (that is, moving backward) toward higher and selective protectionism in agriculture. The industrialized countries should make a meaningful reduction in tariff ceilings by 2005 and strengthen the market access provisions. Tariff peaks should be slashed in the case of major agricultural exports of the developing countries. The Special and Differential Treatment provision should be made more attractive so that developing countries can increase their agriculture.

Conclusion

The production disciplines stemming from the URAoA are unlikely to cause much of an adjustment problem for most developing countries, including Pakistan, because most provide little direct price support to their producers. Many in fact have taxed farmers by keeping farm prices below equivalent world price levels.

The most likely problem will be how to help poorer consumers deal with higher prices, a matter largely outside the purview of the URAoA. This could be tackled by a combination of targeted food assistance supported by domestic resources (generated through some taxation of the increased returns expected from the agriculture sector), as well as external assistance under Article 16. Finally, in light of greater reliance on tariffs in the future, there is some concern that this could lead to an increase in domestic price instability, but which could be mitigated by a variety of approaches including food security stocks and a sliding scale of tariffs.

A review of Pakistan's experience with the implementation of the URAoA shows that it has not defaulted on its obligations and commitments under the URAoA but has gone far ahead of its URAoA requirements. However, owing to the industrialized countries increased protection and subsidies that have denied market access opportunities, whether because of SPS measures or other factors, Pakistan has not realized the expected gains in terms of exports and growth. Pakistan is perhaps correct in supporting the need for fast liberalization of trade in agriculture. The next round of negotiations will certainly prove useful if it attends to these issues raised earlier. In context of the ongoing agricultural negotiations, proposals submitted to the WTO General Council by the Cairns Group, the United States, the European Union, Norway, Switzerland, Japan, Pakistan, countries in transition (Hungary and Bulgaria, for instance), Korea, and the Latin American countries reveal that they have taken their old positions of previous UR multilateral negotiations. Under these circumstances the next round will certainly be a difficult one.

Bibliography

Arshad Zaman, Associates (Pvt.) Ltd. 1997. *Pakistan Industry and Trade Sector Study*. Manila: Asian Development Bank.
Blarel, Benoet, G. Purcell, and A. Valdés. 1999. *Implications of the Uruguay Round Agreement on Agriculture for South Asia: The Case of Agriculture*. Washington, D.C.: World Bank.
FAO (Food and Agriculture Organization). 1998. *Commodity Market Review*. Rome.
GATT Secretariat. 1995. *Report on Trade Policy Review of Pakistan*. Geneva.
Gotsch, Carl, and Gilbert Brown. 1980. "Prices, Taxes, and Subsidies in Pakistan's Agriculture, 1970–76." Working Paper 387. Washington, D.C.
Ingco, Merlinda, and Alan Winters. 1996. "Pakistan and the Uruguay Round: Impact and Opportunities, A Quantitative Assessment." Discussion Paper. World Bank, Washington, D.C.
Majd, Nader. 1995. "The Uruguay Round and South Asia: An Overview of the Impact and Opportunities." Working Paper. World Bank, Washington, D.C.
Pakistan Ministry of Commerce. Various years. *Trade Policy*.
———. 1992. "Position Papers on Uruguay Round and Agriculture." Islamabad.
———. 1995. "Trade Policy Review for GATT Committee." Islamabad.
———. 1998. "Pakistan's Foreign Trade Key Indicators (1997–98)." Islamabad.
Pakistan Ministry of Finance. 1999. *Economic Survey of Pakistan 1998–99*. Islamabad.
Pakistan Ministry of Food and Agriculture. Various years. *Agricultural Statistics*. Islamabad.
Srinivasan, T. N. 1994. "Regional Trading Arrangements and Beyond: Exploring Some Options for South Asia Theory, Empirics, and Policy." World Bank, Washington, D.C.

UNCTAD (U.N. Conference on Trade and Development). 1999. *Preparing for Future Multilateral Trade Negotiations: Issues and Research Needs from a Development Perspective*. Geneva.

UNCTAD/WTO Joint Study. 1997. "The Post-Uruguay Round Tariff Environment for Developing Country Export." Geneva.

WTO (World Trade Organization). 1995a. "Supporting Tables Relating to Commitments on Agricultural Products in Part IV of the Schedule." Report. Geneva.

———. 1995b. "The Results of the Uruguay Round." Geneva.

———. 1995c. *Trading into the Future: Introduction to the WTO*. Geneva.

———. 1996. *Technical Cooperation Handbook on Notification Requirements*. Geneva.

5
India

Ashok Gulati

The Uruguay Round (UR) Agreement on Agriculture (AoA), signed in Marrakesh on April 15, 1994, as a part of the overall agreement, had a built-in provision to review its progress before the end of 1999. It was considered necessary to do so because agriculture was being brought into the world trading system through the World Trade Organization (WTO) for the first time, and it was expected that there would be hiccups in the implementation of this URAoA. It was believed that the URAoA would not achieve any major breakthrough in streamlining large distortions in production and trading of agriculture, except to bring agriculture into the fold of global trading rules.

The new round of trade negotiations is expected to bring greater discipline in agricultural production and trading policies. But, how far is India prepared for agricultural liberalization? What are India's interests and options with respect to URAoA? And what should India put on the negotiating table with a view to maximize its gains and minimize pains?

There is no doubt that this time India is better prepared for negotiations than was the case while signing the URAoA. There has been a debate in the country, and the Ministry of Commerce has met with the industry associations, especially the Confederation of Indian Industry (CII), the Federation of Indian Chambers of Commerce and Industry (FICCI), and the Associated Chambers of Commerce and Industry of India (ASSOCHAM), and with some selected academic institutions, academics, and bureaucrats.

Unfortunately, none of the farmers' organizations was involved in the discussions and nor was there any special effort made to include agroprocessors and exporters in any meaningful way to develop an agenda for negotiations on URAoA. Their representation through industry associations has been rather weak. Nevertheless, India can still put forward a credible agenda for negotiations, provided the homework is done well. For this, India has to have a proper understanding of where Indian agriculture stands vis-à-vis the commitments given under URAoA, and also how the rest of world is adjusting its agriculture to the new set of rules.

Commitments under URAoA and India's Status

There are three basic commitments under URAoA: market access ("tariffication"), domestic support, and export competition. Where does India stand in relation to these three basic commitments?

Tariffication

The URAoA required conversion of all nontariff barriers into equivalent tariff barriers, or "tariffication." Tariffication was meant to reduce the base tariff under a time-bound program; that is, by 24 percent over 10 years in the case of developing countries and by 36 percent over 6 years for the industrialized countries. The least-industrialized countries were exempt from these reductions. In addition to this there was a call to maintain current access opportunities and to establish a minimum access tariff quota, where there was no binding of tariffs. The minimum access tariff quota was to be established at reduced tariff rates for those basic products where minimum access was less than 3 percent of domestic consumption in the base period 1986–88. Minimum access was to be gradually increased to 5 percent of the base period consumption. Tariff quotas at reasonable levels were to facilitate access, and these tariff quotas would be established on a tariff-line-by-line basis.

Tariffication Commitment

In the UR, India agreed to make adjustment in tariff rates for 3,373 commodities/commodity groups[1] at Harmonized System (HS) 6-digit level or commodity subgroups of HS 6-digit HS level,[2] including agriculture and nonagricultural commodities. The bound rates for all the commodities are ad valorem, except for two commodities (HS codes 080211 and 080212) whose bound rates are committed in the form of specific amounts in Rs/kilogram. The committed commodities account for around 65 percent of India's tariff lines (which are defined at HS 6-digit level).

Out of this total of 3,373 lines, agriculture accounts for only about 20 percent (673 lines). Table 5.1 presents these agricultural lines committed by India at 6-digit, or subgroup of 6-digit, by different chapters of HS classification. There are a large number of items that have been committed in the URAoA belonging to commodity groups (by different chapters of HS classification), such as edible vegetables, animal or vegetable fats and oils, and meat and edible meat.

To understand the present state of the tariff rates of the commodities committed in the UR, the UR bound rates should be compared with the present level of India's tariff rates. India levies two main types of custom

India

Table 5.1 Tariff Commitment Made by India in the URAoA

Chapter number	Description	Number of lines
1	Live animals	15
2	Meat and edible meat offal	50
4	Dairy produce, birds' eggs, honey	25
5	Products of animal origin	17
6	Live trees and other plants	13
7	Edible vegetables	57
8	Edible fruit and nuts; peel of citrus	50
9	Coffee, tea, mate, and spices	33
10	Cereals	17
11	Products of the milling industry	34
12	Oilseed and oleaginous fruits	44
13	Lac; gums, resins, and other vegetable secretions	12
14	Vegetable planting materials	11
15	Animal or vegetable fats and oils	51
16	Preparations of meat, fish	16
17	Sugar and sugar confectionery	15
18	Cocoa and cocoa preparation	11
19	Preparation of cereals, starch, milk	16
20	Preparation of vegetable, fruit, nut, etc.	45
21	Miscellaneous edible preparations	15
22	Beverages, spirits, and vinegar	21
23	Residues and wastes from food	24
24	Tobacco and manufactured substitutes	9
29	Organic chemicals	2
33	Essential oil and resinoids	14
35	Albuminoidal substances	8
38	Miscellaneous chemical products	2
41	Raw hides and skins and leather	12
43	Fur skins and artificial fur	9
50	Silk	4
51	Wool, fine or coarse animal hair	10
52	Cotton	5
53	Other vegetable textile fibers	6
	Total	673

Note: Tariff lines at Harmonized System (HS) 6-digit. There were two lines defined as subgroups of HS 6-digit and also includes only agricultural products and is based on final bound rates committed at the Uruguay Round. URAoA = Uruguay Round Agreement on Agriculture.

Sources: WTO; Government of India (1999a).

duties on imported goods: basic custom duty (BCD) and additional custom duty (ACD).

BCD rates are also called "Scheduled Rates of the Basic Custom Duty," which in turn are known as "Statutory Rates" in literature. The ACD equals the excise duty on like articles produced in India. There are two main categories of scheduled rates: the standard rates and the preferential rates. In this chapter, the BCD, or the standard rates (or most favored nation [MFN] rates), only are considered.

The BCD MFN rates for 1999–2000 are generally ad valorem. India has not announced ad valorem rates for 11 commodities (including two from the agricultural sector), but rather a specific amount (in Rs) of custom duty per unit of quantity imported.

India's budget for 1999–2000 has a surcharge on BCD of 10 percent of BCD, in addition to other duties, for all products. In the budget of 1998–99, a special additional duty was announced in addition to earlier announced categories of import duties. The objective of a special additional duty was to offset the sales tax on domestic goods. The rate was 4 percent. However, the effect of this special additional duty will be more than 4 percent, because the special additional duty will be calculated at the aggregated value of the imports, basic custom duty, surcharge, and the additional duty.

The standard rates of duty defined in the schedules, however, do not determine the actual duty rates applicable on different products. The BCD, ACD, surcharge on BCD, and the special additional duty and various exemption notifications issued by the government determine the actual applicable duty rates, which is called the effective duty rates. There are a large number of duty exemptions on BCD[3] as per different notifications by the government. The exemptions may be use-specific, country-specific, commodity-specific, or value-specific. It is not possible to take into account all these exemptions (particularly commodity-specific) in this analysis. Nevertheless, consideration has been given to those exemptions that apply to all items under a tariff heading at HS 6-digit code level. These rates are sometimes called "applied tariff rates" in international literature. In India, the applied tariff rates are generally lower than the corresponding statutory rates for a large number of commodities.[4]

Table 5.2 presents the frequency distribution of a number of UR committed products (or lines), based on the level of difference in India's MFN rates[5] for 1999–2000 and UR final bound rates. The distribution clearly shows that the present levels of India's MFN tariff rates are significantly lower than that of final bound rates for a large number of commodities. Out of 673 products[6] belonging to the agriculture sector, the present level of MFN tariff rates in most of the commodities is significantly less than that of corresponding UR final bound rates. The difference was more than

Table 5.2 Difference in UR Final Bound Rates and MFN Tariff Rates

Range (UR–TR) percentage points	Number of lines
UR–TR > = 75	401
50 = < UR–TR < 75	155
25 = < UR–TR < 50	29
10 = < UR–TR < 25	39
0 = < UR–TR < 10	41
UR–TR < 0	8
Total	673

Note: MFN = most favored nation; TR = tariff rate; UR = Uruguay Round. TR, MFN tariff rates (basic custom duty) as announced in India's budget 1999–2000; UR, UR final bound rates; tariff lines at Harmonized System 6-digit or subgroups of HS 6-digit; includes only agricultural products.
Sources: WTO; Government of India (1999a).

50 percentage points and above for 556 commodities (82.6 percent of 673 commodities). This implies that India has not only honored the commitments of UR bound rates but has substantially reduced the level of MFN tariff rates unilaterally.

Table 5.3 presents the list of the commodities whose present level of MFN tariff rates is higher than the corresponding UR final bound rates. There are only eight tariff lines, most of which belong to the beverages group, where the MFN tariff rates exceed the UR bound rates. In six of these eight tariff lines the difference is 80 percentage points, in one it is 20 percentage points, and in another one (HS 210690; other food preparations not elsewhere specified) 120 percentage points. In this context the UR final bound rates taken here are the ones that have to be committed by March 2004.[7]

The analysis of these results are based on India's BCD, and the 10 percent surcharge announced in the present Indian budget that has not been included in the MFN tariff rates. In case a 10 percent surcharge is also included in MFN tariff rates, the frequency distribution of tariff rate–bound rate will not change significantly.

Quantitative Restrictions Commitments

It was decided in the UR to remove all types of quantitative restrictions (QRs) or prohibitions (other than tariffs), whether maintained through quotas or import-export licenses. India had also agreed to phase out QRs on all commodities except for about 632 commodities for reasons related to security, religion, etc. (at HS 8-digit or 10-digit level). However, India

Table 5.3 Difference between MFN Tariff Rates for 1999–2000 and Corresponding UR Final Bound Rates

HS code	Description	UR bound rate	MFN rate	(UR–TR)
080620	Dried grapes	100	120	–20
210690	Other food preparation not elsewhere specified	60	180	–120
220710	Undenatured ethyl alcohol of an alcoholic strength by volume of 80 percent volume or higher	150	230	–80
220820	Spirits obtained by distilling grape wine or grape marc	150	230	–80
220830	Whiskeys	150	230	–80
220840	Rum and taffia	150	230	–80
220850	Gin and geneva	150	230	–80
220890	Other compound alcohols	150	230	–80

Note: MFN = most favored nation; HS = Harmonized System; TR = tariff rate; UR = Uruguay Round. TR, MFN tariff rate (BCD) as announced in India's budget 1999–2000; UR, UR final bound rates; tariff lines at HS 6-digit or subgroups of HS 6-digit; includes only agricultural products. Based on final bound rates.
Sources: WTO; Government of India (1999a).

maintains QRs on imports of some additional items (around 1,482 tariff lines) under provisions of Article XVIII:B of the WTO. This article recognizes that members whose economies can only support a lower standard of living and are in the earlier stages of development may "apply quantitative restrictions for Balance of Payments Position . . . [and] . . . shall be free to deviate temporarily from the provisions of the other Articles of this Agreement." The provisions relating to balance of payments also provide that a member has to announce publicly time schedules for the elimination of QRs. India presented a case of time schedules for nine years for elimination of QRs. Although it was acceptable to most developing countries, a number of industrialized economies objected to a phased-out period of even seven years. The United States, European Union, Canada, Australia, New Zealand, and Switzerland (and Japan as third party) started the dispute settlement proceedings against India. India reached mutual agreements with all countries except the United States.

Under this agreement, India agreed to phase out its QRs over a six year period (1997–2003). But the United States filed a dispute against India. A panel was constituted in November 1997 to examine the U.S. allegation that the continued maintenance of QRs on India's imports was inconsistent with India's obligations under the WTO agreement. In a 1999 report[8] of the Appellate Body it was recommended that "India bring its balance-of-payments restrictions, which the Panel found to be inconsistent with Articles XI:1 and XVIII:11 of the GATT 1994, and with Article 4.2 of the Agreement on Agriculture, into conformity with its obligations under these agreements."

By April 2001 the government of India had removed all QRs on imports. India has already offered, unilaterally, trade concessions to members of the South Asian Association for Regional Cooperation (SAARC) by withdrawing QRs on all commodities.

In the pre-1990s India's import policy was quite complex, with different categories of importers, various types of import licenses, and many ways of importing. A number of concrete steps were taken during the 1990s to liberalize the import regime. The existing trade policy[9] presents a negative list of commodities, which cannot be imported under Open General License (OGL) (or that the private sector is free to import). This negative list basically is composed of three main categories: prohibited, restricted, and canalized. The prohibited items are, for instance, tallow, fat, ore, oil of animal origin, wild animal, and ivory. A large number of restricted items are consumer goods, and their import is allowed against a license.

To understand the present state of protection by different types of QRs, the import policy of different lines can be further categorized under more groups. Under restricted there is the consumer good; that is, items that are permitted to be imported against license or in accordance with public notice. Then there is the actual user, or imported commodities used by the importer. Last is the special import license; that is, select traders (exporters) freely trade these licenses in the Indian market. This is certainly a soft type of nontrade barrier (NTB), because it is easily available (in market) and an importer has to pay a certain premium. The rate of premium has varied from 1.5 percent to around 3 percent.

Under the canalized category there is a special import license. On the basis of the export-import policy for the year 1999–2000, only 2,114 tariff lines (that is, about 20 percent out of 10,261 tariff lines) are now subject to any type of NTBs. Out of this total of 2,114 lines under NTBs only about 29 percent (606 lines) belong to agriculture (HS 1–24). However, as a percentage of total agricultural tariff lines (1,398) in HS 1–24, those under NTBs (606) comprise 43 percent, which is quite a sizeable number. But out of this 606 agricultural tariff lines under NTBs, only 344 (56.8 percent) are under NTBs owing to balance of payment reasons, while the remaining 262 (43.2 percent) are under NTBs owing to reasons related to security or religion. Thus, the lifting of the balance of payments cover from QRs effectively opens 344 tariff lines of agriculture.

Table 5.4 Different Types of Nontrade Barriers Imposed on India's Imports for Agriculture Sector (HS 1–24), 1999–2000

	Number of lines	
Types of NTBs	Total	UR-bound tariff
No barriers	792	
NTBs	606	
Prohibited	51	
Restricted	518	435
Consumer goods	224	206
Special import license	149	85
Other	145	144
Canalized	37	37
Special import license	8	8
Other	29	29
Total	1,398	

Note: HS = Harmonized System; ITC = Indian Trade Classification (HS); NTBs = nontrade barriers; UR = Uruguay Round. National lines at 8-digit or 10-digit ITC-HS.

Source: Government of India (1998); notifications issued on March 31, 1999, for amendments, in Government of India (1998).

Table 5.4 summarizes this import policy of all Indian agriculture products. Of the total 1,398 agricultural tariff lines (at 8- or 10-digit ITC-HS classification), 792 lines are totally free. Of the remaining 606 lines, 51 are prohibited, 518 are restricted under consumer goods or special import license, etc., and 37 are canalized. Out of these 37 canalized items, 8 can be imported by acquiring special import license. Of the total 518 tariff lines restricted, 435 (84 percent) have bound their tariffs under URAoA. Similarly, all the 37 tariff lines that are canalized at present have bound their tariffs under URAoA.

For all commodities, agricultural as well as nonagricultural, as mentioned earlier, there are in total 2,114 items at present subject to QRs, and India has agreed to phase out QRs on 1,482 items as per agreements with WTO. These national lines are subject to one or another type of QRs owing to balance of payments reasons. All these items (except around 632 items for security, religious, and other reasons) will be phased out by the year 2003 (or 2001).

Table 5.5 summarizes the present state of India's import policy for the products whose QRs will be phased out in the near future. It shows that out of 1,482 identified items, 738 (= 730 + 8) can be imported through special import license. Hence, there are only 744 (= 1,482 – 738) lines subject

Table 5.5 Different Quantitative Restrictions for Products, Still Maintained for Balance of Payment Reasons, 1999–2000

Type of QRs	Number of national lines	Percent share
Restricted	1,471	99.26
Consumer goods	550	37.11
Actual user	2	0.13
Special import license	730	49.26
Other	189	12.75
Canalized	11	0.74
Special import license	8	0.54
Other	3	0.2
Total (QRs)	1,482	100

Note: HS = Harmonized System; ITC = Indian Trade Classification (HS); QRs = quantitative restrictions. National lines at 8-digit or 10-digit ITC-HS.

Source: Government of India (1998); notifications issued on March 31, 1999, for amendments, in Government of India (1998).

to hard-core import policies of restricted items/canalized items. Out of these 744 items, most of them are restricted under the import policy of consumer goods.

Table 5.6 presents the number of agricultural products by four commodity groups (HS sections I–IV) subject to any type of QR owing to balance of payment reasons. Most of these products are evenly distributed among sections I, II, or IV and are restricted owing to the import policy of consumer goods. The detailed results of 344 agricultural products, still subject to QRs for balance of payment reasons, for 24 disaggregate commodity groups (HS 1–24), reveal that the frequency distributions of different types of QRs by different commodity groups is evenly distributed.

To sum up, the above exhaustive analysis of Indian import policy reveals that apart from some restrictive tariff lines, India has unilaterally gone ahead to reduce tariff barriers much below the bound rates of duty under URAoA. Agricultural commodities such as rice and milk (skimmed milk powder) are already committed at zero import duty. For wheat the bound rate of duty is 100 percent, but roller flour mills are allowed to import at zero import duty. Similarly, for pulses the bound rate is 100 percent, but they are being imported under OGL at zero import duty. Sugar is bound at 150 percent import duty but is being imported under OGL at 25 percent duty. Similarly, edible oils, most of which are bound at 300 percent import duty, are open for imports at 15 percent duty.

Table 5.6 Different Types of Quantitative Restrictions for Products, Still Maintained for Balance of Payment Reasons, by Commodity Groups (HS Sections I–IV), 1999–2000

Section	Description	Restricted				Canalized		Total number of items
		Consumer goods	Actual users	SIL	Other	SIL	Other	
I	Live animals, animal products	52	0	67	0	0	0	119
II	Vegetable products	66	0	35	8	8	0	117
III	Animal or vegetable fats and oils	0	0	1	0	0	0	1
IV	Prepared foodstuff, beverages	64	0	40	3	0	0	107

Note: SIL = special import license.
Sources: Government of India (1998); notifications issued on March 31, 1999, for amendments, in Government of India (1998); WTO.

Tariffication Agenda

Given the above analysis of present levels of tariffs, what sort of an agenda with respect to tariffication and market access would serve India's interests? It appears quite sensible that India, along with similar developing countries, should negotiate for a more liberal trade environment in the rest of the world, too. This alone could ensure somewhat easier access to industrialized country markets, many of which have been highly protected. Accordingly, it seems logical that India should demand:

- Abolition of all quotas and quantitative restrictions on imports and exports around the world, except for those countries that have acute balance of payment problems (as covered under Article XVIII-B). In particular, the tariff quotas that are widely applied by industrialized countries must be abolished and replaced by equivalent tariffs at the earliest.
- Replacing all specific rates of import duty by rates on an ad valorem basis.
- Negotiate for ceilings on tariff bindings for any agricultural product at no higher than 50 percent for any country.

Market Access Agenda

Why should India have this agenda for negotiation on market access? The reason is that the industrialized world, most notably countries of the European Union and East Asia, are resistant to provide access for agricultural exports of the developing world. Many of those industrialized countries have not gone for full tariffication of agricultural products. Instead, those industrialized countries have opted for an in-tariff quota system for several commodities, which is restricting the potential gains to the developing world. Several industrialized countries, including Japan, the United States, and those in the European Union, have in place a system of tariff quotas. The U.S. tariff schedule, for example, includes as many as 192 tariff lines to administer product-specific tariff quotas for beef, dairy products, sugar and some sugar products, peanuts, tobacco, and cotton (WTO 1997). Most countries have agreed to progressive reductions in the over-quota tariff rates, and some have also agreed to lower the in-quota rates or raise the concessionary access level. But the quota system is essentially limiting the potential gains for developing countries, and therefore the abolition of quota systems should be the first item on India's negotiation agenda.

Next, developing countries like India have to be bold and aggressive and suggest a cap on the maximum tariff binding at 50 percent on any agricultural commodity by any nation. Many Indian negotiators may be somewhat surprised at this suggestion. They may consider that asking for 300 percent tariff is a great success in negotiations, but in reality it may not be so. For edible oils India negotiated for 300 percent tariff binding and opened up at 65 percent, brought it down to 30 percent, and then to 15 percent. There would hardly be any commodity in Indian agriculture, or for that matter in most of the developing countries, that would require 300 percent protection, and if any commodity does, it is worth working on it through nonprice measures, such as research and development, rather than accord such high levels of protection. The idea behind globalization of agriculture is to reduce price distortions and promote efficient use of resources. But when countries in the developing world like India ask for 300 percent protection, they really lose all the strength in their negotiations with the industrialized world. How can India then say that an industrialized country, for instance, Japan, cannot have 700 percent protection on their rice? And if that is the level of protection accorded to agriculture in the industrialized countries, where is the potential to gain for the developing world? And that is what the actual situation is for many commodities in industrialized countries (for example, the dairy sector).

For tariff line 40210 (milk powder, granules etc., fats < = 1.5 percent), in 1998, the peak tariff rate in the European Union was 99 percent, in Japan 336 percent, in Canada 213 percent, in Korea 211 percent, as against zero in India. Further, for tariff line 40221 (milk powder, granules etc., fats > = 1.5 percent, no sugar), the peak tariff rate in the United States was 58 percent, in the European Union 171 percent, in Japan 557 percent, in Canada 313 percent, in Korea 211 percent, as against zero in India for the same year (1998). Still further, for the tariff line 40229 (other milk powder, granules, etc.) the peak tariff in the United States was 70 percent, in the European Union 199 percent, in Japan 988 percent, in Canada 313 percent, in Korea 211 percent, as against 35 percent in India. Similar examples can be found in other commodities as well, especially sugar and even cereals.

That is why it is suggested that the maximum tariff should not be more than 50 percent on any tariff line (of HS 10-digit level) relating to agriculture. This will help in promoting true comparative advantage in the use of resources at the global level, which often gets blurred owing to huge subsidization of agriculture by the industrialized countries of East Asia, the European Union, and also by Canada and the United States. Only then can it be hoped that this approach would open up some potential for exports of developing countries even to the industrialized country markets, especially for goods such as milk and milk products, grains, or sugar. As far as Indian agriculture is concerned, it has a reasonably good comparative advantage in most of the products, which would emerge even more competitively once import barriers in industrialized countries are reduced and distortions minimized (Gulati and Kelley 1999; Gulati and Narayanan 1999).[10] Some countries, notably those in the European Union, started reducing domestic support prices compared to world prices, but funneled subsidies through the blue box.

There is also another reason for suggesting a cap on 50 percent maximum tariff. The base period for tariffication was 1986–88. During this period world prices in agriculture were quite low. This meant that the tariff equivalent—calculated as the gap between the higher supported internal prices and the then low world prices—was unusually large. The new tariffs that were based on this large tariff equivalent in 1986–88 offer high protection in other years when the world prices are normal. So the process of tariffication on the basis of 1986–88 prices was really "dirty tariffication" (Hathaway and Ingco 1997). As a result, gradual reduction in these high tariffs, as agreed under URAoA, really slows down the process of opening up on the part of the industrialized world. Replacing this entire process by a maximum cap of 50 percent will be in the interest of India and other such developing countries.

Another problem in the present agreement on tariffication relates to uneven tariff cuts across products. Tariff cuts can be undertaken in such a way that there is substantial reduction in tariffs of less-protected products with negligible cuts in tariffs for the highly protected commodities. The result is continued high border protection for several commodities by many countries. In the European Union, for instance, products such as meat, edible offal of animal origin, milk and cream, some cheese, rice, wheat flour, and bran continue to carry tariffs of over 120 percent (WTO 1997). The tendency to concentrate tariff reductions on products with relatively low protection levels, and to minimize reductions on sensitive items, such as dairy and sugar products, applies to basic and processed products alike. Consequently, the potential gains to a country like India remain elusive. India therefore must insist that the 50 percent cap is on each tariff line at HS 10-digit level.

On the issue of renegotiating for zero tariff binding, it may be recalled that under the URAoA India has basically bound its agricultural tariffs at 100 percent for raw commodities, 150 percent for processed agro-commodities, and 300 percent for edible oils. But for a number of commodities[11] the binding rates were very low and in a few cases even zero. These were owing to commitments made by India in the earlier rounds of negotiations.[12] Many of these are sensitive products (such as skim milk powder and rice, two of India's biggest agro-commodities), and it is therefore important that India renegotiates these bound rates to take them to the ceiling of 50 percent, as suggested for all agricultural products.

In conclusion, India's stand on the issue of tariffication could be twofold. First, India should strive to have the system of tariff quotas and other

NTBs abolished. Such restrictions are inimical to India's export interests and do not do justice to the commitment to increased market access. Second, along with complete tariffication India should argue for rapid reduction in the levels of tariffs (in each tariff line rather than the average tariff levels). It is in India's interest to negotiate for a maximum ceiling on tariff bindings at no more than 50 percent. This would naturally mean that India would also have to reduce its tariffs to less than 50 percent on its agricultural imports. This, though contrary to popular opinion, should not be any cause for alarm. Indian agriculture is reasonably efficient and competitive, and will emerge so even more once the domestic support to agriculture in industrialized countries is reduced/abolished.

Domestic Support

Also agreed upon was a reduction in domestic support, which is being quantified through the aggregate measurement of support (AMS). Commitments with respect to domestic support are in terms of annual and final bound rates of current total AMS specified in the member's schedule. The AMS is calculated on a product-specific basis for each basic agricultural product receiving market price support, nonexempt direct payments, or any other subsidy that is not exempted from the reduction commitment ("other nonexempt policies").

Market price support is computed as the gap between a fixed external reference price (based on years 1986–88 is the average free on board [f.o.b.] unit value in a net exporting country and the average c.i.f unit value in a net importing country) in the base year period adjusted for differences and the applied administered price multiplied by the quantity of production eligible to receive the applied administered price. Budgetary payments made to maintain this gap, such as buying-in or storage costs, are not included in the AMS. Nonexempt direct payments dependent on a price gap are computed by using the difference between the fixed reference price and the applied administered price multiplied by the quantity eligible to receive the administered price. Those nonexempt direct payments based on factors other than price are estimated by using budgetary outlays. Other nonexempt measures such as input subsidies or marketing cost reduction measures are measured by using budget outlays. Where this does not reflect the full extent of the subsidy it is calculated as the gap between the price of the subsidized good or service and its representative market price multiplied by the quantity of the good or service. Support that is nonproduct specific is totaled into one nonproduct-specific AMS in total monetary terms.

Subsidies include both budgetary outlays and revenue foregone by governments or their agents. Supports at both national and subnational

INDIA

levels are included. Specific agricultural levies or fees paid by agricultural producers are deducted from the AMS. For each basic agricultural product a specific AMS is established expressed in total monetary value terms. The AMS is calculated as close as practicable to the point of first sale of the product concerned. Those measures directed at agricultural processors are included to the extent that such measures benefit the producers of the basic agricultural products. The AMS for the base period, calculated in the manner above, constitutes the base level for the implementation of the reduction commitment on domestic support.

A country whose product specific and nonproduct specific AMS does not exceed 10 percent of the total value of agricultural product in the case of a developing country (5 percent for industrialized countries) is not subject to any reduction commitments. If, on the other hand, the AMS exceeds the de minimis level, then a developing country is committed to reduce domestic support by 13.3 percent over 10 years and 20 percent for an industrialized country over 6 years. The obligation is on total AMS and within that there is flexibility to choose products covered and extent of support measure and quantity of products that benefit from them.

Ambiguous "AMSiffication"

The procedure for estimating AMS is not foolproof. It has ambiguities. For example, should 1986–88 fixed external reference prices be used even for the years 1995–99? The legal text of the URAoA seems to suggest this, but there may not be any economic logic in that calculation when the world prices have dramatically gone up especially during 1995–97 compared to the 1986–88 period. Since world prices during 1986–88 were quite low, the estimated AMS for that period turned out to be quite high. Reducing that by 20 percent by industrialized countries over six years does not really mean anything when world prices during the mid-1990s went up. Purcell and others (1998) term this process "dirty AMSiffication." Obviously, the estimates of AMS would differ depending upon whether a fixed (1986–88) external reference price or varying reference price is used.

Developing countries like India have another problem in correctly estimating AMS because of the nature of the exchange rate regime. During 1986–88, India followed a fixed exchange rate system. The official exchange rate was about 15–20 percent below the free exchange rate. Such a situation existed in many of the developing countries suffering from a chronic shortage of foreign exchange. Depending upon which exchange rate was used, the estimates of AMS would differ.

The legal text states that the fixed external reference price is customs, insurance, and freight if the country is a net importer and f.o.b. if it is a net exporter. But what if the country were a net importer during 1986–88 but has turned out to be a net exporter during 1995–99? Should the c.i.f. price continue to be the relevant reference price, or should there be a switch to f.o.b. price? If there is a switch to f.o.b. price, should it be the 1986–88 f.o.b. price or the 1995–99 price when that country emerged as a net exporter? Furthermore, how sound is the assumption of taking each country as a price taker in the world market, especially when the country is large?

The URAoA also states that the difference between external reference price and domestic support price should be multiplied by the "quantity of production eligible for support" to estimate product-specific support. In developing countries a substantial portion of production is used for home consumption. In that case should India use total production of the commodity as the relevant quantity or the marketed surplus or the quantity actually purchased by the government agency at the support price? Whichever quantity is used in the numerator it is important to keep in mind that the same quantity is used in the denominator, or else the estimates of AMS would have problems.

In the case of nonproduct-specific support, say, for fertilizers, the issue is: Should India use the budgetary support under the title "fertilizer subsidy" or should it be estimated as the difference between external reference price (fixed or variable) and domestic price paid by the farmers? This is important in India because almost half the fertilizer subsidy shown in the budget is given to fertilizer companies (on a flat rate basis or through a retention price scheme) to cover their high costs of production compared to the import parity prices (Gulati 1999b). Is the farmer being subsidized or is the fertilizer industry?

Similar problems arise in cases of estimating nonproduct-specific support through power supplies to agriculture, canal irrigation, and rural credit. In the case of power, for example, consumption figures for the agriculture sector are worked out on a residual basis with government estimates overestimating the real consumption by a wide margin, anywhere from 20 to 80 percent, depending upon the state. In the case of canal irrigation, should India take the difference between only the O and M costs and recoveries or should it also include amortized capital costs on the cost side? In the case of rural credit, should India take only the concession in the interest rates as the relevant subsidy or also include the likely bad debts? Even if on theory, it comes to an agreement on these issues, it is difficult to obtain accurate information on many of these in developing countries. So the estimates of AMS can vary widely depending upon what definition of nonproduct-specific support is used. The text of URAoA seems to suggest using budgetary figures, but given the distortions in pricing, it may not be correct on pure economic grounds.

Finally, the URAoA (Article 6, paragraph 2) allows for exemption of support (investment subsidies as well as agricultural input subsidies) that are generally given to "low income or resource poor producers" in developing countries to encourage agricultural and rural development as an integral part of the overall development programs. It clearly states that the "domestic support meeting the criteria of this paragraph shall not be required to be included in a member's calculation of its current total AMS." This exemption clause raises a question: Who is a "low income or resource poor producer?" In a country like India, can a farmer cultivating less than 10 hectares or 4 hectares or 2 hectares be a resource-poor producer? By global income standards, even a farmer with 10 hectares of land and Indian levels of yields is perhaps a resource-poor farmer.[13]

If this is accepted, 90 percent of India's nonproduct-specific support should be exempted from AMS calculations. However, even if India were to take a conservative estimate of low income and resource-poor farmers in India, all those with four hectares or less land would fall in this category. This is the size of the holding in India that can be considered as a minimum break-even size, which is necessary for a farm family to make both ends meet. Even on this conservative basis, almost 60 percent of the nonproduct-specific support would be exempt from AMS calculations.

AMS estimates are quite fragile depending upon the treatment given to these issues. India's efforts to estimate AMS under alternative assumptions reveal that in almost all cases, in most of the years, the product-specific support to Indian agriculture is negative, the range is quite wide, anywhere from about –10 percent to –70 percent under different assumptions. The nonproduct-specific support is of course positive and varies from about 1 to 10 percent. If the product-specific and nonproduct-specific supports are added, as the term "aggregate" in AMS suggests, then Indian agriculture in most cases is having negative support or "implicit taxation."

Table 5.7 presents one such estimate of AMS, worked out on the basis of fixed external reference prices (c.i.f.), assuming India is a net importer, and exempting 60 percent of the nonproduct-specific support to account for low income and resource-poor farmers. The product-specific support turns out to be negative for most of the crops in most of the years, adding to a large negative sum, which fluctuated from about –32 percent of the value of agricultural commodities in 1987, touching the trough at –69 percent in 1992, and then recovering to –32 percent in 1997, and then again sliding to –42 percent in 1998.[14] Nonproduct-specific support amounts to 2.25 percent of agricultural produce in 1986 and 4.12 percent in 1997.

Sometimes, this negative product-specific support also raises an issue: Should it be treated as negative or zero? New Zealand objected to India's treating negative as negative. New Zealand wanted this negative product-specific support to be treated as zero. But this does not sound appropriate because nowhere in the URAoA is it stated that the negative product-

Table 5.7 Aggregate Measurement of Support to Indian Agriculture, Selected Crops, 1986–98

Year	Product-specific support	Nonproduct–specific support	Total AMS
1986	–34.29	2.25	–32.04
1987	–32.08	3.20	–28.88
1988	–35.54	3.32	–32.22
1989	–36.97	3.39	–33.58
1990	–31.78	3.36	–28.42
1991	–62.23	3.60	–58.63
1992	–69.31	3.46	–65.85
1993	–54.75	3.14	–51.61
1994	–43.27	3.40	–39.87
1995	–44.09	3.90	–40.19
1996	–45.84	3.62	–42.22
1997	–32.16	4.12	–28.04
1998 (P)	–41.89	3.49	–38.40

Note: AMS = aggregate measurement of support; P = provisional, because it uses some projected values of nonproduct-specific support owing to lack of actual data. All figures are expressed as a percentage of total value of production of selected commodities in Indian agriculture. Selected commodities include rice, wheat, maize, sorghum, bajra, gram, arhar, soyabean, rapeseed and mustard, groundnut, sunflower, and cotton, which comprise about 60 percent of the value of output in the Indian crop sector. The value of production is computed by multiplying quantity of production by applied administered price, procurement prices, or minimum support prices as the case may be.

Product-specific support is computed piecewise as the difference between the applied administered price and a fixed external reference price (of the base period 1986–88) multiplied by the quantity of production. This is aggregated over the products to get total product-specific support. For estimating product-specific support, fixed external reference prices are c.i.f. prices of the selected commodities.

Nonproduct-specific support comprises subsidies on inputs such as power, irrigation, fertilizer, and credit. Power subsidy per unit is the difference between the unit cost of power supplied to the economy and the average tariff for agricultural consumers. Credit subsidy is the amount foregone on account of concessional rates of interest on lending to the agricultural sector. Irrigation subsidy is the difference between operating and maintenance expenses and the total direct receipts of major and medium irrigation works. The fertilizer subsidy is drawn from the budgetary outlays. The nonproduct-specific support for the selected crops has been assumed to account for 0.45 of the total support of this kind to the agricultural sector (assuming that the crops considered account for 60 percent of the total value of crop sector output and that the crop sector itself accounts for 75 percent of the total value of agricultural output; the rest is dairy and livestock). Sixty percent of this is exempted under the provision of low income and resource-poor producers.

The exchange rate used in the comparison is the official exchange rate until 1992 and the Foreign Exchange Dealers of India rates thereafter.

Computations are for calendar year. Rabi crop production in a cropping year is included in the following calendar year whereas kharif production for a cropping year is included in the preceding calendar year. The former includes wheat, gram and rapeseed, and mustard. All other crops fall in the latter category.

specific support is not to be added in working out current total AMS. Moreover it does not sound rational to treat negative as zero. The developing countries with a large mass of poverty often want to keep prices of agricultural products suppressed with a view to keep food within reach of the people. But this results in lower incentives to cultivators. This then forces the governments to extend nonproduct-specific support to farmers. This is somewhat built into the structure of the economy. Therefore there is no logic in counting only the positive and treating the negative as zero, unless the structure undergoes a dramatic change.

The *Trade Policy Review of India* by WTO (1997) puts its product-specific AMS for 19 commodities in 1995–96 at US$29,518 million in the negative. As a proportion of value of production, this was –38.47 percent (WTO 1997), which is somewhat lower than reported in table 5.7 presumably due to differences in commodity coverage. In 1995–96, with the exception of sugarcane, the product-specific support for all the products considered was negative. This is mainly because domestic prices of most of these products are less than the corresponding international reference prices. India's nonproduct-specific AMS is, on the other hand, shown to be positive to the extent of 7.52 percent of the total value of agricultural production (but less than the 10 percent de minimis level for developing countries). This is somewhat higher than reported in table 5.7 because it does not exclude the support to low income and resource-poor farmers. If this adjustment is carried out, then the resulting figure would be close to what is presented in table 5.7.

"AMSiffication" Agenda

Given that India's domestic support to agriculture is negative, what could be in India's interest to take to the negotiating table?

- The ceiling for total AMS should be 40 percent. For each product separately the ceiling should be 30 percent in case of product-specific domestic support, and 10 percent for nonproduct-specific domestic support;
- Reduction commitments on domestic support ought not only be on the total AMS but also on each product-specific support separately, as well as on nonproduct-specific support. India should argue for faster reduction in individual product-specific domestic support rather than for nonproduct-specific support.
- For estimation of total AMS, both product-specific and nonproduct-specific support should be added, which the current agreement states. India must ensure that this is done even if the product-specific support is negative. (Some countries are raising the issue that negative product-specific support should be treated as zero. India must ward off such views.)

- With respect to direct payments, a clear distinction has to be made between the green box and the blue box measures. Green box measures (support to research and extension, environment, and those on equity grounds) alone should be exempt from reduction commitments. The blue box measures, on the other hand, ought to be included in the calculation of AMS and subject to reduction commitments.

Proposed Agenda: In India's Interest?

To see reasons behind the proposed agenda, India should know the level and structure of domestic support as well as this support in other countries. A review of this would automatically reveal why such a bold agenda is being proposed.

As mentioned earlier, and presented in table 5.7, AMS for Indian agriculture remains negative, despite several ambiguities in the estimation of AMS. Since it is below the de minimis 10 percent level, India has no reduction commitment with regard to either total domestic support or product-specific or nonproduct-specific support.

It would therefore be in India's interest to take a bold stand on the issue of total AMS. Currently, reduction commitments are on total AMS, which is the aggregate of product-specific AMS for a number of commodities. This implies that a country can offer substantial domestic support to one or more commodities and yet have an overall total AMS that meets the commitment levels. Reduction commitments do not, therefore, ensure that domestic support measures are free from trade-distorting effects for all commodities. Highly protected commodities such as sugar, meat, and milk show little or no liberalization. Oilseed, fruits, and vegetables, which were less protected, were further liberalized (Hathaway and Ingco 1997). The implication is that for products that have high product-specific AMS, domestic support for that product is still a trade-distorting measure. India should therefore press for reduction commitments on product-specific AMS rather total AMS, arguing for an upper ceiling of 30 percent on product-specific domestic support for any commodity.

Most major industrial countries of the OECD pursued costly trade-distorting agricultural support policies through the 1980s. The level of support to agriculture increased sharply in 1986 when the UR was launched and continued in the 1990s. This increasing trend continued until 1995, when the implementation of URAoA was to begin. For instance, in 1986–88, the producer subsidy equivalent[15] (PSE) for the OECD countries as a whole was 38 percent increasing to 41 percent in 1995. It has been declining ever since. The PSE declined to 34 percent in 1996, remaining at that level in 1997. When the OECD (excluding Hungary, Poland, the Czech Republic, Mexico, and the Republic of Korea) is considered, the PSE level has declined gradually but consistently from 45 percent in 1986–88 to 35 percent in 1996. It remained at 35 percent in 1997 as well.

Despite declines in protection and support to agriculture it remains a fact that several industrialized countries have exceedingly high protection levels. Four broad groups of countries can be identified depending on the extent of protection offered to their agricultural sectors. One group comprises European countries, particularly the countries that belong to the European Union and the European Free Trade Association (EFTA). The European Union has a level of support that is just above the OECD average. The %PSE has been significantly below the 1986–88 level only during 1999–2000. There has been a clear downward trend in market price support, especially since the early 1990s, which can be attributed in roughly equal parts to decreases in producer prices and increases in world prices expressed in ECUs (European currency). In 1997 just over half of the support was in the form of market price support, as compared to more than three-quarters in 1986–88. Direct payments have increased four-fold and now account for nearly a third of all support. The countries belonging to the EFTA have among the highest PSEs in the world. The EFTA was established in 1958 with a view to removing tariffs on goods produced in and traded among member states. The current members comprise Iceland, Norway, Switzerland, and Liechtenstein. High producer prices in these countries are maintained mainly by import restrictions and deficiency payments related to production.

Another group of countries that heavily protects its agriculture is the East Asian group particularly Japan, Korea, and Taiwan. These countries are essentially net importers of agricultural produce. Although there has been liberalization in some agricultural products in Japan, the basic food products continue to be highly protected. In fact agricultural transfers accounted for a greater proportion of GDP than that of agricultural GDP itself. The percentage of agricultural GDP to total GDP was 1.4 percent in 1995 (provisional), while estimated share of transfers in total GDP was higher at 1.8 percent. Protection has merely encouraged inefficient farms. Unlike other major trading countries, in Japan there is no discussion of fundamental reforms for the major commodities through steps to integrate Japanese agriculture with the world market. Liberalization had been restricted by 1990 to beef (which has been tariffied), apple juice, processed dairy products, and other minor products. Japan's PSE has fluctuated for most of the period since 1986–88, but showed declines in 1996 and 1997. The average producer price has developed along a slow downward path, and in 1997 was 10 percent below its 1986–88 level. Around 85 percent of support is market price support, and this share has been remarkably stable over the years.

Yet another group of countries—the United States, the Czech Republic, Hungary, Poland, and Canada—has succeeded in reducing previously high PSEs (Canada, of course, does protect certain sectors significantly). In the United States, for instance, the PSE has fallen by almost half since 1986–88. Recent developments have been marked by the shift from set-aside and deficiency payments for crops to direct income payments. In 1997 domestic prices were on average 9 percent above the world market level. Input subsidies have declined over the last decade, while expenditures on general services and subnational expenditures have increased.

Canada is a net exporter of agricultural produce and is pro-reform. However, Canada, which is also a major importer, has a high PSE and has in place an extensive income support system for its heavily protected domestically oriented agricultural sector. Its protection to import-competing products is particularly noteworthy. Despite this, Canada has striven to bring down its protection levels. This is reflected in the decline in its PSEs particularly after 1994. The downward trend in Canada's PSE was further accentuated in 1997, with the ending of the grain transportation program. Canada's 1997 %PSE is less than half that of 1986–88. The share of direct payments in total support has varied between 10 and 30 percent over the last decade, reflecting a previous practice by the Canadian government to resort to ad hoc payments and temporary payment schemes. Expenditures by provincial governments account for a quarter of the PSE.

The fourth group of countries consists of members of the net food-exporting countries of the Cairns Group.[16] These countries, particularly Australia and New Zealand, have low protection levels and strongly advocate free trade. New Zealand, with a PSE of 3 percent, provides the lowest level of support of all the OECD countries. Moreover, support has been at the same low level since 1991. More than half of the support is in the form of budget-financed general services and the remainder is from market price support resulting from sanitary import restrictions for poultry and eggs. There is close alignment between domestic and world prices. In Australia the PSE was the second lowest in the OECD area in 1997 and saw a gradual decline beginning in the late 1980s and into the 1990s, particularly after 1995. Australia has liberalized most of its agricultural sector. Controls on wheat marketing and sugar imports have been lifted. The composition of Australia's support to agriculture has changed little in the long run. Less than half of Australia's PSE is from market price support, the remainder being provided in the form of input subsidies and expenditures on infrastructure and general services. More than one-third of support is provided at the state level.

This review clearly shows that it is important for India to seek reduction in high domestic support by the industrialized countries most notably the European and the East Asian countries.

Another important issue that India must raise in the forthcoming negotiations is that of the blue box measures. Annex 2 of the URAoA details the basis for exemption of a prescribed list of measures from reduction commitments. The exemptions are of two kinds: those that are referred to as the green box measures and those that are called the blue box measures.

The green box measures essentially involve measures of the nature of funding for research, pest and disease control, training services, extension and advisory services, payments under environmental programs, payments under regional assistance programs limited to producers in disadvantaged regions, payments (made either directly or by way of government financial participation in crop insurance schemes) for relief from natural disasters, and similar forms of support.

The blue box measures refer to direct payments to producers, such as decoupled income support; that is, payments not linked to production, structural adjustment assistance provided through investment aids to compensate for the structural disadvantage through resource retirement programs, government financial participation in income insurance, and income safety-net programs. These relate to income and not to either the level of production or to prices, domestic and international.

Such a wide range of support measures that are exempt from reduction commitments thus offers enormous possibilities for member countries to alter their domestic support structure. It can be done in such a manner that there is apparent reduction in domestic support as measured by the AMS but a corresponding increase in exempt measures like direct payments of the sort mentioned above.

This is evident from the domestic support composition of the OECD countries. Market price support was the overwhelming form of support in 1997 as it was in 1986–88 followed by direct payments and other forms of support. There has, however, been a significant change in magnitudes. For the OECD overall, market price support accounted for 85 percent of all assistance. By 1997 its share was only 62 percent. In contrast to the trend in market price support, direct payments have been growing in importance. This essentially implies that market price support is being increasingly substituted for by direct payments.

Of the four groups of nations just discussed, it is the European group (the European Union and the EFTA) that has marked movements toward direct payments. Declines in the share of market price support have been matched by concomitant increase in the share of direct payments. In the practice of carrying out reforms, these countries have reduced support policies in terms of input subsidies and the system of administered prices, but maintained support to agricultural producers through increased direct payments in forms exempt from reduction commitments.

Despite a general tightening of government budgets in 1997, nearly half of the OECD countries continued to increase their direct payments in national currency terms, either through more funds for existing programs or by introducing new payment measures. The growing use of direct payments supposedly implies a shift away from production-linked measures and toward direct income payments in providing support to farmers.

While almost all direct payment measures have taken place in the context of a decline in output-related price support and have therefore improved market orientation, they have not always reduced the dependency of the agricultural sector on support. Although in terms of resource allocation these programs are supposed to achieve disassociation from production and thereby weaken the policy incentive to increase agricultural production at the margin, they end up encouraging in keeping the farmers in the industry. What these blue box payments do is to cover the fixed costs of the farmer, leaving the farmer to bear only the variable costs. This makes even the most inefficient farmers competitive. Increased production results in these countries exporting more at lower prices harming other competitors who may be more efficient producers of a commodity. The fact that several European economies, notably the EFTA countries and the European Union, are disguising trade-distorting domestic support under the blue box canopy is an issue that India must put forth in strong terms.

Export Competition

Export subsidies were subject to reduction commitments, although several kinds of direct payments were exempted. The export subsidy commitment is either in the form of budgetary outlay reduction commitments or in the form of export quantity reduction commitments.

Direct export subsidies are to be reduced by 36 percent below the 1986–88 level in the case of industrialized countries over the implementation period of six years. The quantity of subsidized exports by the industrialized countries is to be reduced by 21 percent in this period. For the developing countries, commitments involve a reduction of direct export subsidies by 24 percent and quantity of subsidized exports by 14 percent. This is to take place within the span of 10 years. The least developed countries, as before, are not subject to any reduction commitments.

The implications of export subsidies for India is easy to see. It restricts the ability of India's exports to compete with those originating in industrialized countries.

The export subsidies in the URAoA that are subject to reduction commitments include direct subsidies to agricultural producers contingent on export performance; subsidies on agricultural products contingent on their incorporation in exported products; provision on favorable terms of internal transport and freight charges on export shipments (developing countries are exempt from commitments on this form of subsidy provided that it is not used to circumvent reduction commitments); subsidies to reduce the cost of marketing exports of agricultural products excluding export promotion and advisory services (here again, developing countries are conditionally exempt from reduction commitments); sale or disposal for export of noncommercial stocks of agricultural products by the government or its agencies at a price lower than the comparable price charged for a like product by buyers in the domestic market; and payments on the export of an agricultural product that are financed by virtue of governmental action whether or not a charge on the public account is involved, including payments financed from the proceeds of a levy imposed on the agricultural product concerned or on an agricultural product from which the exported product is derived.

Export subsidies not listed (including export credits, export credit guarantees, or insurance programs) can be used, but not in a manner that results in or threatens to lead to circumvention of reduction commitments nor shall noncommercial transactions be used to circumvent such commitments.

As far as India is concerned, agricultural exporters in India do not get any direct export subsidies. India provides income tax exemptions for profits from agricultural exports under Section HHC of the Income Tax Act (India). Apart from this there are subsidies on costs of freight on export shipments of floriculture exports and also of vegetables and fruits. Since these payments are exempt from reduction commitments for developing countries India is not required to reduce these subsidies. India has however capped its export subsidies and is required to notify the WTO on its direct export subsidies once every two years.

India's concerns however lie elsewhere; that is, the high level of export subsidization by some of the industrialized countries. In the period 1986–90 the world's top five users of export subsidies for any given major product accounted for almost the total of such subsidies in the world and for almost all commitments for reduction. For example, of the total export subsidies on wheat in the world, the share of the top five users (the United States, the countries in the European Union, Canada, Turkey, and Hungary) was 95 percent. For rice the figure was 100 percent, and those subsidizing their rice exports most were Indonesia, the European Union, Uruguay, the United States, and Colombia. For most of the products, the European Union is the largest user of export subsidies particularly for sugar and dairy (Hathaway and Ingco 1997).

India's Proposed Agenda for Export Subsidies

It would be in India's interest to demand:

- Complete elimination of export subsidies by the industrialized countries, particularly the European Union (the dairy sector in particular) and Eastern Europe.
- Press for a line-by-line reduction commitment on export subsidies if India cannot succeed in getting all export subsidies eliminated. At present, the chief drawback of the rules on export subsidy is that commitments are defined over commodity aggregates rather than over individual lines.
- Savings in export subsidies in one year, in monetary terms or quantity terms, must not be permitted to be carried over to the next year.

Today, despite reduction commitments on export subsidies, several industrialized countries continue to make extensive use of export subsidies as has been in the past.

Even though the high world prices during the past few years have made the export subsidy limits less constraining, especially for grains, a number of countries reached their permitted subsidy limits for some commodities in 1997. Many times unused subsidy allowances from previous years were used to permit subsidized exports in excess of the annual limit. While carryover is part of the agreement, it could reduce the effect of the discipline over the implementation period. The European Union exhausted the allowable volume (but not the budgetary) limits for subsidized exports of cheese, was close to the limit for beef, but remained well under the limits for butter and skim milk powder.

Between 1996 and 1997 export refunds for cheese were reduced by 23 percent for processed cheese and between 14 and 45 percent for other types of cheese (OECD 1998). But refunds for butter increased by 18.8 percent, 16.7 percent for skim milk powder, and 4.6 percent for the whole-milk powder. Since August 1997, however, export refunds for all dairy products were reduced by 5 percent. Export subsidy allowances for some commodities were rolled over from previous years, particularly for beef. As a result of lower world prices, the European Union reinstated export subsidies for grains. In the United States no export subsidies were paid for crops, but those for dairy products increased sharply.

Export subsidies have been less important for processed than for basic agricultural products in the past. The export subsidy commitments under the URAoA constrain exports of certain food products containing subsidized agricultural raw materials, such as those incorporating dairy components, sugar, and cereals. Some countries have resorted to greater use of arrangements allowing duty-free entry of agricultural raw materials for processing if the final products are re-exported (OECD 1998).

India's Negotiating Strategy: A Review

What does this review of the three basic clauses of URAoA say in terms of a possible negotiating strategy for India during the next round? First, as a negotiating strategy for URAoA, India should start from a position of strength because it is not distorting its agriculture to the extent the industrialized world is. Agriculture is reasonably efficient in the global context, and if it could streamline its domestic policies then it has potential to gain from the emerging world scenario.

India must demand removal of all distortions in agricultural policies ranging from quotas to domestic support, not only at product aggregate levels but also at product-specific levels of ITC-HS 10-digit classification. This would expose the extremely high levels of protection on certain commodities used by some industrialized countries. The major thrust of the tariffication or "AMSiffication" agenda should be to move from product aggregates to product specifics, and to put a ceiling of no more than 50 percent in case of tariffs and 30 percent in case of AMS on any commodity.

Second, in terms of India's allies it appears that India's interests would be closer to the overall interests of the Cairns Group, and the ones that are in line with the basic spirit behind the WTO rules. From India's standpoint, therefore, it would pay to support or join the Cairns Group. The Indian sugar industry has seen this as an opportunity. Without the formal backing of the Indian government, the sugar industry declared that it will join with the members of the Cairns Group in demanding abolition of sugar quotas as well as subsidies being given in the industrialized countries (*Economic Times* 1999). It is the first time that any Indian industry has taken an independent stand in the context of negotiations. The sugar industry hopes that with the Cairns Group as a formidable fourth power (after the United States and the European Union) it can succeed in securing provisions that would unshackle and open up sugar markets in industrialized countries (the United States and the European Union, in particular). Similar views have been expressed by the Indian dairy industry through industry associations. These are steps in the right direction, and it is to India's benefit to align with the Cairns Group and through greater bargaining power demand for genuine liberalization of agricultural markets.

Food Security and the New Trade Agenda

Trade liberalization in agriculture is going to be slow, whether it is in the case of Japan, the European Union, or India. Food is a sensitive item, and given an option, most countries would like to produce a major part of their needs, and trade only at the margin. In fact, most of the industrialized countries want to be self-sufficient and also be net exporters, no matter what the costs are. It is this desire and pursuit of self-sufficiency in food that creates economic distortions in production of agricultural commodities around the world. As was discussed, Switzerland, Norway, Japan, and Korea heavily subsidized their agriculture by almost 70 percent of the value of agricultural produce in 1997. The European Union subsidizes by more than 40 percent, Canada by 20 percent, and the United States by about 16 percent.

Trade liberalization under WTO, *if it succeeds*, aims to contain and cut those costs and promote more efficient use of resources at the global level. Theoretically, it is feasible to do so given the revolutionary developments in information technology and transportation during the last couple of decades. But, given the concerns of the past, many countries may not be willing to trade food security, despite the high costs of production or stockpiling of food. They would do better to tread with caution. The Indian position on food security is no different. In fact several net importing countries, particularly the developing and the underdeveloped, have already voiced their concern over food security. The URAoA acknowledges this to be a legitimate concern stating that countries "may experience negative effects in terms of the availability of adequate supplies of basic foodstuffs from external sources on reasonable terms and conditions, including short-term difficulties in financing normal levels of commercial imports of basic foodstuffs."[17]

India's Apprehensions

What are India's apprehensions with regard to liberalization of agricultural trade, especially in foodgrains and food security? First, because India is a large country it would disturb the world markets unduly. The world prices will probably increase on India's entry as an importer, and dip when India exports. Second, spikes and troughs in world prices of basic foodgrains such as rice and wheat, transcending to domestic markets, would hit the poor consumers and producers badly. Third, liberalization of trade in agriculture will induce farmers to shift from cereals to cash crops, and thereby create scarcity of food in the country at a macro scale, which is not desirable.

So the prescription may be to not put much reliance on world markets for food, hold large stocks under government control, and ensure that farmers keep producing foodgrains in sufficient quantities. Driven by these apprehensions, an idea was floated in government circles that India should ask the WTO or the Food and Agriculture Organization to pay for the cost of holding food stocks in India for the sake of global food security. It also emphasized the need to insulate domestic food markets from world markets through canalization, by retaining the monopoly of the Food Corporation of India (FCI) to import foodgrains.

Another idea that was discussed concerned asking for exclusion of domestic support to farmers in developing countries from any reduction commitments to ensure food security. In fact India has already raised concerns regarding food security, and said, that "the developing countries need to be allowed to provide domestic support in the agricultural sector to meet the challenges of food security and to be able to preserve the viability of rural employment, as different from trade distortive support and subsidies presently permitted by the Agreement."

Many of these concerns and prescriptions appear legitimate, but a deeper probe reveals that these concerns are overly cautious and involve huge costs, and therefore may not be worth pursuing. It may be better to look for alternative instruments that are more cost effective in protecting the interests of the poor than the existing instruments.

For instance, the world market for wheat is about 100 million tons, and normally India imports/exports less than 3 million tons. It does not disturb the world market in any major way. If India enters with a demand of 10–15 million tons of wheat imports, in the short run it will disrupt the world market. But, if India stays in the market as a large and regular importer, the supply response will come in the medium run, and markets will find a new equilibrium.

In the case of rice, where the world market is about 22 million tons, India's entry with 5 million tons of imports or exports may create a big response in the world market. This argument is valid because India and China are not fully aligned with world rice markets as yet, and their domestic prices are anywhere between 20 and 40 percent below world prices.

Supposing that these two countries gradually align their domestic markets with world markets, then the small world market of 22 million tons today becomes a market of more than 200 million tons tomorrow. It is like a sea, and a few million tons of imports/exports will cause only ripples, which will be passed on with the ever running waves. Thus, integration of domestic markets with world markets is likely to contain the wild fluctuations by simply enlarging the size of market.

Sugar is another case where freer trade will contain fluctuations in world prices when compared to the situation that prevails at present. But sometimes, even in a sea there are high tides that may hit the large mass of poverty. And it is this concern, quite a legitimate one, that India needs to worry about. Is keeping huge stocks in the name of food security an answer to this problem? What is the cost of food security policies being followed today? Are there some other alternative instruments that are more cost effective in achieving food security? In order to respond to these questions, it is essential to understand the framework within which India's food security system operates.

Modus Operandi of India's Food Security System

There are basically four dimensions of India's food security system:

- Public procurement of foodgrains through fixing of a minimum support/procurement price. This provides some element of security to farmers and induces them to sustain production levels.
- Public distribution system, which is a system of delivery of cheap food that is supposed to protect consumers against volatility of prices. For most of the period of its existence, since 1939, it never had poor people as its target group. Efforts are now on to target that group.
- Storage and buffer stock operations, where the Indian government maintains food stocks in keeping with the requirements of a prescribed minimum norm for buffer stocking. This minimum stock is supposed to take care of food security in case of any number of national emergencies. An operational stock is required to supply the public distribution system. And there is a market intervention stock for release of goods into the open market to help moderate the open market prices.
- Regulation of trade in foodgrains in the form of legal controls on hoarding and aspects of internal trade, such as zoning or levy. This is apart from the restrictions on external trade.

Both the federal and the state governments participate in the procurement and distribution of foodgrains. Direct interventions in the foodgrains market are through the FCI acting on behalf of the federal government.

The procurement operations of wheat, paddy, and coarse grains are voluntary, at least in theory.[18] Farmers sell grain to the FCI or state agencies at a minimum support price fixed by the government on the basis of yearly recommendations of the Commission for Agricultural Costs and Prices. Rice is collected by way of statutory levies on rice millers and dealers. State governments fix the percentage levy with the approval of the federal government and varies from 75 percent in the Punjab and Haryana to 50 percent in Andhra and 25 percent in Karnataka.[19] The procurement of rice depends therefore on the amount of paddy milled by rice millers or dealers so that no targets for procurement can be fixed. Levies are used for sugar as well. Sugar is bought from the mills at a levy price less than the open market price at which the rest of the sugar is sold. The levy on sugar mills is 40 percent, with some relief for new mills.

The FCI carries out the storage, movement, and distribution of the procured output. Beside this, some states have food and civil supply corporations or cooperative marketing agencies that purchase and sell on behalf of the FCI. Most of the procured output is supplied to the states at a uniform issue price for their public distribution system. It is the FCI that issues foodgrains to the public distribution system based on federal government–prescribed allocations. The state governments draw on their quotas from the FCI and distribute them to buyers through a network of fair price shops. Foodgrains are also allocated from the federal pool as part of the remuneration to various employment programs (including those undertaken off-season) and relief works during times of drought and floods. Therefore, apart from supplies to the public distribution system, the FCI also provides foodgrains to the states for antipoverty programs such as the Jawahar Rozgar Yojana.

Cost of the Present Food Security System

Since food security is the motivation for India's tightly controlled agricultural markets particularly for cereals, any discussion of the former is inextricably linked to the latter. It is therefore relevant to discuss cost of food security in terms of the costs of government intervention in agricultural markets.

The direct budgetary cost of this whole system of governmental intervention in agricultural markets is measured as the food subsidy. Food subsidy is essentially the gap between the economic cost of the FCI and the average realization by the FCI based on the issue prices of the public distribution system. The issue price of the FCI is usually less than the cost incurred by it and this difference is met by the federal government.

It is true that India's food subsidy has been rising over the decades, and this was a continuing trend even in the 1990s (table 5.8). The subsidy per quintal of rice has increased from Rs139.11 in 1991–92 to as high as Rs419.62 in 1998–99. The increase is even more dramatic for wheat: from Rs131.46 per quintal in 1991–92 to Rs474.82 per quintal in 1998–99 (table 5.9). The

Table 5.8 Foodgrain Subsidy, 1991–99

Fiscal year	Subsidy (Rs million)
1991–92	2,850
1992–93	2,800[a]
1993–94	5,537
1994–95	5,100[a]
1995–96	5,377[a]
1996–97	6,066[a]
1997–98	7,500
1998–99	9,000

a. Includes sugar subsidy.
Note: Rs = rupees.
Source: Government of India (1999b).

Table 5.9 Subsidy on Rice and Wheat: Food Corporation of India, 1991–99

Fiscal year	Economic cost (per quintal)		FCI average sales realization (per quintal)		Consumer subsidy (per quintal)	
	Rice	Wheat	Rice	Wheat	Rice	Wheat
1991–92	390.79	497.04	251.68	365.58	139.11	131.46
1992–93	504.10	585.27	279.63	442.40	224.74	142.87
1993–94	532.03	665.10	355.88	500.42	176.15	164.68
1994–95	551.17	694.71	407.89	600.75	143.28	93.96
1995–96	583.95	762.82	411.94	613.34	172.01	149.48
1996–97	640.16	847.69	433.20	610.57	206.96	237.12
1997–98	800.50	940.40	395.87	610.80	404.63	329.60
1998–99	807.95	1076.00	388.33	601.18	419.62	474.82

Note: FCI = Food Corporation of India.
Source: Government of India (1999b).

increase was substantial in the latter half of the 1990s. The trend in food subsidy represents an increasing fiscal burden on the government. Price controls ensure a basic floor price to the farmer, but these prices have also been maintained to keep the government's food subsidy low. Since 1994–95 the government has been trying to align domestic prices of wheat and rice at least with their export parity levels. This has led to increases in the minimum support price. But not allowing commensurate increases in the issue prices has resulted in significant increases in government expenditure on food subsidies. It is doubtful whether this growing food subsidy can be sustained fiscally for too long.

Of particular importance to the growing costs to the FCI is the excessive build up of stocks. Indian policymakers have devised some norms, which vary from 18 million tons on October 1 to 24 million tons on July 1, for keeping some minimum stock of foodgrains in the name of food security.[20] These stocks feed the public distribution system as well as keep a buffer for any emergency. The actual stocks with the government, however, on an average for the last five years, are about 50 percent higher than these norms (table 5.10), entailing a cost of about Rs90 billion in excess of the norms. This is a huge cost borne ultimately by the taxpayers for uneconomic management of food stock policy. It is this mismanagement of buffer stocking policy that leads to diseconomies of scale in the operations of FCI (Gulati et al. 1996). Asking the WTO or the Food and Agriculture Organization to bear such costs of inefficiency is being too naïve in negotiations. Such a policy leads to embarrassing mountains of foodgrains on the one hand and stark poverty on the other.

Table 5.10 Central Foodgrain Stocks and Minimum Buffer Stocks, 1994–99 (million metric tons)

Beginning of the month	Norms			
	Wheat		Rice	
	Minimum	Actual	Minimum	Actual
July 1994	13.1	17.5	9.2	13.3
July 1995	13.1	19.2	9.2	16.4
July 1996	13.1	14.1	9.2	12.9
July 1997	13.1	11.4	9.2	11.0
July 1998	13.1	16.5	9.2	12.0
July 1999 (P)	14.3	22.5	9.2	11.0

Note: P = provisional.
Source: Government of India (1999b).

Table 5.11 Foodgrain Allocation and Offtake under the Public Distribution System and the Targeted Public Distribution System, 1991–99 (million tons)

	Wheat		Rice	
Year	Allocation	Offtake	Allocation	Offtake
1991–92	10.36	8.83	11.36	10.17
1992–93	9.25	7.85	11.48	9.69
1993–94	9.56	6.09	12.41	9.10
1994–95	10.91	5.11	13.32	8.01
1995–96	11.32	5.81	14.61	9.75
1996–97	10.71	9.35	15.10	12.04
1997–98	10.11	7.08	12.83	9.90
1998–99	8.36	5.14	10.76	7.07

Note: Provisional allocation up to January 1999; offtake up to November 1998.
Source: Government of India (1999b).

The buildup of stocks is often linked to high procurement prices and rising issue prices. In fact, a comparison of the quantities of foodgrain allocation to the public distribution system and the offtake (table 5.11) reveals that the offtake from the public distribution system has been consistently below the allocated quantities right through the 1990s. The implications of excess stock are easy to see. The storage of these excess stocks unnecessarily increases the share of carrying costs. Of the total economic cost of the FCI only 12.26 percent was accounted for by carrying costs in 1992–93. By 1994–95 it accounted for 44.09 percent of the total economic cost, and in later years it is likely to be even more.

Cost Effectiveness of the Public Distribution System

When considering the working of the public distribution system, there are serious inefficiencies here as well. Faulty targeting in terms of leakage to the nonpoor, regional mistargeting, leakage of supplies to the open market, and the cost-ineffectiveness of the transfer of income through the public distribution system are issues that have been discussed by many.[21] In terms of economic cost of this type of public distribution system to transfer income to the poor, it is one of the highest. Studies have shown that in order to transfer one rupee worth of income support to the poor, it costs Rs5.37 through the public distribution system, Rs6.35 through the Andhra rice scheme, Rs2.28 through the Jawahar Rozgar Yojana, Rs1.85 through Maharashtra's Employment Guarantee Scheme, and Rs1.80 through Integrated Child Development Services (Dev and Ranade 1999). Given this cost profile of several programs aimed at providing food security, it is worth rethinking the present structure of the public distribution system with a view to achieve food security in a cost effective manner.

Trade Liberalization, Crop Diversification, and Food Security

Food security in terms of producing cereals more than the effective demand is not going to be a problem in India, at least for the next 10 years, even under liberalized agriculture. In fact it was under insulated agriculture in the late 1980s and early 1990s when high protection accorded to edible oils/oilseed led to a shifting of about 7 million hectares away from cereals and other crops to oilseed when problems emerged on the cereal front. Starting with the rationalization of protection in edible oils in 1994–95, and carrying it through 1999, protection on edible oils has been largely removed. The present import duty on edible oils is just 15 percent, with a notable exception of coconut oil. This has led to a surge in imports of edible oils of about 3.5 million tons during the oil year 1998–99 (October–September), which is more than 30 percent of the domestic requirement. On the other hand, during 1994–95 to 1998–99, wheat and rice prices have been given a sizeable lift to come near to their export parity levels. The result is that the relative incentive structure has now been corrected in favor of cereals.

As a result, it can be expected that the expansion in the oilseed area will slow down and may partially revert back to cereals. Enhanced incentives to cereals are likely to increase cereal production, as is demonstrated by the 1998–99 foodgrain production, which surpassed 200 million tons, the highest ever in the history of India, leading to bulging stocks with the FCI. Thus, it appears that having largely removed the distortion in pricing of edible oils in relation to cereals, India is now likely to remain comfortable on the cereal front, provided reasonable investments keep flowing to the agricultural sector.[22]

The real problem of food security, however, is of economic access to food. And to solve that problem, the solution should be sought not in following a restrictive trade or price policy but in a well-defined income support policy, be it employment generation programs, restructuring of the existing public distribution system targeted toward the poor, or introduction of inflation indexed food stamps. On the trade front, introduction of futures markets, nonrestrictive trade, using tariffs whenever needed, allowing the private sector to hold stocks, and import/export freely in competition with the parastatal will better serve the purpose of food security, and will be economically more efficient than the existing system. Government intervention should be through the instrument of tariffs, and that too should be at the margin. But most of these policy issues belong to the domestic domain, and may increasingly come in conflict with external policies as agriculture proceeds under the WTO's new rules.

Other Issues for the Millennium Round

The issues of tariffication (market access), domestic support, export subsidy, and food security are by no means the only issues that will come up in the new round of negotiations. There are several other issues, such as sanitary and phytosanitary measures, intellectual property rights, and the issue of state trading enterprises, that have powerful implications for Indian agriculture. These are just touched upon because these issues also need better preparation on the part of the negotiators.

Sanitary and Phytosanitary Measures

Sanitary and phytosanitary measures refer to any measures that are undertaken to protect the life or health of plants, animals, and humans within the territory of a member country from risks that arise from the entry, establishment, or spread of pests, diseases, and disease-causing or disease-carrying organisms or to prevent or limit other damage within the territory of the member country from entry, establishment, or spread of pests (WTO 1995b).

Sanitary and phytosanitary measures include all relevant laws, decrees, regulations, requirements, and procedures including inter alia product criteria, processes and methods of production, testing, inspection, certification and approval procedures, quarantine treatments including relevant requirements associated with the transport of animals and plants, risk assessment methods and procedures, and packaging and labeling requirements directly related to food safety.

According to the Agreement on the Application of Sanitary and Phytosanitary Measures (Article 2), members have a right to take sanitary and phytosanitary measures deemed necessary for the protection of human, plant, and animal life. These must be based on scientific principles and supported with scientific evidence. Such measures must not constitute a disguised restriction on international trade and must not discriminate between members where similar conditions prevail, including between their own territory and that of other members. The Agreement also states that the members shall harmonize their sanitary or phytosanitary measures in accordance with certain common international standards, guidelines, and recommendations wherever possible.

While there is a risk that trade liberalization could increase the spread of plant and animal diseases into other countries, enhancing the need for appropriate regulation, there is also a risk that necessary regulation for food safety or environmental purposes might act as NTBs. In order that this does not happen, the following steps need to be taken:

- Harmonization of regulations, as well as the protection of intellectual property rights and labels of origin.
- Alignment and simplification of regulations within countries will facilitate these efforts. Some of the new regulatory issues can also be addressed through industry-led quality schemes.
- Transparent and science-based risk analysis as the basis for regulation.

This particular provision has important ramifications for India's exports. The need is therefore to invest in infrastructure in food-processing and related industries and to tighten laws to ensure that products meet international sanitary and phytosanitary standards, and to guard against its misuse by importing countries. It is ironic to note that the progress in this direction has been slow in India. And it will soon be the situation that many of India's agro-exports will face problems on this front. Already this problem has surfaced in India's horticultural products.

India, which produces almost 60 percent of the world's mangoes, cannot export them to the United States because the United States requires vaporized heat treatment of mangoes, and until recently India did not have this facility in the country. India's grape exports often are criticized owing to high pesticide residues. Even egg powder exports suffer from pesticide residues that are said to have traveled through maize feed. It is likely that India's dairy exports will also receive similar complaints. Peanut exports in 1999 are said to have been affected, compared to 1998, primarily owing to a high degree of aflatoxin. Solutions to these problems require a better understanding of the role of the Codex Alimentarius Commission, upgrading of production, and post-harvest technologies, keeping in mind the food safety standards that prevail at the global level. This would require not only large investments but also education among producers, processors, and exporters, and it is going to be a long drawn out effort on the part of the developing world.

The developing countries may ask for a longer period for its implementation, but it is unlikely that lower standards of sanitary and phytosanitary measures will be acceptable to the industrialized world. A better option for the developing world would be to ask for the technology at concessional rates to help achieve these standards at an early date.

Intellectual Property Rights

It is perhaps in this area that developing countries are most disadvantaged. This has been mainly due to the "patent illiteracy" of these countries when the Trade-Related Aspects of Intellectual Property Rights (TRIPS)

Agreement was formulated. It is crucial for India to ensure that developing country interests are not adversely affected on account of lack of preparedness.

There are eight sections in the Agreement of Intellectual Property Rights. They comprise copyright and related rights, trademarks, geographical indications, industrial designs, patents, protection of undisclosed information, control of anticompetitive practices in contractual licenses, and layout designs of integrated circuits. Of particular importance for the agricultural sector are the sections on geographical indications and patents.

Geographical indications are indications that identify a good as originating in the territory of a member or a region or locality in that territory where a given quality, reputation, or other characteristic of the good is essentially attributable to its geographical origin. Members shall provide the legal means for interested parties to prevent the use of any means in the designation or the presentation of a good that indicates or suggests that the good in question originates in a geographical area other than the true place of origin in a manner that misleads the public as to the geographical origin of the good (TRIPS Article 22, Section 3).

TRIPS Article 27 states that patents shall be available for any inventions, whether products or processes, in all fields of technology, provided that they are new, involve an inventive step, and are capable of industrial application. What can be excluded from patentability are diagnostic, therapeutic, and surgical methods for the treatment of humans or animals, plants and animals other than microorganisms, and essentially biological processes for the production of plants or animals other than nonbiological and microbiological processes. But members shall provide for the protection of plant varieties either by patents or by an effective *sui generis* system or by any combination thereof. Article 28 confers the owner of such patents the following exclusive rights: Where the patent is for a product, a patent holder has the right to prevent third parties without the owner's consent from making, using, selling, offering for sale, or importing for these purposes that product. Where the subject matter is a process, the patent holder has the right to prevent third parties without the owner's consent from the acts of using, offering for sale, selling, or importing for these purposes at least the product directly obtained by that process.

There are indications that these two clauses in the agreement have powerful implications for developing countries like India. For instance, people in India and Pakistan were surprised when they found that a Texas-based company got a patent to sell basmati rice in the United States, especially since the name "basmati" has been associated with the aromatic variety of rice grown in the foothills of northern Uttar Pradesh, the Punjab (in India and in Pakistan), and Haryana. So the patenting of U.S. rice as *basmati* was in direct conflict with Article 22 of TRIPS, which gives members the right to protect geographical indicators. But the argument made by Rice Tec was that *basmati* is a generic name. This lead to litigation. Similarly, W. R. Grace and Co. got a patent for the "anti-fungal properties" of neem and was selling neem oil in Europe. A petition was filed against this patent saying that this property of neem has been known in India for centuries and local people have been using neem as a cheap source of medicine. Similar cases are expected, such as for tamarind, turmeric, bitter gourd, and even brinjal (eggplant). And more will come in the years to follow.

This raises a fundamental question: Can the industrialized countries patent produce of agriculture or their special properties, which are known and have been used in the developing world for a long time but have not been recorded in any legal system? While it would take years, if not decades, before this issue is appropriately settled, India's immediate concern with regard to TRIPS should be twofold. On the one hand, India needs to take stock of its indigenous plant knowledge, codify it, and protect it through an appropriate domestic law to ensure that indigenous producers are adequately protected and no one preempts India in patenting what is due to producers in India. The other is to keep check on violations of provisions, such as geographical indications, so that India's export potential is not undermined.

It becomes a challenging task for any developing country when it comes to framing laws to protect plant varieties (or their medicinal uses). The time frame given to developing countries to implement this was January 1, 2000. However, the implementation period has been extended.

India seems to be heading toward a *sui generis* system to give protection to plant varieties as well as to rights of farmers, communities, and breeders. The proposed legislation was expected to be brought to the Parliament before the end of 1999. However, legislation is still pending. The basic guiding principles behind this legislation are likely to be the following:

- A variety can be protected/patented if it clears the "DUS testing" (that is, it can be proved that the variety seeking protection is "distinct, uniform, and stable."
- A new organization, for instance, a "Plant Varieties and Farmers' Rights Protection Authority," may be created for testing and registration of all such new varieties.
- Legislation to ensure farmers' rights may give full freedom to farmers to save, use, exchange, share, and sell their farm produce of the protected variety. The only restriction on the farmers is that they cannot sell these seeds under any commercial brand in the market. Farmers' rights are likely to be given priority in Indian legislation, because it recognizes farmers' contributions over centuries in saving, conserving, and improving these seeds, which they would do even in the future.

- Legislation may involve some methods of sharing the benefits with communities to recognize the contribution of communities and groups of farmers in conserving and improving plant varieties through the selection process.
- Legislation to recognize the contribution of past researchers as well as those likely to come will give free access to researchers to use the protected varieties for further research.
- Legislation to reward the breeders in governmental research institutions may come up with some "benefit sharing" scheme between the breeders and the institutions.
- Legislation to ensure proper accounting may propose compulsory licensing of all protected plant varieties with the proposed authority.

While it is expected that such a *sui generis* system may give enough incentives to breeders and private companies to do research, it will take a long time before this issue of TRIPS can be amicably settled. The coming years will witness attempts at bio-piracy and increased litigation. The developing world, which is bio-rich but resource poor, will have to be on the alert.

State Trading Enterprises

State trading enterprises (STEs) are understood to include "governmental and nongovernmental enterprises, including marketing boards, which have been granted exclusive or special rights or privileges, including statutory or constitutional powers, in the exercise of which they influence through their purchases or sales the level or direction of imports or exports."

To ensure transparency in the activity of STEs members are required to notify such enterprises to the Council for Trade in Goods for review by the Working Party to be set up on behalf of the Council for Trade in Goods. STEs can be operated in a way that creates serious obstacles to trade, and this demands that there be some sort of regulation and negotiation that are mutually advantageous to reduce those barriers to free international trade. Whenever a member country maintains a state enterprise or grants exclusive or special privileges (formally or in effect) to any enterprise, the enterprise shall in its sale and purchase involving exports and imports use the principle of nondiscriminatory treatment. It shall act based on such commercial considerations as price, quality, availability, marketability, transportation, and other conditions of sale and purchase and shall afford other enterprises adequate opportunity to compete for participation in such purchases or sales (Article XVII, GATT 1947).

Imports of products for immediate or ultimate consumption by the government and not otherwise for resale or use in the production of goods for sale are outside the purview of this Agreement. A member that may have reason to believe that its interest is being undermined by the operations of an STE in another member country can request the latter to supply information about its operations related to the carrying out of the provisions of this agreement.

In India, the biggest concern in this regard is for the FCI, which has a monopoly on imports of foodgrains, and does not give equal opportunity to other competing parties in imports as well as in domestic procurement. The levies on rice and sugar are just two examples of violation of the principle of "equal opportunity to competing parties." Further, the FCI does not really work on commercial principles. Its economic losses get concealed under the title "food subsidy." Given the provisions of WTO, the modus operandi of the FCI may come up for review. Besides, as QRs on imports of foodgrains are abolished, and private parties allowed to import foodgrains, the operations of the FCI may become increasingly incompatible with the WTO provisions. It is better for India to begin early action in this area to align its functioning on WTO provisions. This will help India prune the FCI, which is also in the interest of the people of India, notwithstanding stiff opposition from the FCI employees. But to make the FCI compatible with WTO provisions, India will need a strategy for restructuring its safety net, especially the public distribution systems. As mentioned in the section on food security, it may be worth introducing food stamps in urban areas, and launching the Employment Guarantee Scheme in rural areas for constructing infrastructure. Such measures will be more cost effective in providing income support to the poor, and then it may be somewhat easier to trim the FCI.

There are some other STEs that also may come up for review one day: the State Trading Corporation, the Mineral and Metals Trading Corporation, the National Agricultural Cooperative Marketing Federation of India, and some commodity boards, such as the Coffee Board. India needs to undertake a thorough review of the functioning of these commodity boards to ensure that they are compatible in the new unfolding environment under WTO.

Conclusion:
Reform Domestic Policies for Smooth Transition

- Ensure free movement of all agricultural commodities across the country. Abolish movement restrictions by the federal government as well as by the states, often imposed under the Essential Commodities Act.
- Abolish government levies on all agri-products, such as rice, sugar, and molasses.
- Abolish Maharashtra's cotton monopoly procurement scheme.

- Abolish stocking limits on private trade and allow and encourage investments by the private sector in creating modernized bulk handling and stocking facilities.
- Abolish all selective credit controls on private trade for stocking.
- Abolish the ban on futures markets for the remaining agri-commodities (the introduction of futures markets in cotton and edible oils and oilseed is a welcome step).
- Abolish or prune the Essential Commodities Act.
- Abolish the small-scale industry reservation for all agro-products (most notably in the edible oils industry).
- Abolish the remaining licensing controls on the agro-processing industry, most notably the Milk and Milk Products Order (de-licensing of the sugar industry is highly welcome and a bold step).
- Abolish the retention price scheme in the fertilizer industry.
- Restructure the public distribution systems to cater only to the poor and introduce food stamps in metropolitan areas.
- Resurrect and enlarge the Tariff Commission to encompass the Bureau of Industrial Costs and Practices, the Commission for Agricultural Costs and Prices, and antidumping offices (this would help in a smooth transition of domestic price policy to take into account the global price matrix).
- Ensure sanitary and phytosanitary standards in agricultural products and strengthen the legal framework for it and also its enforcement.
- Create and implement a legal framework to give due protection to intellectual property rights in agriculture research.

India, like many other developing countries, has had heavy government intervention in the functioning of the economy, including agriculture. Although agriculture has been the biggest private sector enterprise, it is also ridden with restrictive government policies, which are likely to become incompatible with the emerging scenario under WTO. If appropriate changes in domestic policies are not carried out in time, then it is likely to lead to higher economic costs and greater pains in restructuring.

Some policies need the urgent attention of policymakers with a view to minimizing the pains of restructuring and to maximizing gains. An agenda to change many of these domestic policies has been suggested based on the research work done earlier. It is the delay in undertaking domestic policy reforms that often leads to strong opposition to external liberalization. Here it is presumed that globalization of agriculture is going to be a reality, though it will take some time, and may have quite a few problems. It is against this backdrop that the domestic policy contradictions are listed here, and some changes proposed.

In conclusion, as far as India's negotiating stand at the next round is concerned, it is important to realize that it should negotiate from a position of strength. To this end there must be a greater interaction between the government and the industry and academics. To maximize the benefits that India can get out of the forthcoming negotiations, India needs to be an active participant rather than a passive spectator because India has much more to gain than to lose, at least in agriculture. But strength of arguments in the negotiations depends upon how well decisions are reached and how well a country uses its strengths and acumen when dealing with other countries, both those countries that have similar interests and those countries that do not.

Endnotes

1. There is a one commodity group where the commitment is offered for a subgroup of HS 4-digit level.
2. Tariff rates for India are defined at HS 6-digit level.
3. Similarly, the ACD is subject to various exemption notifications.
4. The level of applied tariff rates (if different from statutory rates) in most of the other countries is higher than the corresponding level of statutory rates.
5. Without taking ACD, SCD, and SAD.
6. This analysis did not consider a few commodities because the definition of HS codes at 6-digit level changed from the pre-UR round period to the post-UR period.
7. Except for those commodities, which are subject to ceiling binding.
8. WTO (1999).
9. The detail of India's import policy is published in Government of India (1998) at regular intervals. This document defines the import policy of all the products (or national lines) at HS 8-digit or 10-digit level Indian Trade Classification. At present, the import policy is defined for around 10,280 products (or national lines).
10. If there are doubts, consider the domestic prices in some of these countries at the beginning of URAoA. In South Korea, in 1995, the domestic prices for soybeans was 720 percent higher than the world prices. For barley, the figure was 419 percent; maize and beef prices within Korea were 343 percent and 309 percent of the world prices, and for rice the figure was 286 percent (WTO 1997). The situation was not very different even in 1999.
11. The products for which tariffs are bound at 0 percent are milk (in powder, granules or other solid forms, of a fat content, by weight, not exceeding 1.5 percent), milk (not containing added sugar or other sweetening matter), spelt wheat, rice (in the husk, paddy or rough, husked-brown, semi-milled or wholly milled, broken), grain sorghum, and millet.
12. Zero tariff bindings for some commodities like rice, plums, fresh grapes, and dried skim milk were committed in 1947 (Geneva Protocol 1947); maize, millet, and spelt were bound at zero at the Torquay Protocol, 1951; sorghum at the Geneva Protocol in the Dillon Round, 1962.

13. The average yield of foodgrains in India, which dominate the Indian cropping patterns, is less than 2 tons per hectare. Assuming the average yield to be 2 tons, and an average price of Rs5,500 per ton in 1999–2000, and out-of-pocket expenses at about 50 percent of the gross revenue, the net income per hectare turns out to be Rs5,500. Given a crop intensity of 1.3, a 10 hectare plot can get an annual net income of Rs71,500 (Rs5,500 × 1.3 × 10 = Rs71,500). Given an average family size of at least five in rural areas, this translates to a per capita income of Rs14,300 or just US$329 at the rate of Rs43.5 to a US dollar.

14. It is assumed that India is a net exporter of some commodities, especially, for instance, rice, so the product-specific support would be different (less negative) as the reference price would be f.o.b. and not c.i.f. Nevertheless, it still remains negative, and on the whole the AMS also turns out to be negative.

15. PSEs are aggregate measures of support. PSEs summarize the effects of different forms of governmental programs and intervention in a single number. This method is superior to other tools like nominal or effective rates of protection since these often account for only a small proportion of the transfers between the government and the producers of agricultural commodities.

PSEs can be represented in many forms depending on the sort of comparison to be made. Two in particular are appropriate and suitable for cross-country comparisons. The first measure divides the PSE by the value to the producers and is multiplied by 100 to get the percentage PSEs. It presents the PSEs relative to the size of the farmers' gross revenue. The other is PSE per unit of output of a commodity where the PSE is divided by the level of production. This measure reflects the subsidies provided by the government for the production of a unit of output. For the purpose of this chapter, percentage PSEs (%PSEs) are considered rather than PSE per unit of output.

Symbolically, PSE can be defined as:

$$\%PSE = \text{total transfers/value to producers}$$
$$= \{Q * (P_d - P_w * X) + D + I\} / (Q * P_d + D)$$

where

Q is the quantity produced
P_d is the producer price in domestic currency units
P_w is the world price in world currency units
X is an exchange conversion factor
D is direct government payments

I is indirect transfers through policies such as input subsidies, marketing assistance, and exchange rate distortions.

The value of %PSE could be negative or positive depending upon whether the domestic price is less than or greater than the world reference price and whether other payments by the government are able to compensate the farmers for the "implicit tax" in case domestic price is lower than the reference price.

In interpreting the PSEs and analyzing trends in the same, a few points are to be noted. It is important to note that changes in world prices, exchange rates, or domestic production can alter the PSE even if the government policies were to remain the same. In particular, exchange rate fluctuations are rather pronounced for some countries, and to interpret PSE changes disregarding exchange rate fluctuations would be erroneous. Moreover, all transfers do not have the same weight in the %PSE calculation. Transfers from price support programs (the effects of which are included in P_d) as well as direct payments (D) appear in both the numerator and the denominator. Indirect transfers (I) on the other hand appear only in the numerator. This implies that a country can lower the PSE without changing total transfers to producers merely by shifting transfers from indirect programs to price support programs or direct payments.

16. The Cairns Group consists of 18 developing and industrialized countries including Argentina, Australia, Bolivia, Brazil, Canada, Chile, Colombia, Costa Rica, Fiji, Guatemala, Indonesia, Malaysia, New Zealand, Paraguay, Philippines, South Africa, Thailand, and Uruguay.

17. Paragraph 2 of the "Decision on Measures Concerning the Possible Negative Effects of the Reform Program on Least Developed Countries and Net Food-Importing Developing Countries."

18. In practice, however, in years of lower production, government often imposes movement restrictions in surplus states to ensure that the open market price collapses to the floor price announced by the government. This enables the government to procure foodgrains for the public distribution system.

19. Basmati rice in the Punjab and Haryana is exempt from levy obligations.

20. Earlier, these norms were between 41.5 million tons to 22.3 million tons.

21. R. Radhakrishna and K. Subbarao (1997).

22. If India wants to attain self-sufficiency in all agricultural products, or even in major ones, for instance, foodgrains, oilseed, cotton, and sugarcane, as many of the experts and policymakers in India strongly feel, the only way is to dramatically increase public/private investments in agriculture, especially in having a reliable irrigation source. India may attain self-sufficiency in these products, and India may be more efficient in their production than imports, but still it would not be availing gains of comparative cost advantage. Given the nature of world trade at present, India need not jump to a zero-one situation, but could carve out a policy with due caution. In the case of cereals India may like to produce within ±10 percent of the domestic requirements, and in the case of pulses and sugar this margin could be ±15 percent, and in the case of edible oils and cotton ±25 percent of the domestic requirements. This would give sufficient buffer to the domestic economy, and also try external trade at the margin to take advantage of the differences in comparative costs of production.

Bibliography

Dev, S., and S. Mahendra. 1999. "Persisting Poverty and Social Insecurity: A Selective Assessment." In K. S. Parikh, ed., *India Development Report 1999*. New Delhi: Oxford University Press.

Economic Times. 1999. "Sugar Industry Joins Free Market Lobby." June 9.

Government of India. 1998. *Export and Import Policy of India, April 1997–March 2002, ITC (HS) Classifications of Export and Import Items, August 1998*. New Delhi.

Government of India. 1999a. *Custom Tariff of India, 1999–2000*. New Delhi.

Government of India. 1999b. *Economic Survey 1998–99*. New Delhi.
Gulati, Ashok. 1999a. "Negotiating for Agriculture in the WTO." *The Economic Times*. September 8.
Gulati, Ashok. 1999b. "Towards Rationalization of Fertilizer Subsidy: Case of Urea under an Open Economy Environment." Paper presented at Workshop on Agricultural Policy. NCAER-IEG-World Bank, April 1999, New Delhi.
Gulati, Ashok, and Tim Kelly. 1999."*Trade Liberalization and Indian Agriculture.*" New York: Oxford University Press.
Gulati, Ashok, and Sudha Narayanan. 1999. "Indian Agriculture in the Global Economy: What Should India Negotiate in Seattle and Why?" Report. Indian Institute of Foreign Trade, New Delhi.
Gulati, Ashok, et al. 1996. "Self-Sufficiency and Allocation Efficiency: Case of Edible Oils." *Economic and Political Weekly* (India). 31:A15–A24.
———. 1998. "Indian Agriculture in an Open Economy: Will It Prosper?" In Isher Judge Ahluwalia and I. M. D. Little, eds., *India's Economic Reforms and Development: Essays for Manmohan Singh*.
Hathaway, Dale E., and Merlinda. D. Ingco. 1997. "Agricultural Liberalization and the Uruguay Round." In Will Martin and Alan Winters, eds., *Uruguay Round and the Developing Economies*. New York: Cambridge University Press.
Indira Gandhi Institute of Development Research. 1997. *India Development Report, 1997*. Mumbai.
IMF (International Monetary Fund). 1992. *Issues and Developments in International Trade Policy*. Washington, D.C.
Kelly, Margaret, and Anne Kenny McGuirk. 1992. *Issues and Developments in International Trade Policy*. Washington, D.C.: IMF.
OECD (Organisation for Economic Co-operation and Development. 1998. *Producer and Consumer Subsidy Equivalent, 1998*. Paris.
Purcell, G., B. Blarel, and A. Valdés, eds. 1998. *Implications of the Uruguay Round Agreement for South Asia: The Case of Agriculture*. Washington, D.C.: World Bank.
Radhakrishna, R., and K. Subbarao. 1997. "India's Public Distribution System: A National and International Perspective." Discussion Paper 380, World Bank, Washington, D.C.
WTO (World Trade Organization). 1995a. *Schedules on Goods*. Geneva.
———. 1995b. *Legal Texts of the Uruguay Round*. Geneva.
———. 1997. *Trade Policy Review: Various Countries*. Geneva.
———. 1999. "India: Quantitative Restrictions on Imports of Agricultural, Textile and Industrial Products." Report of the Appellate Body, Geneva.

Index

Additional custom duty (ACD), India, 192, 231n3, 231n5
Ad valorem tariffs, 3, 14
Aggregate measurement of support (AMS), 2, 8, 34n1, 180–82; AMSiffication, 203–8, 215; Bangladesh, 11, 25, 66, 90n41; India, 9, 10t1.3, 34–35nn2–3, 202–8; Pakistan, 14, 25, 162, 163–64t4.11, 184, 185
Agricultural Development Bank of Pakistan, 150–51
Agricultural Development Finance Corporation, Pakistan, 150
Agricultural growth rate: Bangladesh, 38, 39t2.1, 40t2.2, 86nn2–3; Pakistan, 142–48; Sri Lanka, 97–104
Agricultural inputs, 40t2.2, 42, 67t2.18b, 87n11
Agricultural outputs, 67t2.18a
Agricultural Prices Commission, Pakistan, 161t4.10
Agro-ecological zones, Pakistan, 142
Agro-processing industries, 63, 74, 90n35
Amber box measures, 71, 72
AMS. *See* aggregate measurement of support
AMSiffication, 203–8, 215
Applied tariff rates, 192, 231n4
Australia, 124–25

BADC. *See* Bangladesh Agricultural Development Corporation
Balance of Payments provision, 7, 194–95, 197t5.5
Balance of trade, Pakistan, 176t4.17, 176t4.18, 177–78t4.19, 179–80t4.20

Bangkok Agreement, 117
Bangladesh: agricultural reforms, 2, 51, 53, 54t2.11, 55, 56–57t2.12, 58–59t2.13, 89nn27–28; agriculture and food sector, 38, 39t2.1, 86nn1–5; AMS, 11, 25, 66, 90n41; bound tariff rates, 3t1.1, 63, 65t2.17, 66, 90n37; credit, 63, 64t2.16, 66, 89nn31–32; distribution system, 42, 43, 87n13; domestic policies, 10–11, 12–13t1.4, 35nn5–6, 41–42, 86nn6–8, 87nn9–12; domestic supports, 23–25t1.6, 63, 66–68, 90nn41–43; EPC, 89n28; EPRs, 11, 12t1.4, 33tA1.1, 35n6, 45, 48t2.5, 50, 53, 83–84tA2.3, 85tA2.4, 90n35; exchange rate, 10, 35n5, 50, 51t2.8, 52t2.9, 88–89nn25–26; exports, 23–25t1.6, 25, 66, 90nn38–39; features of agricultural trade, 53t2.10; fertilizer sector, 41, 68, 72, 86nn6–8, 87n9; food security, 19, 40t2.2, 42–44, 87nn13–17, 88nn18–20; GDP, 38, 39t2.1, 62t2.15, 72, 86nn1–3; HS codes, 45, 49t2.6, 50, 76tA2.1a, 76tA2.1b; imports, 51, 54–55t2.11, 58–59t2.13, 69t2.19, 70, 90n35; irrigation, 41, 68; labor force, 38, 86n1, 97f3.1; manufacturing sector, 72, 91n51; market access, 23–25t1.6, 25, 68, 69t2.19, 90n44, 91n45; NPRs, 11, 33tA1.1, 35n6; policy options and recommendations, 72–75, 91–92nn51–55; pricing policies and incentives, 10–11, 12–13t1.4, 14, 35nn5–6; product-specific supports, 11, 35n6; QRs, 25, 45, 50t2.7, 72–73, 91n54; SPS measures, 21, 71; STEs, 17,

Bangladesh *(continued)*
  43, 44*t*2.3, 69–70; tariffs, 6, 45–50, 66,
  78–82*t*A2.2, 88*nn*21–24; and TRIPS
  Agreement, 22, 70; U.N. Food
  Program, 108*t*3.3; unweighted tariffs,
  45, 46*t*2.4a, 47*t*2.4c, 48*t*2.5, 50, 53,
  88*n*21, 90*n*37; and URAoA, 63–72,
  90*n*37, 91*nn*46–50, 91*nn*52–53;
  weighted tariffs, 45, 46*t*2.4b, 47*t*2.4c,
  52*t*2.9, 88*n*21
Bangladesh Agricultural Development
  Corporation (BADC), 41, 42
Bangladesh Ministry of Commerce,
  71–72
Basic custom duty (BCD), India, 192,
  231*nn*3–4
Basmati rice, 167, 168, 226–27, 233*n*19
Bhutan, U.N. Food Program, 108*t*3.3
Big onions, 96, 102
Blair House Accord, 185
Blue box measures, 2, 185, 208, 211, 212
Board of Investment, Sri Lanka, 121
Bound tariff rates, 2, 25, 74; Bangladesh,
  3*t*1.1, 63, 65*t*2.17, 66, 90*n*37; India,
  3*t*1.1, 191, 191*t*5.1, 192–93, 194*t*5.3;
  Pakistan, 3*t*1.1, 152

Cairns Group, 187, 210, 215, 233*n*16
Canada, 91–92*n*55, 200, 210
Ceiling binding, 231*n*7
Cereal production, 223, 233*n*22
Cesses and surcharges, 123*t*3.10
Ceylon Fisheries Cooperation, 107
Chili production, Sri Lanka, 102
CIS. *See* Commonwealth of Independent
  States
Coconut Development Authority (CDA),
  Sri Lanka, 114, 123*t*3.10
Coconut Development Board, Sri Lanka,
  114
Coconut sector, Sri Lanka, 100, 114, 124,
  125
Codex Alimentarius Commission, 27,
  126, 225
Colombo, Sri Lanka, 98
Commission for Agricultural Costs and
  Prices, India, 218
Commonwealth of Independent States
  (CIS), 98, 124

Community intellectual rights, 28
Consumer price index (CPI), 31–32
Consumption: Pakistan, 147, 182–83; Sri
  Lanka, 97
Cooperative Wholesale Establishment
  (CWE), Sri Lanka, 17, 103, 110–11,
  136*t*A3.7, 137*t*A3.8
Cotton Export Corporation, Pakistan,
  176
Cotton sector, Pakistan, 168, 171*t*4.13
Council for Trade in Goods, India, 228
Countervailing duties, 125
Credit: Bangladesh, 63, 64*t*2.16, 66,
  89*nn*31–32; Pakistan, 150–51, 165; Sri
  Lanka, 116
Crocodile mammoty market, 112
Cross-boarder trade, 50, 88*n*24
Cultivated land: Bangladesh, 42, 87*n*12;
  India, 205, 232*n*13; Pakistan, 142,
  144*t*4.2; Sri Lanka, 96, 133*t*A3.3
Customs duties. *See* tariffs
CWE. *See* Cooperative Wholesale
  Establishment, Sri Lanka
Czech Republic, 210

Dairy industry: India, 214; Sri Lanka,
  104–5, 106*f*3.7, 135*t*A3.5
Decomposing of prices, 31–32
Decoupled income supports, 211
de minimis rule: India, 9, 208; Sri Lanka,
  16
Developing countries: and market
  access, 1, 199–202; necessity for
  involvement in trade reform, 1; and
  patents, 22, 226–27; tariffication of
  nontariff barriers, 2; and TRIPS, 27; *see
  also names of specific countries*
Direct payments, 211–12
Dirty tariffication, 125, 138*n*3
Dispute settlement proceedings, 185, 194
Distribution systems, 19; Bangladesh,
  42–43, 87*n*13; India, 218, 219, 222–23,
  222*t*5.11
Domestic supports, 211; Bangladesh,
  23–25*t*1.6, 63, 66–68, 90*nn*41–43; and
  food security, 18, 27, 217; India,
  23–25*t*1.6, 202–3, 208; Pakistan,
  184–85; Sri Lanka, 23–25*t*1.6
Dowlah, C.A.F., 38–94

INDEX

Duty drawback schemes, Bangladesh, 62
Duty exemption schemes, India, 8–9

East Asia, 200
Eco-labeling issues, 71
Economics: agriculture and growth in Pakistan, 142–48; role of agricultural trade in Sri Lanka, 109
ECUs, 209
Edible oils, 223, 233n20
Effective exchange rate for imports (EERm), Bangladesh, 50, 52t2.9, 62
Effective exchange rate for exports (EERx), Bangladesh, 62, 64t2.16
Effective protection (EP), 30
Effective protection coefficient (EPC), 15, 30, 89n28, 130t3.12
Effective protection rates (EPRs), 8, 34n1; Bangladesh, 11, 12t1.4, 33tA1.1, 35n6, 45, 48t2.5, 50, 53, 83–84tA2.3, 85tA2.4, 90n35; India, 33tA1.1; Pakistan, 33tA1.1; South Asia, 33tA1.1; Sri Lanka, 33tA1.1, 128
Effective subsidy coefficient of agricultural consumers, 130t3.12
Egg production, 106
Emergency Food Assistance, Sri Lanka, 108–9
Emergency food shortages, 44, 88n20
Employment programs, 219
End-user concessions, Bangladesh, 47t2.4c, 50, 88n23
Enhanced Structural Adjustment Program (ESAP), Bangladesh, 38, 41, 72, 91n46
Environmental issues: Bangladesh, 70–71, 91n50; see also sanitary and phytosanitary measures
EP. See effective protection
EPC. See effective protection coefficient
EPP. See export parity price
EPRs. See effective protection rates
Equilibrium exchange rate, Bangladesh, 50, 51t2.8, 88–89nn26
Essential Commodities Act, India, 229
European Free Trade Association (EFTA), 209
European Union, 73, 91–92n55, 105; and basmati rice, 167; export subsidies, 213, 214, 216; and food aid, 124–25; supports to agriculture, 209; tariffs, 199, 200
Exchange rates: Bangladesh, 10, 35n5, 50, 51t2.8, 52t2.9, 74, 88–89nn25–26; ECUs, 209; India, 203; Pakistan, 14; real exchange rates, 8, 50, 88n25; Sri Lanka, 14; XPB, 63, 89n33
Exemptions, 117–20, 192
Export competition: Bangladesh, 23–25t1.6, 25; India, 23–25t1.6, 25; Pakistan, 23–25t1.6, 25; Sri Lanka, 22, 23–25t1.6, 25, 26
Export credit, 63, 64t2.16, 66, 89nn31–32
Exporters, duty concessions for, 121
Export parity price (EPP), 161t4.10, 162
Export performance benefit (XPB), Bangladesh, 63, 89n33
Export processing zones, 8–9, 62, 89n30, 185
Export Promotion Bureau, Pakistan, 166, 167
Export promotion schemes, 62
Exports: anti-export bias, 10, 62; cesses and surcharges, 123t3.10; coconut products, 100; decline in agriculture's share, 63, 89n34; EERx, 62, 64t2.16; fisheries, 107; fruits, 168, 171t4.13; incentives and institutional supports for, 121, 130t3.12; poultry meat, 106; prohibitions and restrictions in, 165–66; spices, 115; and SPS requirements, 20–21; tea, 97–99; see also exports *under names of countries*
Export subsidies, 1–2, 212; Bangladesh, 64t2.16, 66, 72; India, 213–14, 216; industrialized countries, 26; overview, 212–13; reductions in, 121, 165; Sri Lanka, 26, 122t3.9; under URAoA, 214
External supply shocks, and food security, 20

Famine, 41
Farmers, 148–51, 205, 232n13
Farmers' rights, 28
FCI. See Food Corporation of India
Fertilizer sector: Bangladesh, 41, 68, 72, 86nn6–8, 87n9; Pakistan, 149; Sri Lanka, 115, 124

INDEX

Fiber Mill Modernization Scheme, Sri Lanka, 114
Fisheries industry: Bangladesh, 71; Pakistan, 145, 146t4.5, 185; Sri Lanka, 106–7, 115, 135tA3.6, 138n2
Food and Agriculture Organization, 16, 20, 221
Food aid: Bangladesh, 43, 87n16; impact of URAoA on, 124–25; Pakistan, 182; Sri Lanka, 108–9
Food Commissioners Department, Sri Lanka, 103
Food Corporation of India (FCI), 17, 26, 217, 218–21, 229
Food crops, 147
Food-For-Education Program, Bangladesh, 44
Food-for-work programs, 109
Foodgrains: Bangladesh, 42–43, 87nn13–15; domestic production of, 71; imports, 70, 217, 229; India, 232n13; Pakistan, 147; procurement and distribution of, 19, 218–19, 222t5.11, 222–23, 233n18; production of in Bangladesh, 38, 40t2.2, 86nn4–5; subsidies, 219t5.8
Food processing infrastructure, 225
Food production, 20, 43, 44
Food rationing programs, Bangladesh, 87n14, 87n16
Food safety. *See* sanitary and phytosanitary (SPS) measures
Food security, 17, 18–20, 27; Bangladesh, 19, 40t2.2, 42–44, 87nn13–17, 88nn18–20; costs of, 219–23; and crop diversification, 223–24; and domestic supports, 18, 27, 217; impact of URAoA on, 127–28, 129t3.11; India, 26, 27, 216–24; overview, 215; Pakistan, 182–83; Sri Lanka, 107–8, 110; and trade liberalization, 223–24
Food stamps, 223
Food stocks: Bangladesh, 19; India, 218, 221–22, 223, 233n20; Sri Lanka, 136tA3.7
Forestry, Pakistan, 145, 146t4.5
Freight concessions, 90n38
Fruits, export of, 168, 171t4.13
Futures markets, 27

Garment industry, Bangladesh, 62, 89n29, 91n50
GDP. *See* gross domestic product
Globalization, 200
Global System of Trade Preferences (GSTP) Agreement, 117, 121
Grading and Marketing Agricultural Produce Act of 1937, Pakistan, 167
Green box measures, 16, 25, 66, 71, 181–82, 208
Gross domestic product (GDP): Bangladesh, 38, 39t2.1, 62t2.15, 72, 86nn1–3; Japan, 209; Pakistan, 142, 144t4.2, 145, 146t4.4, 147; Sri Lanka, 96, 109f3.9, 128, 132tA3.2
GSTP. *See* Global System of Trade Preferences Agreement
Guarantees, 66, 89n31; Bangladesh, 66; Sri Lanka, 121
Gulati, Ashok, 34–35n2, 189–234

Harmonized System (HS) codes, 27; Bangladesh, 45, 49t2.6, 50, 76tA2.1a, 76tA2.1b; India, 7, 190, 191t5.1, 194t5.3, 196t5.4, 197t5.5, 198t5.6, 201, 231nn1–2, 231n9; Pakistan, 152
Health and safety. *See* sanitary and phytosanitary (SPS) measures
Horticultural products, 20, 148, 225
HS. *See* Harmonized System codes
Hungary, 210

Implicit taxation, 8
Import parity price (IPP), 161t4.10, 162
Imports, 2, 4–5t1.2; Bangladesh, 51, 54–55t2.11, 58–59t2.13, 69t2.19; by CWE, 110; by STC, 112; controls of, 3; dairy products, 135tA3.5; duty rates, 116; EERm, 62; fisheries, 107, 135tA3.6, 138n2; food and foodgrains, 136tA3.7, 229; impact of URAoA on, 124, 137tA3.10; and market access, 69t2.19; milk products, 105, 105t3.2, 106f3.7, 135tA3.5; prices, 183; and SPS measures, 21; sugar, 102–3; wheat, 103f3.6; *see also* imports *under names of countries*

Index

Import substitution policies, 2, 8; Bangladesh, 70, 90n35; India, 10
Income: farmers in India, 205, 232n13; impact of URAoA on, 127; Pakistan, 148–50
Income support policies, 223
India, 75, 203, 208–12; agriculture policies, 2, 148–51; AMS, 9, 10t1.3, 34–35nn2–3, 202–8; bilateral trade arrangements, 3; cultivated land, 205, 232n13; dairy industry, 214; distribution system, 218, 219, 222–23, 222t5.11; domestic policies, 8–10, 23–25t1.6, 34–35nn2–4, 202–3, 208, 229–31; EPR, 33tA1.1; exports, 23–25t1.6, 25, 213–14; food security, 18, 26, 27, 216–18; (HS) codes, 7, 190, 191t5.1, 194t5.3, 196t5.4, 197t5.5, 198t5.6, 201, 231nn1–2, 231n9; imports, 193–97, 231n9; irrigation, 233n22; licensing requirements, 9, 195, 196, 197, 198t5.6; market access, 23–25t1.6, 25, 199–202; nonproduct-specific supports, 25, 202–5, 206t5.7, 207; NPRs, 33tA1.1; NTBs, 195, 196, 196t5.4; product-specific supports, 25, 203–5, 206t5.7, 207, 208, 215, 232n14; protection of plant varieties, 227–28; QRs, 7, 25, 26, 193–97, 198t5.6, 229; SPS measures, 20, 224–25; STEs, 16–17, 26, 229; tariff rates, 3t1.1, 6–7, 191, 191t5.1, 192–93, 194t5.3; tarrification, 190–93, 199; trade reform, 28; and TRIPS Agreement, 22; U.N. Food Program, 108t3.3; and URAoA, 215
Indigenous knowledge, 28
Indirect taxes, Bangladesh, 11, 12t1.4
Indonesia, 105, 168
Industrialized countries: agriculture supports, 209; direct export subsidies, 212; dominance of trade negotiations, 1; export subsidies, 26, 213, 214; and market access, 70, 199–202; tarrification of nontariff barriers, 2; and TRIPS Agreement, 22
Industrial sector: Bangladesh, 10; Pakistan, 11; promotion of, 8; Sri Lanka, 14
Ingco, Merlinda D., 1–37

Input subsidies, Pakistan, 162
Institutional measures, Bangladesh, 73–74
Intellectual property rights (IPRs), 21–22, 27–28; Bangladesh, 70; India, 225–28; *see also* TRIPS Agreement
Interest rates: Bangladesh, 64t2.16; Pakistan, 165
Internal supports, in Sri Lanka, 113–16
International Monetary Fund (IMF), and trade policy in Bangladesh, 71–72
Investment subsidies, 90n41
Inward-processing programs, 26
IPP. *See* import parity price
IPR. *See* intellectual property rights
Iran, 166
Irrigation: Bangladesh, 41, 68; India, 233n22; Pakistan, 142, 144t4.2; Sri Lanka, 115–16

Japan, 168, 199, 200, 209
Joint ventures, Bangladesh-China, 86n7

KAFCO, Bangladesh, 86n7, 87n9
Kandiero, Tonia, 1–37
Kelegama, Saman, 96–140
Khan, Safraz, 141–88
Kiriya Milk Industry, Sri Lanka, 104, 105
Korea, 200, 209, 231n10

Labor force: Bangladesh, 38, 86n1, 97f3.1; Pakistan, 144t4.2; Sri Lanka, 96, 132tA3.1
Labor Force Survey, Bangladesh, 86n1
Land use: India, 223; Pakistan, 146; Sri Lanka, 96, 133tA3.3
Leakage, foodgrains, 222
Licensing requirements: India, 9, 195, 196, 197, 198t5.6; Pakistan, 6, 160; Sri Lanka, 110, 120–21
Livestock, Pakistan, 142, 145, 146t4.5, 147

Maize, 120, 147
Mangoes, 225
Manufacturing sector: Bangladesh, 72, 91n51; Pakistan, 142; Sri Lanka, 15
Marine resources, 106–7
Market access, 26, 125; Bangladesh, 23–25t1.6, 25, 68, 69t2.19, 90n44, 91n45;

Market access *(continued)*
India, 23–25*t*1.6, 25, 199–202; Pakistan, 23–25*t*1.6, 25; Sri Lanka, 23–25*t*1.6, 25; and tariffs, 2–7; to industrialized countries, 70; *see also* tariff rates; tariffs
Market prices, and food security, 19–20
Market price supports, 162, 209, 211
Marrakesh Agreement of 1994, 73, 183, 186
Mechanization, promotion of, 151
Milk industries: Pakistan, 147; Sri Lanka, 104*t*3.1, 104–5
Milk Industry of Lanka Co., Ltd., Sri Lanka, 104–5
Ministry of Commerce, Pakistan, 165
Monopolies: on foodgrain imports, 229; *see also* state trading enterprises (STEs)
Most favored nation (MFN): India, 192–93, 194*t*5.3; and market access, 90*n*44
Multilateral trade negotiations, 73
Multi-Purposes Cooperative Societies, Sri Lanka, 112–13

National Accreditation Body, Sri Lanka, 126
National Dairy Development Board of India, 105
Natural disasters, and food security, 19
Neem oil, 227
Nepal, U.N. Food Program, 108*t*3.3
Nestlé Lanka Ltd., 104
New Comprehensive Rural Credit Scheme, Sri Lanka, 116
New generation issues, 73
New Zealand, 105, 205
Nominal exchange rates, Bangladesh, 64*t*2.16
Nominal protection (NP), 8, 29–30, 34*n*1
Nominal protection coefficients (NPCs), 9, 35*n*4; Pakistan, 13*t*1.5, 29–30, 161*t*4.10; Sri Lanka, 130*t*3.12
Nominal protection rates (NPRs), 9, 35*n*4; Bangladesh, 11, 33*t*A1.1, 35*n*6; India, 33*t*A1.1; Pakistan, 11, 13*t*1.5, 33*t*A1.1, 35*n*7, 160, 161*t*4.10, 162, 163–64*t*4.11; South Asia, 33*t*A1.1; Sri Lanka, 14–15, 33*t*A1.1, 128
Nonexempt direct payments, 202

Nonproduct-specific supports, 9, 10*t*1.3, 34–35*nn*2–3; India, 25, 202–5, 206*t*5.7, 207; Pakistan, 162, 163*t*4.11
Nonstructural policies, 148
Nontrade barriers (NTBs), 2; Bangladesh, 71; India, 195, 196, 196*t*5.4; Pakistan, 6, 152, 160, 184; Sri Lanka, 25; tariffication of, 69
Notified crops, 41
NP. *See* nominal protection
NPCs. *See* nominal protection coefficients
NPRs. *See* nominal protection rates

OFC. *See* other field crops
OGL. *See* open general license, India
Oilseed areas, 223
Open general license (OGL), India, 197, 198*t*5.6
Operative tariff rates, Bangladesh, 78–82*t*A2.2
Organisation for Economic Co-operation and Development (OECD), 91–92*n*55, 208–9, 210, 211
Other field crops (OFC), Sri Lanka, 100–103

Paddy Marketing Board (PMB), Sri Lanka, 111
Paddy sector: India, 218; irrigation of, 115–16; Sri Lanka, 97, 98*f*3.2, 111, 113, 115–16, 128
Pakistan, 2, 6; aggregate measurement of support (AMS), 14, 25, 162, 163–64*t*4.11, 184, 185; balance of trade, 176*t*4.17, 176*t*4.18, 177–78*t*4.19, 179–80*t*4.20; consumption policies, 147, 182–83; credit, 150–51, 165; domestic policies and incentives, 11, 13*t*1.5, 14, 35*n*7, 184–85; economic growth, 142–48; EPR, 33*t*A1.1; exports, 23–25*t*1.6, 160, 168–69, 170*t*4.12, 171*t*4.13, 175*t*4.16, 176*t*4.17, 177–78*t*4.19; fisheries industry, 145, 146*t*4.5, 185; food security, 19–20; GDP, 142, 144*t*4.2, 145, 146*t*4.4, 147; HS codes, 152; imports, 169, 172–73*t*4.14, 174*t*4.15, 175*t*4.16, 176*t*4.18, 179–80*t*4.20; irrigation, 142, 144*t*4.2;

Index

labor force, 144t4.2; licensing requirements, 6, 160; manufacturing sector, 142; market access, 23–25t1.6, 25; nonproduct-specific supports, 162, 163t4.11; NPCs, 13t1.5, 29–30, 161t4.10; NPRs, 13t1.5, 33tA1.1, 35n7, 160, 161t4.10, 162, 163–64t4.11; NTBs, 6, 152, 160, 184; plant breeders' rights, 22; product-specific supports, 11, 14, 162, 163t4.11; QRs, 26, 152, 155–56t4.7, 165; SPS measures, 21, 166–68; state trading enterprises, 17; tariff rates, 3t1.1, 152, 153–54t4.6, 157–59t4.8, 160t4.9; trade reform, 28–29; U.N. Food Program, 108t3.3

Pakistan Horticulture Export Development Project, 148

Parastatals, 43, 68

Patents, 226–27

%PSE, 30–31

Pesticides, 20, 149, 225

Plantation crops, Sri Lanka, 96

Plant Protection Act, Sri Lanka, 127

Plant varieties, protection of, 22, 126–27, 227–28

PMB. *See* Paddy Marketing Board, Sri Lanka

Poland, 210

Population: Pakistan, 144t4.2; Sri Lanka, 96, 132tA3.1

Potato crop: and market access, 68; Sri Lanka, 96, 101f3.4, 101f3.5, 102, 111, 120–21; tariff equivalents for, 6

Poultry sector, 106, 147

Poverty: antipoverty programs in India, 219; Bangladesh, 19, 42; developing countries, 207; food-based, 42

Power supplies, 204

Preferential trading arrangements, Sri Lanka, 117

Preshipment inspection for imports, 45, 88n22

Prices, 181; and AMS, 203; Bangladesh, 67t2.18b; decomposing of, 31–32; domestic pricing policies, 26; food crops, 148–50; guaranteed price schemes, 110, 111–12; impact of URAoA on, 124, 128; imports, 183; increases in, 71; India, 202; Pakistan, 148–50, 176t4.17, 176t4.18, 177–78t4.19, 179–80t4.20; rice, 43, 87n17; Sri Lanka, 131

Prima Ceylon Ltd., Sri Lanka, 103, 111, 120, 138n1

Private trade, in Bangladesh, 70, 91n47

Processed agricultural products, 63, 90n35

Producer subsidy equivalents (PSEs), 30–31, 208–10, 232–33n5

Production: foodgrains, 38, 40t2.2, 86nn4–5; measures linked to, 212; Pakistan, 148–50, 180–82; policy options in Pakistan, 180–82; schemes for limiting, 181, 185; subsidies for, 25

Product specificity, obscurity of, 185

Product-specific supports, 9, 10t1.3, 34–35n2; Bangladesh, 11, 35n6; India, 25, 203–5, 206t5.7, 207, 208, 215, 232n14; Pakistan, 11, 14, 162, 163t4.11; Sri Lanka, 15

Program Food Aid, Sri Lanka, 108–9

Project Food Aid, Sri Lanka, 108

PSEs. *See* producer subsidy equivalents

Public distribution systems: Bangladesh, 19, 42, 43, 87n13; India, 218, 219, 222–23, 222t5.11

Public Foodgrain Distribution System, Bangladesh, 19, 42, 43, 87n13

QRs. *See* quantitative restrictions

Quality control, 167

Quantitative restrictions (QRs), 25; Bangladesh, 25, 45, 50t2.7, 72–73, 91n54; India, 7, 25, 26, 193–97, 198t5.6, 229; Pakistan, 26, 152, 155–56t4.7, 165; removal of, 28; Sri Lanka, 121, 123, 130

Quarantine regulations, 126–27

Quota restrictions, Pakistan, 166

Real exchange rates, 8, 50, 88n25

Red meat production, 106, 147

Red onions, 120

Reform Programme on Least-Developed and New Food-Importing Developing Countries, 183, 186

Rice: Bangladesh, 38, 41, 42, 86n4, 87n12; basmati rice, 167, 168, 226–27, 233n19; export subsidies, 213; India, 218, 219,

Rice *(continued)*
 233*n*19; market for, 43; output, 42, 87*n*12; Pakistan, 145, 146*t*4.5, 147, 165, 168, 171*t*4.13; Sri Lanka, 97, 98*f*3.2, 111–12, 113, 124, 128; and world markets, 217
Rice Export Corporation, Pakistan, 176
Rice Exporters Association, Pakistan, 167
Rice Tec, 227
Rubber sector: prices, 124; Sri Lanka, 99–100, 99*f*3.3, 115, 123, 124, 125

S&D. *See* special and differential provisions
SAARC. *See* South Asian Association for Regional Cooperation
Safeguard provisions, 186
Sanitary and phytosanitary (SPS) measures, 20–21, 27, 131; Bangladesh, 21, 71; India, 224–25; overview, 225; Pakistan, 166–68, 185–86; URAoA impact on, 126–27
Sanitary and Phytosanitary Measures Agreement, 20–21, 131, 167, 185–86
SAPTA. *See* South Asian Preferential Trading Arrangement
Scheduled Rates of the Basic Custom Duty, 192
Seattle Ministerial Conference, 1999, 70
Second generation issues, 70, 71
Seed Amendment Act of 1997, Bangladesh, 42
Seed and Planting Material Center, Sri Lanka, 116
Seed Rules of 1998, Bangladesh, 42
Seed sector, 70; Bangladesh, 41–42, 68*t*2.18c, 87*n*10, 116; high yielding varieties, 149; post-URAoA implementation, 127; Sri Lanka, 116, 117
Shadow exchange rate, 90*n*39
SIL. *See* special import license, India
SLECIC. *See* Sri Lanka Export Credit Insurance Corporation
SLEDB. *See* Sri Lanka Export Development Board
SLSI. *See* Sri Lanka Standards Institution
Small Holdings Tea Development Project, Sri Lanka, 114
Smuggling, 50, 75, 88*n*24, 91*n*45, 166

South Asia: bound and post-UR applied tariff rates, 3*t*1.1; reform under URAoA, 23–25*t*1.6; *See also names of individual countries*
South Asian Association for Regional Cooperation (SAARC), 108*t*3.3, 125, 195
South Asian Preferential Trading Arrangement (SAPTA), 117
South Korea, 231*n*10
Soybeans, 231*n*10
Special and differential (S&D) provisions, 21, 181; Pakistan, 185–86; Sri Lanka, 126, 131
Special import license (SIL), India, 9, 198*t*5.6
SPS. *See* sanitary and phytosanitary measures
Sri Lanka, 14, 97, 168; commodities, 97–104, 129*t*3.11, 134*t*A3.4; cultivated land, 96, 133*t*A3.3; CWE purchases, 136*t*A3.8; dairy industry, 104–5, 106*f*3.7, 135*t*A3.5; Department of Customs, 123*t*3.10; domestic policies, 14–16, 23–25*t*1.6; EPC, 15, 130*t*3.12; EPR, 33*t*A1.1, 128; exports, 23–25*t*1.6, 25, 26; fertilizer sector, 115, 124; fisheries industry, 106–7, 115, 135*t*A3.6, 138*n*2; food security, 20, 107–8; GDP, 96, 109*f*3.9, 128, 132*t*A3.2; implementation of Uruguay Round, 113–23; imports, 15–16, 110, 117, 118–19*t*3.8, 120–21, 137*t*A3.10; irrigation, 115–16; labor force, 96, 132*t*A3.1; licensing requirements, 110, 120–21; manufacturing sector, 15; market access, 23–25*t*1.6, 25; NPRs, 14–15, 33*t*A1.1, 128; overview, 96; poultry and meat industries, 106; product-specific supports, 15; QRs, 121, 123, 130; role of agricultural trade in economy, 109; rubber sector, 99–100, 99*f*3.3, 115, 123, 124, 125; seed sector, 116, 117; STEs, 103, 110–13; tariffs, 3*t*1.1; trade reform, 28; U.N. Food Program, 108*t*3.3
Sri Lanka Export Credit Insurance Corporation (SLECIC), 15–16, 121
Sri Lanka Export Development Board (SLEDB), 15–16, 121, 123*t*3.10

INDEX

Sri Lanka Standards Institution (SLSI), 126
Sri Lanka State Trading Corporation (STC), 17, 112
Sri Lanka Tea Board, (SLTB), 123t3.10
Standard of living, India, 194
State-owned enterprises, and fertilizer production, 41
State trading enterprises (STEs), 16–17, 26; Bangladesh, 17, 43, 44t2.3, 69–70; foodgrains, 43; India, 26, 229; operations of, 34; Pakistan, 176; Sri Lanka, 103, 110–13
Statutory Rates, 192, 231nn3–4
STC. *See* Sri Lanka State Trading Corporation
STEs. *See* state trading enterprises
Structural Adjustment Program (SAP), 38, 41, 72, 91n46, 181–82
Subsidies: coconut sector, 114, 114t3.7; exports, 62–63, 64t2.16, 115; fertilizer, 115; fisheries, 115; food and food crops, 44, 88n19, 149–50, 219–21; India, 202; inputs, 162; interest, 116; irrigation, 115–16; other export crops, 115; Pakistan, 14; production, 25; rubber sector, 115; tea sector, 113t3.6; urea, 41, 86n8; *see also* export subsidies
Subsistence farmers, Pakistan, 148–50
Sugarcane, 207
Sugar sector: India, 215, 218; and market access, 68, 91n45; Pakistan, 145, 146t4.5, 147; Sri Lanka, 102–3, 124; tariff equivalents for, 6; and world markets, 217
Sui generis system of plant protection, 22, 227, 228
Support notifications, Pakistan, 25
Support price programs: Bangladesh, 11, 12t1.4, 35n6; India, 9, 10t1.3, 34–35nn2–3; Pakistan, 11, 13t1.5, 14, 35n7, 162, 163–64t4.11

Taccavi loans, 150
Taiwan, 209
Tariff quotas, and market access, 190
Tariff rates: Bangladesh, 6, 45–50, 66, 78–82tA2.2, 88n21; bound and applied, 2–7, 25, 74, 192, 231n4; India, 6–7, 192–93, 194t53; three-band structure, 3; uniformity of, 184
Tariffs: ad valorem, 3, 14; Bangladesh, 45–50, 51, 53, 66, 78–82tA2.2, 88nn21–24; changes in Sri Lanka, 117, 118–19t3.8; dirty tariffication, 125, 138n3; India, 190–93, 199; Pakistan, 152, 153–54t4.6, 157–59t4.8, 160t4.9; Sri Lanka, 116–23; zero tariff binding, 201, 231nn11–12; *see also* bound tariff rates; nontrade barriers (NTBs)
Tariff Value Set, Bangladesh, 88n22
Tea Board, Sri Lanka, 99
Tea Factory Development Scheme, Sri Lanka, 113–14
Tea Research Institute, Sri Lanka, 99
Tea sector: Pakistan, 169; Sri Lanka, 97–99, 113–14, 124
Tea Small Holdings Development Authority, Sri Lanka, 99, 113–114
Thailand, 100
Trade-distorting measures, 208
Trade Policy Review of India, 207
Trade-Related Aspects of Intellectual Property Rights Agreement. *See* TRIPS Agreement
Trading Corporation of Bangladesh, 68
Trading Corporation of Pakistan, 17, 152, 176
Trading rights, Sri Lanka, 111
Transparency, 25
TRIPS Agreement, 21–22, 27–28; Article 27.3, 91n49; Bangladesh, 22, 70; India, 225–28
Tubewells, 151

United Arab Emirates, 98
United Nations Conference on Trade and Development (UNCTAD), 73
United States: dumping of rubber stocks, 100; farm income, 73, 91–92n55; food aid, 108, 124–25; milk products, 105; PSEs, 210; and tariffs, 199, 200
Unweighted tariffs, Bangladesh, 45, 46t2.4a, 47t2.4c, 48t2.5, 50, 53, 88n21, 90n37
U.N. World Food Program, 108–9, 125

URAoA, 1–2, 165, 182–83, 187, 211; and AMS, 203–5; Bangladesh, 63–72, 91*nn*46–50, 91*nn*52–53; consumption policy options, 182–83; and domestic policies, 66–68, 90*nn*41–43, 183; and exports, 66, 90*nn*38–39, 165–66; food aid and security, 124–25, 127–28, 129*t*3.11, 216; impact on incomes, 127; impact on prices, 128; implementation in India, 190–93, 199–208, 215; implementation in Pakistan, 151–60, 165–66, 180–86; implementation in Sri Lanka, 123–28, 137*t*A3.9; nominal protection rates, 160, 161*t*4.10, 162, 163–64*t*4.11; and production policies, 180–82; reform in South Asia, 23–25*t*1.6; seed sector, 127; and SPS measures, 126–27, 166–68; tariffs and tariff bindings under, 4–5*t*1.2, 7, 190–93

Urea, 41, 86*n*6, 86*n*8, 97*n*9

Urea Crisis of 1995, 41, 86*n*6

Uruguay Round: implementation in Sri Lanka, 113–23; tariff rates, 190–93

Uruguay Round Agreement on Agriculture. *See* URAoA

Value-added tax: Bangladesh, 78–82*t*A2.2; Pakistan, 145, 146*t*4.4, 165; Sri Lanka, 98

Voluntary preshipment schemes, 45, 88*n*22

Warehouses, Bangladesh, 62

Water rates, Pakistan, 149

Weighted tariffs, 6, 45, 46*t*2.4b, 47*t*2.4c, 52*t*2.9, 53, 88*n*21, 90*n*37

Wheat grain and flour sector: Bangladesh, 38, 86*n*5; export subsidies, 213; and food subsidies, 219, 220*t*5.9, 221; India, 219, 220*t*5.9, 221; Pakistan, 146*t*4.5, 147, 150, 162, 163*t*4.11, 169; Sri Lanka, 103–4, 111, 124, 138*n*1; and world markets, 217

World Bank: end-user concessions, 88*n*23; and trade policy reform in Bangladesh, 71–72; urea crisis, 86*n*6

W.R. Grace and Co., 227

XPB benefits, 63, 66, 89*n*33, 90*n*39

Zero tariff binding, 201, 231*nn*11–12